"This book is a rare combination of articles from well-known psychoanalysts from all over the world. They share their complex views on psychic bisexuality, dealing in depth with psychoanalytic theory, very interesting developments on early psychic life, on Freud's cases, and contemporary clinic. This book captures the essence of the complex issue of psychic bisexuality in our societies, and of the stimulating work of psychoanalytic technique with contemporary patients. This is a brilliant book, exciting and very accessible: a good combination of education and psychoanalytic thinking."

Christine Anzieu-Premmereur, MD, PhD, Assistant Clinical Professor in Psychiatry at Columbia University, Overall Chair IPA COCAP

"In publishing this book, the editors have succeeded in bringing together a collection of esteemed authors from different regions of the world who invite the reader to explore the complex question of the feminine and the masculine, both of which are intricately linked to the concept of psychic bisexuality. The richness of this book also lies in the deep respect and sensitivity with which each author listens to their patients and follows them in the conundrums of the unconscious processes that underlie the vicissitudes one encounters when confronted with questions that touch the most intimate part of one's identity and sense of femininity and of masculinity, leading to a better understanding of their suffering. Particularly today, in a contemporary world where diversity and respect for the other are under threat, this book enriches the reader by offering the opportunity to discover, or rediscover, the concept of psychic bisexuality from different cultural psychoanalytic traditions, providing new ideas to help us better understand our patients who question gender, sexual identity, femininity and masculinity."

Katy Bogliatto, MD, Training Psychoanalyst from the Belgian Psychoanalytical Society, IPA Vice-President

"Starting from the notion that the field of sexuality today is undergoing profound changes that could be compared to a 'landslide', this book by many eminent authors, admirably edited by Ana Teresa Vale and Nadja Tröger, investigates the background for a cultural phenomenon that can be seen as constituting the nucleus of the dramatic changes within the present time: psychic bisexuality. To sum it up, the attention on psychic bisexuality could be considered a movement against dominance: the 'primacy of genitality', viewed still by Freud as the most advanced, and in this way most mature form of psychosexuality, to reign over the partial drives, has today lost its place and meaning in sexual practices as well as in psychoanalytic theory. Instead, the rediscovery of the concept of psychic bisexuality as it is extensively elaborated in this book, is seen as a liberation by the younger generation. It opens up a path for a new psychoanalytic understanding of the spread of sexual practices that were before considered improper or even pathological.

The authors of this book explore the possibilities clinically and expand into new theories. I can highly recommend reading this book to all who are involved with the training of candidates, but more even with young people of both sexes in their search for orientation in sexual life, intimacy and love."

Rotraut De Clerck, Training Psychoanalyst from the German Psychoanalytic Association, Chair of the EPF Group Psychoanalysis in Literature – Literature in Psychoanalysis, Consultant IPA Culture, and COWAP European Co-Chair

Revisiting Psychic Bisexuality

Revisiting Psychic Bisexuality: The Feminine Within explores the complexities of psychosexual development from a psychoanalytic perspective, challenging traditional ideals and theories.

Viewing the feminine and the masculine as an interdependent dyad in the human psyche, this book examines the construction of identity, as well as the sexual identification process. Considering inter- and intrapsychic dynamics, the chapters explore the relationship between analyst and analysand, looking at how various perspectives on the identification process of the masculine and feminine can challenge the analytic process. Focusing on classic and contemporary psychoanalytic theories, the chapters approach the phenomenon of psychic bisexuality as a mediating and mental function and work to find a model that fits with contemporary psychoanalysis and life in the twenty-first century. Based on the universal idea that each element of the analytic pair carries inside his/her idiosyncratic experience of the feminine/masculine relationship, and that the analytic pair is engaged in an ongoing unconscious communication, the global cohort of contributors invite psychoanalysts working today to expand their viewpoints and move beyond the traditional psychoanalytic frame to better help their clients.

This book is an invaluable resource for all mental health practitioners, as well as those in education and social care, looking to reflect on the vicissitudes of psychosexual development.

Ana Teresa Vale is a clinical psychologist and psychoanalyst living and working in Lisbon, Portugal. She was COWAP's European representative between 2021 and 2025, and a member of the editorial board of the *Portuguese Psychoanalytic Journal*. She is co-editor of the book *Pregnancy, Assisted Reproduction and Psychoanalysis*, published by Routledge in 2025.

Nadja Tröger is a clinical psychologist and psychoanalyst living and working in Lisbon, Portugal. She is the COWAP link for the Portuguese Psychoanalytical Society and a member of the editorial board of the *Portuguese Psychoanalytic Journal*.

Psychoanalysis and Women Series

Series Editor: Paula Ellman
Previously Frances Thomson-Salo

The Psychoanalysis and Women book series grew from the work of the International Psychoanalytical Association Committee on Women and Psychoanalysis (COWAP). Publications further the conversations on women, sexuality, gender, men, and psychoanalysis, and intersections with diversity and cross-cultural experience. We value written exchanges between psychoanalysis and related disciplines of gender studies, anthropology, sociology, politics, philosophy, arts and activism. We encourage contributions from all regions, allowing for global perspectives and different creativities on topics relating to women, gender and sexuality. The series editorial board is comprised of Paula Ellman (Editor-in-Chief, North America), Carolina Bacchi (North America) Sara Boffito (Italy), Lesley Caldwell (UK), Amrita Narayana (India), and Paula Escribens Pareja (Peru).

Titles in the series:

Changing Sexualities and Parental Functions in the Twenty-First Century
Changing Sexualities, Changing Parental Functions
Candida Se Holovko

Psychoanalytic Explorations of What Women Want Today
Femininity, Desire and Agency
Margarita Cereijido, Paula L. Ellman and Nancy R. Goodman

The Desire and Passion to Have a Child
Psychoanalysis and Contemporary Reproductive Techniques
Patricia Alkolombre

Independent Women in British Psychoanalysis
Creativity and Authenticity at Work
Elizabeth Wolf and Barbie Antonis

For further information about this series please visit: https://www.routledge.com/Psychoanalysis-and-Women-Series/book-series/KARNACPWS

Revisiting Psychic Bisexuality

The Feminine Within

Edited by
Ana Teresa Vale and Nadja Tröger

Routledge
Taylor & Francis Group

LONDON AND NEW YORK

Designed cover image: Getty Images © Ada daSilva

First published 2026
by Routledge
4 Park Square, Milton Park, Abingdon, Oxon OX14 4RN

and by Routledge
605 Third Avenue, New York, NY 10158

Routledge is an imprint of the Taylor & Francis Group, an informa business

British Library Cataloguing-in-Publication Data
A catalogue record for this book is available from the British Library

ISBN: 978-1-032-95357-1 (hbk)
ISBN: 978-1-032-95355-7 (pbk)
ISBN: 978-1-003-58448-3 (ebk)

DOI: 10.4324/9781003584483

Typeset in Times New Roman
by Taylor & Francis Books

Contents

MONA CHAHOURY CHARABATY

Foreword

The Psychoanalysis and Women book series grew from the work of the International Psychoanalytical Association Committee on Women and Psychoanalysis (COWAP). The International Psychoanalytical Association (IPA)/Routledge series furthers global perspectives and different creativities on topics related to women, gender and sexuality, and psychoanalysis, considering intersections with diversity and cross-cultural experience.

This volume offers an original point of view on the area of gender, the feminine, the masculine, and psychic bisexuality, both within a historical perspective and taking into account current thinking in psychoanalysis.

Viewing the feminine and the masculine as an interdependent dyad in the human psyche, the authors investigate how sexuality is experienced and perceived both internally and externally, and they explore the multiple ways in which this is reflected in the consulting room and in the relationship between analyst and analysand, looking at how various perspectives on the identification process of the masculine and feminine can challenge the analytic process.

The authors' approach values the richness of contemporary perspectives by grounding and dialectically integrating them with the history of psychoanalytic theory, always considering how the dimensions of masculinity and femininity are part of the unique expression of subjectivity. This allows us to see and enhance the transformative and creative aspect of the continuously changing dynamic of the infinite combinations of representations and identities.

From working with gender-fluid identities, alternative family dynamics and people undergoing gender transition, the global cohort of contributors invite psychoanalysts working today to expand their viewpoints and move beyond traditional psychoanalytic work.

The book is divided in two sections. The first one, "Power, difference and complementarity," assembles five chapters from different authors under the umbrella of the relationship between masculine and feminine in its several forms. The second section, "Challenges in the construction of a gender and sexual identity," composed of seven chapters from different authors, focuses on the enigmatic aspects of gender and sexual identity and explores the clinical value of the concept of psychic bisexuality.

The interplay between the theory and the clinical brings depth to the chapters and relevance to psychoanalysts, mental health practitioners, and academics in areas of gender and women studies.

The Psychoanalysis and Women book series editorial board represents all regions of the IPA with six editors collaborating as a team from Goa, London, Lima, Milan, San Francisco, and Washington, DC. We are women writers and editors active in psychoanalysis both regionally and in the IPA. We encourage single author and multiple author book proposal submissions to our IPA-Routledge book series on topics of women, gender, femininity, and masculinity. We offer our close-up consultation and guidance in the crafting of the book proposals, and throughout the writing and publishing process.

The Women and Psychoanalysis Book Series Editorial Board
Carolina Bacchi
Sara Boffito
Lesley Caldwell
Paula Ellman (Editor-in-Chief)
Paula Escribens Pareja
Amrita Narayanan

Editors' and contributors' biographies

Editors

Ana Teresa Vale is a clinical psychologist and a psychoanalyst living and working in Lisbon. She is an associate member of the Portuguese Psychoanalytic Society, teaching in her society's training program. She is currently an assistant on the editorial board of the *Portuguese Psychoanalytic Journal*. She has been a part of COWAP since 2012, having started as the link between COWAP and the Portuguese Society and was COWAP's European representative between 2021 and 2025, and as such she has facilitated study groups on infertility and assisted reproduction, participated in the organization of international COWAP conferences, and has worked on COWAP panel organizations in the European Psychoanalytical Federation (EPF) and IPA meetings. She participates regularly in national and international psychoanalytic events where she has on several occasions presented her work. She is co-editor of the book *Pregnancy, Assisted Reproduction and Psychoanalysis* with Renata Viola Vives (Routledge, 2025). Email: ana.t.vale@gmail.com

Nadja Tröger is a clinical psychologist, psychotherapist, and psychoanalyst. She is an associate member of the Portuguese Psychoanalytic Society, member of the EPF and of the IPA. She was representative of the International Psychoanalytical Studies Organization for Portugal from 2014 to 2017. She was also part of the COWAP Portuguese Study Group and is currently COWAP link for the Portuguese Psychoanalytical Society, as well as an assistant on the editorial board of the *Portuguese Psychoanalytic Journal*. Email: nadja.troeger@gmail.com

Contributors

Luz Abatángelo Stürzenbaum has a degree in literature and psychology and a PhD in psychology from the Complutense University of Madrid. She is a full member of the Asociación Psicoanalítica de Madrid (APM), full member with didactic functions of the Asociación Psicoanalítica Argentina (APA),

member of the EPF, and member of the IPA. She was also COWAP liaison member for the APA from 2008 until 2012 and she is currently COWAP's European representative. A specialist in children and adolescents by the IPA, she worked as a supervisor in the Juvenile Psychopathology Service of the Hospital José de San Martín of the University of Buenos Aires and of the Rivadavia Hospital of the city of Buenos Aires. She was also professor at the University of Belgrano (Argentina) and is currently professor in the master's program on psychotherapy at the University of Alcalá de Henares. She was co-editor of *Aportes de los autores argentinos a la estructuración del aparato psíquico* (Letra Viva, 2016) and has written several papers for different psychoanalytic journals and books.
Email: luzmariastur@gmail.com

Silvia Raquel Acosta, PhD, is an associate member of the Asociación Psicoanalítica de Cordoba (Argentina) and of the Portuguese Psychoanalytic Society. She was a full professor for 15 years on the doctoral and master programs in psychoanalysis at Universidad del Salvador in Argentina. She currently serves as Overall Chair for the IPA Gender and Sexual Diversity Studies Committee (S&GDSCo). She was Assistant Director of the *Revista Portuguesa de Psicanálise* (*Portuguese Psychoanalytic Journal*) and scientific secretary of the Annual of the *International Journal of Psychoanalysis* (*IJP*) in Spanish. For her work, she has received the Psychoanalytic Research Exceptional Contribution Award, the award Training Today (IPA), as well as other awards for her academic and clinical work in the field of clinical psychology and psychoanalysis. She has published several scientific papers on clinical psychoanalysis with adults and adolescents, and she is the editor of several books on sexual diversity and gender in Spanish and in English. The book *Polimorfismos*, with Leticia Glocer and Jean Marc Tauszik, was published in 2021 by Editorial Letra Viva in Spanish, and she is currently co-editing a Routledge–S&GDSCo series based on the same subject, *Polymorphisms, Technomorphisms and Resistances to the Difference.*
Email: centrodrac@gmail.com

Conceição Tavares de Almeida is a clinical psychologist and psychoanalyst with a master's in psychopathology. She is a training and supervising member of the Portuguese Psychoanalytic Society and of the IPA. She is currently COWAP's Overall Chair (2025–2029) and she was IPA European board representative between 2021 and 2023. She is currently the President of the Portuguese Society board, having also been vice-president and scientific secretary of the same board. She was co-chair of IPSO Portugal and link for COWAP in Portugal. She is senior officer at the General Directorate of Health and former advisor for Child and Youth at the National Mental Health Program (2012–2022). She has been involved in scientific working groups, lectures, supervision, and training activities and has taken part in numerous organizing committees of national and international events. She is

a published author in several scientific publications on clinical research and health policy guidelines.
Email: conceicaotavaresdealmeida@gmail.com

Dana Amir, PhD, is a clinical psychologist and a training and supervising member of the Israel Psychoanalytic Society. She is full professor and head of the interdisciplinary doctoral program in psychoanalysis and "Zramim" Postgraduate Psychoanalytic Psychotherapy Program at Haifa University. She is also part of the department of Counseling and Human Development at the same university. She is editor-in-chief of *MA'ARAG – The Israeli Annual of Psychoanalysis* and a published author in several journals and books on psychoanalysis. She is a published poet. She was awarded literary as well as academic prizes, including six international psychoanalytic awards.
Email: dana.amir2@gmail.com

Cláudia Aparecida Carneiro is a PhD candidate in clinical psychology and culture at the University of Brasília. She is a psychologist and psychoanalyst, as well as associate member of the Psychoanalytic Society of Brasilia, affiliated with the IPA. She teaches at the Institute of Psychoanalysis "Virginia Leone Bicudo" of the Psychoanalytic Society of Brasilia (federal city) (SPBsb) and member of the Working Party Committee of the IPA. She is part of the editorial team of the *Calibán Journal* of the Psychoanalytic Federation of Latin America.
Email: claudiacarneiro@hotmail.com

Mona Chahoury Charabaty is a psychoanalyst and a founding member for the Lebanese Association for the Development of Psychoanalysis, where she is a training and supervising member and currently president. She continues to hold the position of Training and Supervising Member. She is a full member of the IPA. She is a lecturer at St. Joseph's University of Beirut, where she holds seminars about borderline pathologies, interpretation, and psychoanalytic traditions. Her professional experience also extends abroad: she was a member of the CPPQ in Canada and served as an Expert for the Tribunals while practicing in Montreal.
Email: chahoury.mona@gmail.com

Eliana Rigotto Lazzarini is a postdoctorate in psychology, holds a PhD and master in psychology from the University of Brasília, and is professor in the Department of Clinical Psychology at the Institute of Psychology, University of Brasília. She is a member of the Laboratory of Psychoanalysis of Subjectivation Processes (Lapsus).
Email: elianalazzarini@gmail.com

Ester Palerm Mari, MD, is a clinical psychologist and training and supervising member of the Spanish Psychoanalytic Society (SEP), a component society of the IPA. She was a member of the SEP's board of directors from 2008 to 2012. Since 2019 she has been the president of SEP. She is a COWAP member and a COWAP European consultant.
Email: palerm.mari@gmail.com

Rosine Perelberg is a psychoanalyst, training and supervising member of the British Psychoanalytic Society, visiting professor at the Psychoanalysis Unit, University College of London, and corresponding member of the Paris Psychoanalytical Society. Her books include *Psychoanalytic Understanding of Violence and Suicide* (Routledge, 1999), *Female Experience: Four Generations of British Women Psychoanalysts on Work with Women* (co-edited with Joan Raphael-Leff, Anna Freud Center, 2008), *Time, Space and Phantasy* (Routledge, 2008), *Murdered Father, Dead Father: Revisiting the Oedipus Complex* (Routledge, 2015), and *Psychic Bisexuality: A British-French Dialogue* (Routledge, 2018). In 2007 she was named one of the ten women of the year by the Brazilian National Council of Women.
Email: rperelberg@perelberg.com

Barbara Stimmel, PhD, is an assistant clinical professor of psychiatry at Mt. Sinai Medical School. She is training and supervising member and faculty of the Contemporary Freudian Society (CFS) in New York, and also belongs to the IPA. She was a former president of the Contemporary Freudian Society, former associate secretary of the IPA, she was program chair for the IPA Berlin Congress, member of the IPA Committee on Culture, she currently is also North American co-chair of the Committee on Aging.
Email: barbara.stimmel@mssm.edu

Ângela Vila-Real is a clinical psychologist and psychoanalyst. She is an associate member of the Portuguese Psychoanalytic Society and is currently part of the Society's board of directors. She holds a PhD in psychology from the University of Oporto, and was for many years assistant professor at the University Institute of Psychological Social and Life Sciences (ISPA) in Lisbon, and president and founding member of IA (Identidades e Afectos, an association for clinical and gender studies). Her main interest is in trans identities.
Email: angelavila-real@sapo.pt

Chapter 1

Introduction

Ana Teresa Vale and Nadja Tröger

As one looks upon the waves of time, humankind's origins and evolution seem to depend on a never ceasing dichotomy, being one of its most intriguing and enigmatic aspects, the field of psychic bisexuality. Psychic bisexuality implies the feminine and the masculine as unavoidable elements of psychic organization, rooted in the difference between the sexes. The feminine and masculine in each individual are in a unique and continuous articulation, thus undergoing a constant transformation process. But is it necessary to invoke bisexuality in order to understand more profoundly the vicissitudes of the feminine and the masculine? Furthermore, is it possible to capture the feminine without the masculine or vice versa?

Across all cultures, the dimensions of the feminine and the masculine find a particular way of expression, whereby the division and distinction between them may be rigid, or on the contrary dissolved, fluid, and/or liquidated, above all, in unconscious life, where dreams show a continuous mutability through infinite combinations of representations. In each individual, the feminine and the masculine correspond to a very subjective experience that constitutes one of the central aspects of this book.

The development of different life spheres, the progress of science and new technologies that entail new possibilities of self-reinvention, and the increasing ways of acting upon external and concrete realities, give rise to controversial psychosexual phenomena that exceed the scope of a binary system built on genital organization. If there ever was a way of regarding feminine and masculine as immobile entities, one is faced in present times with interchangeable positions that contribute significantly to the continuous shaping of sexual identity and its unconscious representations.

For the psychoanalytical clinical practice, this development requires new ways of untangling the complexities of psychosexual development. Presuming that one cannot exist without the other, thus viewing the feminine and the masculine as an interdependent dyad in the human psyche, this book explores various forms of how the contemporary psychoanalyst seeks to listen to the feminine and the masculine. As the ongoing identification process represents an unavoidable question in each one's (sexual) identity, similar and different

DOI: 10.4324/9781003584483-1

forms of integrating and articulating the feminine and the masculine are at stake in the transference/countertransference field.

Defining psychic bisexuality is difficult not only due to its inherent duality of psychological and biological dimensions, but also because the meaning of the feminine and the masculine are hard to apprehend and are specific to each culture and each individual. In this book, psychic bisexuality is understood particularly as a constitutive and organizing function of the psychic mind of every human being, participating on a meta-psychological level in the development and shaping of each one's psychic space. This psychic function occurs through the infinite possibilities of intrapsychic dynamics between the feminine and the masculine as abstract entities, as well as through the multiple and continuous unconscious identification processes that gain density and form within psychic growth.

Since Freud, psychic bisexuality has in the past decades become a subject of discussion. Freud himself approached bisexuality from different angles throughout his life, yet without exploring this matter to his full comprehension (Ferraro, 2001; Perelberg, 2018). He thereby opened space for a diversity of reflections on bisexuality that has not only enriched psychoanalytic thinking, but also unleashed passionate discussions and controversies that range, especially in Western contemporaneous societies, from the appreciation of the concept of psychic bisexuality to the impetus of its – at least partial – banishment (Rapoport, 2019).

The allusion to a fate that results from the physically visible on the outside, opposed to a hidden and unknown place on the inside, provides the ground for a tension between the concrete and the abstract, between the external reality of solid matter and the internal dimension, with its very own laws and layers.

Whereas Freud oscillated between the biological and psychic layers of bisexuality, David (1975) focused on its creative aspect, thereby shifting the concept to a metaphoric level that confers a mediatic role on psychic bisexuality. From a terminological point of view, this author emphasizes the conjunction of opposites expressed in the meeting of *bi* (two) with *sex*, which comes from *separe* (to separate), and which reflects, in its semantic richness, the infinite variety contained in bisexual phantasmatics.

According to David, in psychoanalysis, bisexuality is related to psychic organizations that depend on many factors and cannot be seen as merely linked to the vestigial presence in an individual of a particular gender of certain characteristics of the other gender. The author proposes the concept of a pregenital (pre-oedipal) psychic bisexuality, one that describes early introjection of sexual differentiation and emphasizes the bisexuality's positive and creative aspects inherent to the unfolding of desire, phantasy, and internal object, that are embedded in the mother-infant's interplay (David, 1975, 1992).

The mediating quality of bisexuality is expressed in a bifacial way. On the one hand, the difference between the sexes in external reality can be transposed to an imaginary interior and, consequently, to phantasmatic life and dreams. On the other hand, psychic bisexuality manifests itself as a united duality of feminine and masculine traits.

As bisexuality is evolving into a meta-psychological concept, new lines of theoretical thoughts are drawn, which contribute significantly to a more profound understanding of the psychic and sexual integration process, having important clinical implications. Furthermore, these new perspectives develop along with important social and cultural changes that relate to self-determination and emancipation. In that sense and according to Schaeffer (2011), the articulation between the feminine and the masculine corresponds to a mental creation that entails acknowledgement and acceptance of otherness, whereas the phallic/castrated dichotomy sustains social structures and power relationships. Considering the relationship between active – passive and feminine – masculine, Pederson (2018), suggests that the distinction between active and passive is independent of the distinction between masculine and feminine. Furthermore, according to the author, there are both male and female positions at both poles, resulting in four basic libidinal configurations.

The shift of psychic bisexuality to a symbolic level allows for working psychoanalytically in two different, yet interconnected ways, that may complement each other. The first concerns the identification with unconscious feminine and masculine representations, that trace back to the early introjection process. With respect to the ongoing work of transference and countertransference, psychic bisexuality is continuously present, insofar as each element of the analytic pair carries inside his/her idiosyncratic experience of the feminine/masculine relationship, which is engaged in the unconscious communication of the analytic pair. The second way relates to psychic bisexuality as a mediatic and mental function.

Both perspectives are intimately related to intrapsychic dynamics and can therefore be regarded as being crucial for the transition from a bi- to a tri-dimensional space that invokes the notion of thirdness.

The analytic third or intersubjective third, as conceived by Ogden (2004), arises as a third subjectivity that implies a dialectical relationship between the individual subjectivities of the analytic pair and intersubjectivity. Both the subjectivity of the analyst and that of the analysand are mutually engaged within what he defines as a *primary intersubjectivity* or primary undifferentiation, a pre-subjective and intersubjective level of existence that allows the singularities of each of the subjects in the analytic pair to emerge. The intersubjective third comprises duality and is simultaneously engendered by it, because it is the consequence of the dynamics resulting from the "experience" of the third by each of the subjects in the analytic pair, and not just the relationship between subjects.

In analogy with the transition from bi- to tri-dimensional psychic space, this development of intersubjectivity opens space for a new perspective on the transference-countertransference field.

The notion of the third manifests itself throughout this book in manifold ways. Of course, first and foremost, it is inherent to psychoanalytical function, which is revealed through the elaboration of psychic bisexuality by the analytic pair, as illustrated by several of the clinical vignettes the reader will find in the book. While the unconscious communication of the analytic pair is unfolding, each subjective experience of the feminine and the masculine contributes to the *rêverie* process, allowing for a fluidity of feminine and masculine representations. Consequently, internal representations can be submitted to complex transformation processes toward new emotional experiences.

Nevertheless, the notion of polarity remains important for psychoanalytic thinking. With respect to the relation between bisexuality and development, various authors emphasize psychic bisexuality in a pre-genital spectrum within the primal homosexual mother-daughter relationship (primary femininity), where a binary logic contributes to the structuring of psychic bisexuality through the rhythms of coming and going, inside and outside, receptivity and penetration, which unfold in the early mother-infant relationship (Fiorini, 2018; Gibeault, 1993).

In Winnicott's work, the idea of a feminine/masculine duality in both sexes appears in association with different psychic qualities, being the "pure feminine elements" related to the experience of "being," whereas the masculine elements refer to psychic properties of "doing" (Winnicott, 1971).

Taking into account the possibilities of psychic dynamics in a tri-dimensional space, the third is considered in different theoretical conceptualizations of psychic bisexuality that, on the one hand, conceive the third to exist in the psychic space of the mother in a configuration of primitive triangulation, as it is to be found in the concepts of "*father as mother*" (Ogden, 1987), or in a conception of the negative according to Green's contribution through the figure "*the other of the object*" (Green, 1999).

On the other hand, and regarding psychic bisexuality as a mental function, the third is an indispensable element in its mediatic function. In this context, Bion (1970) conceives of psychic space as an unknowable universe that is based on the interrelational presence of the dual elements, container and contained, which are designated by the female and male symbols ($\female$ and $\male$), that exceed sexual implications by being apprehended as hypothetical entities. Intra- and interpsychic life are generated in a constant oscillation between $\female$ and $\male$, whose relationship is mediated by the positive and negative quality of emotional links (Bion, 1970).

Following this line of thinking, but conferring to the notion of the third an even greater expression, Birksted-Breen (1996) comprehends the *a priori* knowledge as to be related not only to the breast, but also to the penis, conceiving a model of a tripartite world of the mother. For the author, containment implies a maternal function – receiving empathically the baby's/analysand's projections – as well as a paternal function – taking a perspective on this – so that containment entails the aspect of bisexuality. The binary logic is surpassed insofar as that the opposites (masculine and feminine, good and bad, inside and outside, etc.) can be viewed from an encompassing perspective, rather than only from a mutually exclusive one. The structuring and linking function of the penis in the mother's mind constitutes the notion of a mental bisexuality that contrasts with the phallus, which Birksted-Breen relates to a pre-symbolic mode of thinking.

The approach to bisexuality as a mental function that traces back to the origins of psychic life, allows for a more profound understanding of the unconscious communication process unfolding in the analytic pair, harboring the pre-symbolic and structuring levels.

Finally, the relation between psychic bisexuality and gender identity is considered, whereby the latter has become increasingly debated in contemporaneous societies, as self-determination can be expressed through different forms of self-experience and even materialized by undergoing a concrete transformation of the body. One of this theme's fundamental problem lies perhaps in the circumstance that earliest psychoanalytic reflections preceded a clear differentiation between sex and gender, so that, unlike psychic bisexuality, it is difficult to approach gender identity without the notion of splitting or dichotomy. If gender identity implies the sense of femininity or masculinity as ground-building for the belief of being feminine or masculine, it seems closer to the need for a conscious circumscription than to the ambiguity and paradoxical phenomena of unconscious life. In this line of thought, psychic bisexuality is challenged by the vicissitudes of a gender identity that is not congruent with stereotyped references that build the ground for common social and cultural beliefs.

This book originally began in December 2019, when the COWAP Conference titled "The Feminine Within" was held in Lisbon. This conference brought together a number of colleagues, many of them authors of the chapters in the book, to discuss the concept of psychic bisexuality in the light of the contemporary world and then current psychoanalytic thought. The organization committee immediately started to gather the material, and we take the opportunity to thank our colleagues Edviges Guerreiro, Maria Conceição Simões, Conceição Tavares de Almeida, Ângela Vila-Real, and Teresa Abreu, who initiated this process.

But, as we all know, the COVID-19 pandemic hit the world a few months after the conference and disorganized many plans, disrupting many projects, not to mention the personal lives of all of us. The book project was put on hold for a certain time, and it was only in 2024 that the current editors took it up again. But time had passed, and the material needed a fresh editorial look, which we offered, in collaboration with the Women and Psychoanalysis Book Series Board, who we also thank for all the support and effort put into the making.

The book is divided in two sections – Part I, "Power, difference, and complementarity," assembles five chapters from different authors under the umbrella of the relationship between masculine and feminine in its several forms – from a situation where the two are opposed to one another, to a hierarchical relationship where one is deemed to be superior to the other, to the possibility of complementarity, where one enriches the other and as such both may grow. The second section, Part II, "Challenges in the construction of a gender and sexual identity," is composed of seven chapters from different authors. It focuses on the conundrums of gender and sexual identity and how the concept of psychic bisexuality may help the contemporary analyst to navigate this complex but timely topic.

Part I opens with Conceição Tavares de Almeida's chapter, Chapter 2, titled "Mind the gap: Reflections on the feminine and psychic bisexuality," where the author postulates that psychic bisexuality is always present in the transference-countertransference relationship, summoning the analyst's gender and sexual identity. Focusing on how the feminine is built in a dialectic relationship with the masculine, the clinical vignettes are particularly poignant, showing the analyst at work with these very delicate issues of identity and self-representation.

In Chapter 3, "Psychic bisexuality in the construction of subjectivity," Cláudia Aparecida Carneiro and Eliana Rigotto Lazzarini take the notion of psychic bisexuality in its mediating function in subjective processes and in the construction of individual autonomy. Psychic bisexuality is understood as an organizer of identificatory movements that participate in the construction of the person's uniqueness, his/her internal space, the possibility of integrating (or not) internal objects, and the recognition of the third. The authors take an overview on how psychic bisexuality is built throughout human life, revisiting classic as well as contemporary psychoanalytic authors.

In the next chapter, Chapter 4, titled "The feminine side of the force: The elaboration of the feminine identity," by Ana Teresa Vale, we find a reflection on the elaboration of psychic bisexuality in analysis, which will necessarily engage the analyst's unconscious representations and her own psychic bisexuality. The author presents a moving case of a patient in her twenties, that comes to analysis with a strong unconscious conviction that men are strong, and women are weak; therefore, she maintained a bisexual representation of herself, believing unconsciously that she could be both. Struggling to find her own answers to the meaning of feminine and masculine, and what kind of relationship they may establish with each other, as the analysis unfolded the patient ended up finding her own power as a woman.

In the same vein, Barbara Stimmel, in Chapter 5, "Bisexuality: Freud and Woolf meet," postulates that the fantasy of being both man and woman is present in all of us and gains an important meaning for creativity of any kind. Overlapping Virginia Woolf and Sigmund Freud, the author holds that Woolf was the first to talk openly about the existence of homosexual longing in all women (in psychoanalytic terms, we could think of it as primary homosexuality), parallel to Freud's conception of bisexuality as a building block of human condition.

Part I ends with Chapter 6, Rosine Perelberg's "Passion and melancholia, red and black: The vicissitudes of the sexual in an analytic process," where psychic bisexuality is linked to the uncanny, both fascinating and frightening, in the sense that sexuality is only incompletely transformed into psychic reality. In this chapter, we can follow the analyst working with the profound unconscious layers of the sexual and its connection to melancholic aspects of the feminine, that find their way into the transference-countertransference relationship through the repetition compulsion.

Part II, "Challenges in the construction of a gender and sexual identity," opens with Chapter 7, "Crossing borders: Persona, mask, who am I?" by Mona Chahoury Charabaty, focusing on the issues of borders and their crossing, limits and their transgression, identity, and identification. Using a clinical vignette, the author lets us inside the mind of the analyst working in the session, trying to get in touch and understand the experience and unconscious representations of a patient coming from a different community than her own. Calling forth her psychic bisexuality, her experience of growing up as a girl, her own representations of men and women, and of the relationship between them, the analyst allows the patient to express all the suffering, hatred, repression, and frustration she harbored, which for the patient was linked to her being a woman.

In Chapter 8, "Integration of the feminine and the masculine in the analysis of a woman," Ester Palerm Mari explores the use of the internet, namely dating apps, by men and women, proposing that the way people interact with these reflects their unconscious representation of the masculine and the feminine, and of the relationship between them. Through a clinical vignette, where we can follow the evolution of a woman in analysis, we can see how the patient's use of the dating apps and her expectations and understanding of the interactions happening in this context, will evolve and change during the course of the analytic process, mainly linked to the transformation of her self-representation, her psychic bisexuality, and her unconscious representations of the parental couple.

In Chapter 9, "Masculinity as appearance," Silvia Acosta explores the relationship between unprocessed grief and transgenerational trauma in enabling or hindering the maturation process of an adult male's sexuality. The author argues that previous traumas and rigid family mandates may hinder the elaboration of psychic bisexuality, which in turn may promote the experience of a dissociated sexual life and a conflicting expression of identity. The author illustrates the conundrums of the construction of the masculine identity with a case presentation.

Luz Abatangelo Stürzenbaum offers us her reflection on today's clinical practice in Chapter 10, "Psychic bisexuality and its pulsional vicissitudes," highlighting the shortcomings of binary thinking to address some manifestations of psychic suffering in contemporary patients. Coming from a Lacanian perspective, the author postulates that the concept of psychic bisexuality gives us a broader view on the choice of object, the processes of identification, masculine and feminine representations, and the possible ways in which all these elements may be articulated. A clinical vignette is portrayed, where there is a homosexual choice of object, which does not prevent the putting into action of heterosexual motions, which in turn come as a response to a certain kind of psychic suffering.

"When I look into your eyes: An approach to psychic bisexuality in the case of role reversal" is the title of Chapter 11 by Nadja Tröger, who explores the situation of role reversal, taking into account the notion of ambiguity as an equivalent of undifferentiation. The author reflects on the possible articulation between the vicissitudes of the ambiguous parts that inhabit the mother's psyche, leaving the patient stuck or even lost in the integration process of psychic bisexuality. Through a clinical vignette, we are able to see how, within the psychoanalytic relationship, this feeling of in-between may become more differentiated, thus opening space for creating representations that can be put to use for working through the individual's identification process.

Ângela Vila-Real brings us Chapter 12, "Of gender and bisexuality," based on the author's clinical experience with transgender patients. Reflecting on the countertransferential dynamics triggered during sessions with two of her patients, the author postulates two possible relations between gender and bisexuality, with different unconscious meanings and different functions concerning identity. In both, differences seemed to be traumatic, but in one patient gender issues seemed to arise secondarily to an intense castration anxiety, while in the other there was a clear differentiation of a paradoxical nature, linked to an early gender organization.

Part II, and the book, end with Dana Amir's chapter, Chapter 13, on "A chronicle of mother-daughter envy: Elena Ferrante's *Lost Daughter*." The author states that gender dichotomy is probably the primary dichotomy internalized in human thinking, which acts as a prototype for all the later dichotomies, inaugurating dichotomous thinking in general. This dichotomy always harbors rigid, saturated elements, along with more flexible, unsaturated ones. Analyzing the protagonist of Elena Ferrante's *Lost Daughter*, Leda is seen as a woman trapped in the excesses of gender dichotomy, without any capacity to create a more flexible gender space that could allow free and creative internal and external movement. The entrapment within gender dichotomy explains, in the author's interpretation, the occurrences described in the book.

This book offers a multifaceted discussion of the concept of psychic bisexuality and its application in today's psychoanalytic practice, with multiple points of view coming from authors from different cultural backgrounds and diverse psychoanalytic traditions. Simultaneously, the book embraces an intersubjective perspective in psychoanalytical clinical practice, which is expressed through various descriptions of each author's individual elaboration of the countertransference process. This diversity opens the field to an array of points of view that enriches our understanding of such a complex concept, and of the complex phenomena we face as analysts nowadays. Nonetheless, the common ground remains untouched, with the importance every author gives to unconscious processes and to the need to better understand psychic suffering, in order to help our patients to navigate this delicate issue of identity.

References

Bion, W. (1970). *Attention and interpretation*. Karnac Books.

Birksted-Breen, D. (1993). *The gender conundrum: Contemporary psychoanalytic perspectives on femininity and masculinity*. Routledge.

David, C. (1975). La bisexualité psychique – Éléments d'une réévaluation. *Revue Française de Psychanalyse*, 39 (5–6), 694–856.

David, C. (1992). *La bisexualité psychique*. Éditions Payot.

Ferraro, F. (2001). Vicissitudes of bisexuality: Crucial points and clinical implications. *The International Journal of Psychoanalysis*, 82: 485–500.

Fiorini, L. (2018). *Deconstructing the feminine: Psychoanalysis, gender and theories of complexity*. Routledge.

Gibeault, A. (1993). On the feminine and the masculine: Afterthoughts on Jacqueline Cosnier's book Destins de la féminité. In D. Birksted-Breen (Ed.), *The gender conundrum: Contemporary psychoanalytic perspectives on femininity and masculinity* (pp. 166–181). Routledge.

Green, A. (1999). *The dead mother*. Routledge.

Ogden, T. (1987). The transitional oedipal relationship in female development. *The International Journal of Psychoanalysis*, 68, 485–498.

Ogden, T. (2004). The analytic third. *Psychoanalytic Quarterly*, 73 (1), 167–195.

Pederson, T. (2018). *The economics of the libido: Psychic bisexuality, the superego and the centrality of the Oedipus complex*. Routledge.

Perelberg, R. (2018). *Psychic bisexuality: A British-Frenh dialogue*. Routledge.

Rapoport, E. (2019). *From psychoanalytic bisexuality to bisexual psychoanalysis: Desiring in the real*. Routledge.

Schaeffer (2011). *The universal refusal: A psychoanalytic exploration of the feminine sphere and its repudiation*. Routledge.

Winnicott, D. ([1971] 2011). Transitional objects and transitional phenomena. In L. Caldwell & A. Joyce (Eds.), *Reading Winnicott* (pp. 99–103). Routledge.

Part I

Power, difference, and complementarity

Chapter 2

Mind the gap

Reflections on the feminine and psychic bisexuality

Conceição Tavares de Almeida

Introduction

Sitting at the breakfast table, bathed in the sweet softness of an autumn Sunday morning, my youngest son, then 11 years old, unleashes his provocation as a riddle: "Mum, do you know that I've got something you don't?" Emboldened by the curricular science program and concerned by the first signs of puberty, he's telling us of his discovery concerning the difference between the sexes, one that he regards as an advantage of the male over the female. Prompted by our indifference to his theory, he repeats himself and tries to rope his older brother into the argument for support, who, in response to his puerile insistence, says only: "Can't you see that they're the same thing? Men and women. It's all the same thing! The difference is only on the outside; inside we're all the same."

At that moment, apart from feeling reassured that I hadn't raised my children poorly, I felt inspired by this snapshot of daily life to think about psychoanalysis, theory, and clinical practice.

A series of factors, as much personal as professional, have contributed to the development of my interest in this subject: being a woman, becoming a mother during training, undergoing two analyses, the first with a man and the second with a woman, and experiencing the same situations in my practice (being the second analyst for women who had started their treatment with a male colleague). Yet it is not only this ... Within psychoanalytic themes, questions about creativity, subjectivity, intuition, and vulnerability have always worked as attractors and, with time, have gained consistency, weight, and context. All this led me to perceive the analytical meeting as a ground on which a battle of strength is simultaneously a generator and a result of representations, not isolating the transferential and countertransferential dynamics from this understanding.

In May 2015, at the *75th Congrès de Psychoanalystes de Langue Française*, titled "Le sexual infantile et ses destins," using a countertransferential dream as a source, the theme was addressed in the work "Identité de genre dans la paire analytic." There, the dream element of "shaving the beard" served as a

DOI: 10.4324/9781003584483-3

motto to reflect on the dimensions of gender and generation, as much in terms of development as of challenges in the analytical process. It was interesting to think how analytical listening, from a narrative about a trivial fact from the masculine universe, evoked thoughts in the psychoanalyst that are singularly linked to questions of gender and psychic bisexuality.

Psychic bisexuality, a classical concept revived by its current relevance, is called forth in the current public and clinical conversation, which is precisely where the roles of men and women and their consequences in the labor market, education, sexuality, conjugality, fertility, and parenthood, are challenging us to make sense of new configurations.

The ideas developed and defended in this work are supported by clinical research, whose selection followed the criteria of free association, often from a common element that brings relevance to the listening of the contents in question. Similarly, the "beard" associations arise surrounding aspects related to both identity issues and feminine and masculine cultural classic representations, such as the choice of one's name, motor vehicles, mysterious boxes, and beauty accessories. The intention is to reflect on how feminine and masculine psychoanalytical concepts are present in both sexes and how these aspects are integrated in the psychoanalyst, according to his/her gender, as well as his/her feminine or masculine analytical function, throughout the analysis.

Psychoanalysis and the feminine

Psychoanalysis has always been controversial. At the time, Freud's discoveries regarding the unconscious and sexuality shocked sensibilities with their boldness and, a century on, some of his ideas surrounding the feminine and sexuality run the risk, for some, of seeming outrageous, and, for many, outdated. However, the essence of his legacy remains a fracturing thought at its origin, subversive in its destiny. This continues to be the place of psychoanalysis: questioning, unease, and listening in search of meaning.

What if psychoanalysis refers to the clinic and, in this way, to the (inter) subjective? What is its setting in social and cultural space? Times call for intervention in a transversal space directed to the differing plans and manifestations of the human phenomenon. The challenge of thinking of the social context positions us as agents to the service of a citizenship that does not deny its disruptive vocation or its humanist ethic and whose tools provide us with access to the understanding of both the external and the internal, favoring the mutual enrichment of both. One may ask: What does this have to do with the actual concept of psychic bisexuality?

From the way health policies shape our perception of mental health narratives and landscapes, fantasies about the relational matrix that makes up our world and the resulting identities are the space where representations are permanently forged. In our favor, we possess a tool that gives us access to these raw materials in a configuration open to repetition and transformation.

Let us return to the social fabric – violence, intimacy, and femininity. The facts and figures speak for themselves: violence within couples and crimes against women are in the order of the day. In this multi-causal phenomenon, unconscious beliefs tend to repeat, ideas transported through time, preconceptions rooted in our minds and ritualized in our traditions.

In "Confusion of Tongues," Ferenczi ([1933] 1992) looks afresh at the problem of trauma to propose an explicative model on the effect of the psychic violence perpetrated by an adult on a child. Not so much in opposition to Freud's ideas but more as a complementary dialogue, mutually rich and fertile, making for a "good primal scene," Ferenczi calls attention to the impact of the environment in forming an individual. In the conceptual framework, it becomes a precursor to the object relations model, which later, through concepts of projective identification, broadens the knowledge of the phenomena of identification and unconscious communication and its influence regarding technique through the study of countertransference.

This chapter introduces the notion of identification with the aggressor as a form of psychic violation, whose devastating effects will not be felt so much as a defensive value but as one of survival, which explains the perpetuation of the abuse. In the author's view – whereby there are three underlying steps of a mental operation: identification/introjection, confusion, and denial – it seems easy to make a connection with the proposal that Virginia Ungar, in her lecture "From the Glass Slipper to the Glass Ceiling" (2019), presented to us regarding the mechanisms of self-regulation whereby a woman's place is maintained, transmitted, and converted by women themselves, through unconscious and self-prophetic beliefs. In the same way, it is not hard for us to extrapolate the model on trauma and psychic violation from its private sphere to the social and cultural space with regard to women, where shame and guilt dull and darken both desire and ambition, like a shadow of the malign object, to which they remain loyal. In parallel, they often act with rage and rivalry that cannot be exercised otherwise in the relationship with their children, strengthening, in an unconscious, transgenerational way, the model of identification.

Virginia Ungar parallels these two levels to explain how they are self-perpetuating. In the social reality of today, which is still strongly patriarchal, misogyny rules, stereotypes persist, and inequalities exist. On the internal level, myths and fantasies associated with the woman's role reiterate the phallocentric model, justifying its inequality as an unchangeable condition (Ungar, 2019).

In free association, the word "glass" placed two more elements into the equation: glass bell and glass ceiling. The image of *snow globes* came to my mind, decorative objects that populate the fantasy of children and that are a kind of aquarium where space invites us to a safe place and time has stopped: shake this globe, and a type of snow will fall and magically cover its imprisoned interior. This world, the stronghold of childhood, made me think of the expression "glass bell" as a protective yet limiting continent of the primal and maternal object. This element led me to *Citizen Kane*, the rise and fall of a powerful man with "glass ceilings," a masterpiece of cinema where the vulnerability of the relationship with childhood is condensed into that image of the snow globe. The climax of the trauma in this object, embedded in the mysterious name "Rosebud" (Kane's childhood sled), is a conjuring of the feminine, erotic/transgressor, and the maternal/traumatic, lost, and idealized primary object.

On the other hand, one can associate "glass ceilings" with the biblical representation that becomes the core of a civil moral, in which we shouldn't throw stones since everyone has their vulnerability. This precursor is a Christian reference to respect for others, according to which all people are equal in the face of good and evil. In psychoanalytical terms, glass ceilings could correspond to the development of a depressive position, relinquishing pathological projective identification in an integrating movement of strength and fragility, of envy and gratitude.

Virginia Ungar refers to fairytales' rich symbolism and matrixial function or identifications. On the subject of "Sleeping Beauty," I highly recommend the "Maleficent" cinematographic version to all those who have not seen it. In it, there is a return to the sense of primary love and hate contained in narcissistic and Oedipal issues naturally underlying the classic version, repairing the primary conflict in which the "true first love" is, effectively, the link to the primal maternal feminine. Surviving archaic drive destructiveness, the lost mother is genuinely the stepmother who can be returned to the realm of the good enough, internal, and generous object that shapes identifications in terms of nurturing one's narcissism and, in turn, influences the quality of object relations and subsequent investment (Almeida, 2019).

But how are these elements expressed in psychoanalytic practice? The implicit condemnation of women to a place of submission, the rivalry that is horizontally established with other women, or the fear of vacillating or failing, and the shame associated with the emotional expression are some of the elements that we hear or intuit in the patients' narratives, sometimes taking the form of counterphobic movements, exhibitory behavior, or melancholic accusations. The feminine as a social and semantic category is frequently taken as weak, a symbol of castration, jealous, sneaky, frivolous, and often denied, rejected, and contradicted. In that symbolic order, there is a tendency for the introjection of guilt and an alien struggle that, if there is no access to an elaboration, allows for the identification with the aggressor, as well as the alienating projection of that fragility, and of that unbearable denial.

Case I

Victor presents himself as "bisexual," referring to the orientation of his desire. At the same time, he admits that this statement expresses his confusion over his identity, something he hopes to resolve. His name's choice follows his mother, Victoria, with whom he was compared throughout his childhood. Although presenting themselves as a traditional family, he finds the parents' marriage "a farce," which probably hides homosexual issues within both of them. Both were born from an unknown father and had a problematic bond with their mother (abandonment and controlling relationships). Trapped by his transgenerational heritage, the feminine and masculine identifications seem compromised by continued unspoken transgenerational conflicts, attaining both the physical and psychic levels. Listening to his suffering gives substance to the idea of grief as a struggle, since his internal world, populated by malign objects, finds itself in a constant battle.

Initially, his dreams show a maternal continent with intense rawness, partial and fragmented elements of internal organs, decapitations, and mutilations. Throughout the analysis, these elements transform into feminine and masculine elements generally in conflict, in a rough triangulation, namely through identifications at shallow levels (clothes, tasks) or through choices he must make. In a recurring dream in which he is being pursued, he rides a powerful motorbike, but he encounters a wall so steep that he must climb it or go around. In this affliction, the possibility later arises of climbing it in an elevator, but this presents him with a problem of connection: motorbike, elevator, himself. Later, in dreams, a child appears who he has to protect or save. The child is initially a boy but later changes into a girl. Later, he's with his mother, who takes care of both boys and girls simultaneously, with less stress. In a second dream, he wants to come to the session but gets lost in the streets and has to ask for help from his father to find his bearings. In the third one, he bumps into an actor in the street, whom his mother likes very much, who compliments his hairdo and masculine appearance, which surprises yet consoles him.

Despite the apparent suffering, the acknowledged need, and the indisputable advances in his process, Victor's adhesion to analysis was always hindered by enormous suspicion as to the unconditionality of the connection to the analyst and doubt of her interest in him. Interpreting these aspects, Victor initially reacted defensively through the trivialization or the intellectualization of the nature of that bond. The fear of destructiveness and the archaic feminine and maternal identifications were always a point on the horizon that I kept indicating. At the same time, we navigated "the coast," something that was preventing us from exploring deeper waters while planting seeds and pointing the way.

Psychoanalysis and psychic bisexuality

Freud ([1905] 1955) believed psychic bisexuality to be innate. Since, in all children, there is the desire to possess the genital organs of both mother and father, the renunciation of androgyny might be seen as a narcissistic wound. Later, the conceptualization surrounding the importance of the primal scene (Freud, [1912] 1998) would become central to the understanding of narcissism. This loving scene between parents at the beginning of life organizes the feeling of inclusion/exclusion, enunciating the identification destination.

For Klein (1952), the preparatory phantasms of the "primal scene" are etched into the psyche from the beginning. Initially, in a schizoid-paranoid position, the child will understand the necessity of the frustrated object's gratification as malign, in an incipient form of triangulation. Later, in forming the depressive position, the child will internally create the fantasy of the fertile couple (concerning both the idea of alliance and that of eroticism) as benign, able to welcome in and care for a child, a triangular function now subject to being introjected and subject to identification.

In modern psychoanalysis, starting from the most complex and broadest conceptual model of mental life, feminine and masculine categories go beyond a binary Cartesian logic, supported by the conscious perception of the differences in anatomy between the genders. Recent authors (Ogden, 1992; Faimberg, 2005; Guignard, 1996) agree that, instead of complementing each other, by default, these aspects seem to coexist in an intimately correlated way, mutually redefining each other. In the same way, the analyst's work goes beyond overcoming *imagoes*, attempting change concerning the functioning of instances and representations. The interpretation has the effect of reformulating psychic movements around new representations.

Faimberg (2005) proposes the "Oedipal configuration," distinguishing, on the one hand, the recognition of the relationship of the parents founded in differences, namely sexual, and, on the other hand, the interpretation that the subject makes of these differences. It is during the early relationship with the mother that children build the basis of their psychic bisexuality. We allow in this construction a primary level that returns to undifferentiation, to origin, to identity in terms of emotional dependence, and a secondary level that questions the unknown, that contains the triangular configuration and emotional differentiation that the "other" represents. The phantasmic presence of the other gender in the internal, maternal world will probably act as a founder of triangulation and of the possibility of the organization of psychic bisexuality. The idea of the "father-in-the-head-of-the-mother" (Ogden, 1992) is an essential element in objectifying psychic life and the adhesion to new investments and the creative matrix of future memories, in the sense of Bion.

Guignard (1996) argues that the basis of psychic bisexuality lies in the way that the mother experiences her sexuality, which includes mental space for the father, in that he represents the difference present in the understanding of the "primary feminine." But the failure of this process also depends on the way that the child combines their fantasies, namely jealousies, regarding the connection between the couple, as well as their ability to renounce the qualities and privileges of the other sex. Suppose the perception of this revelation is confusing, conflictual, devalued, or attacked. In that case, the child introjects a disharmonious couple, incompatible, destructive, or a non-couple, compromising the integration of the heterosexual aspects and the creation of a depressive position regarding these aspects.

Listening to transference, through the analysis of countertransference, allows the analytical meeting to work as a third party, conferring it the value of construction instead of repetition. If not as such, either the gender of the analyst would be crucial in the analysis of male/female patients, according to the subjective experience through identifications, compromising access to the complementary, or this access would take root in a presumption of the neutrality of the analyst, whose asepsis would favor, in the exclusion of difference, the phantasy of child omnipotence.

Case 2

Sofia came to me due to a generalized anxiety with episodes of panic. In her story, she presents herself as someone who was denied access to her father, describing a mother who constantly competed with her. As an intern, she struggles to get recognition from her tutor, competing with her male and female colleagues. Crying, she talks of her masculine and feminine representations, based on her fears that sway between being too competitive or too seductive, and how both solutions prompt feelings of guilt. I offer her the box of tissues that, by coincidence, are divided into two colors, and as they are pulled out, you can see that they are either blue or pink. Realizing this, Sofia comments and laughs. Interested in knowing more about psychoanalysis, she started a course to learn about it, guided by a male teacher. She then dreams of stabbing her stepmother – who is a psychologist – in the back and, in the same session, referring to the course, she makes a Freudian slip and says "appointment" instead of "class."

In the following session, she dreams of having five sessions per week, which switch between that teacher and me. At that point, I suggested that we begin an analysis. Later on, she speaks of her desire and fear of one day becoming a mother and tells me about the name choices for her children, realizing that if she has a girl, it's her paternal grandmother's name, which makes her feel uneasy. That weekend, Sofia gets confused about whether she has taken the contraceptive pill or not and wonders if she could be pregnant. She dreams that she is in a pharmacy with two women to do a pregnancy test, and she is presented with two options: a conventional test and a mysterious wooden object, a type of chest with unknown contents, that intrigues her greatly.

Case 3

Clara's father died in a car accident. The theme of grief is one of the most significant aspects of her analysis, particularly as she uncovers a transgenerational issue linking a series of tragic accidental losses of men in her family. Accessing her father, however, has always been a difficult task, complicated by the ambivalence present in mother-daughter relationships. In a dream, Clara navigates a path filled with riddles and obstacles on a motorcycle driven by her mother, where the purpose of the journey shifts from escaping a threat to embarking on an exhilarating adventure. While recounting this dream, Clara emphasizes the immense pleasure that arises from trust in that relationship, manifesting as a primal sensation of "heat in the belly from skin-to-skin contact." Having experienced a troubled marriage thus far, largely due to her guilt over Oedipal conflicts, processing transference and countertransference has enabled her to integrate ambivalence, rivalry, and compassion with both men and women, fostering stronger connections. In a subsequent dream, three generations of women appear, and she faces an intriguing yet troubling box whose key is held by her current husband.

The identifying issue calls on the different qualities of the feminine and masculine, according to the sex and gender identity of the analytical pair. The work on identifications of the primary maternal object is the increasingly complex matrix of acquisitions, combined with the relationship between gender and the parental couple. Or rather, whether it is a boy or a girl, identifications become complex according to the biological nature, as with representation and more or less unconscious phantasmatics, which are active in the relationship with the other. If we call for a model of psychic sexuality more in line with Freud, we find a lot of conflicting phenomena involved in childhood sexual development. Bionian literature allows us to understand that the identifying models are not yet complete in those classifications and that feminine and masculine, maternal and paternal, are mental functions and categories of apprehension of external reality and transformation of internal reality, according to the container-contained model.

Both models are essential in clinical practice. The analyst must attune themself to the nature of the identifications transferred to the analytical space, using the quality of affect at stake in the session and the process as an indicator. They must position themself in terms of the conflict present in the material, adjust their listening, and choose the valuable interpretation.

Case 4

Ramiro is a young man, 24 years of age, who grew up in a small city, where he was always an excellent student, and now he has come to Lisbon to begin a promising business career. He develops a depressive state, with some anxiety, but shows rapid improvements and a notable capacity for insight. While criticizing his roommate, he says, "I don't know why I'm not a mother yet." We laugh together, recognizing and delving into the psychic truth and possibilities of identification with the maternal object this Freudian slip reveals.

In this sense, the bisexuality of the analyst is unavoidable, always being summoned to the relationship. Transferential listening of pre-genital or more Oedipal material, for example, calling for different needs in questions of love, aggressiveness, and conflict, has a necessarily different translation. The projection onto the analyst of the maternal/paternal representations depends on whether the analysand is male or female, the transferential/countertransferential atmosphere, and the way both sexes or functions combine in the analytical space, which are the construction blocks of bisexuality. In this sense, freedom, plasticity, authenticity, and honesty toward the other are absolute prerequisites for emotional growth.

The feminine and psychic bisexuality

Listening to patients' psychic bisexuality resonates with the analyst's emotional experience. By analyzing their countertransference, the analyst becomes immersed in the scene, connecting with their original phantasms: pre-genital, primal scene, and childhood sexual identifications. From this perspective, the analyst can perceive the flaws in maternal and paternal identification (Ogden, 1992).

In this framework, the analyst is presented as a relational object in both its actual and sexualized dimensions, that is, capable of expressing themself and their gender identity. Thus, femininity and masculinity serve primarily as mental functions that facilitate the formation of new thoughts. Within the context of analysis, interpretation/penetration or listening/containment refers to the combination of elements that enable change.

Similarly, it can be argued that the foundational triangulation of otherness and difference exists within the analyst and the analytical situation through the K link. More specifically, the primary loyalty of the analytical pair is to the truth. From Green's (1993) perspective, the work of the negative stimulates the symbolic inscription of difference and its essence. Consequently, the potential for healing and transformation encompasses not only the internal representations of binary pairs related to objects (feminine/masculine, maternal/paternal) and identifications (primary/secondary, narcissistic/object) but also the actual object that exists within a multidimensional dynamic that flows through the interaction of two unconscious minds.

On the other hand, gender differences in transferential relationships are influenced by identifications based on perceptual aspects, sensory realities, or more imagined constructs. Therefore, through transference, women, in their interactions with the analyst, show the potential for identification rooted in gender identity, which is more clearly supported by perceptual elements of reality. In men, this identifying movement inevitably recalls the paternal *imago* introjected within the analyst.

Case 6

Serafim, who has been in analysis for over five years, dreams of a woman in a "lovely blue dress." Only during free association does he recall the aesthetic impression made, as the analyst had been wearing blue the day before. Only then does Serafim, who is homosexual, tell me about an aspect of his childhood that had been consciously hidden until then: "I always found women very beautiful and always felt fascinated by the female sex; as a child, I was very curious and wanted to try on my mother's clothes, but the terror of her finding out paralyzed me." Bringing this issue to the transferential space, Serafim confessed,

> I always thought you're a beautiful woman; I never dared to compliment you, nor even to mention it for fear that you would say that, after all, I'm not homosexual or that, after all, I want to be a woman because that's something I never wanted! I am certain that I am a homosexual man, and I'm fine like that.

Intersubjective relationships are always triangular, founded on affect and its representations. We accept, therefore, a psychic flexibility whereby the roles are not confined to perceptive evidence but overlay each other in a permanent construction of pictograms, according to Ferro (2009).

Nevertheless, it is fundamental to take into account that the actual construction and consolidation of gender identity depends on the unconscious vicissitudes of that same process, in which the connection of the woman to the feminine by way of maternal or paternal recognition (and vice versa) allows different levels of identification and compromises in the construction of one's identity. Childhood omnipotence, maintained by the strength of avoiding the reality testing, more than keeping it forbidden, aims to protect from becoming aware of one's narcissistic inferiority.

Thus, from the glass bell, a childhood place, protected and eternal recourse of sensitivity, tenderness, abandonment, and the need for containment, to glass ceilings, aware of one's fragility, of an autonomy constructed from interdependence, a precursor of reciprocity and mutual respect. If this glass recovers its specular capacity, in the sense of updating the container-contained function, whereby the feminine and masculine combined are, in their difference, that which nourishes and allows us all to be who we are, in the uniqueness that, in placing us on the same level, allows for intimacy to become universal.

Some words carry the weight of time. However, despite unconscious determinism, the knowledge that psychoanalysis offers the possibility of change also comes with the responsibility of choice. While the traumatic forces of the outside world can be inflexible and intransigent, a lack of limits and references in excessive permissiveness may lead to equally destructive outcomes. We observe phenomena in the social sphere that tend to establish extreme positions, sometimes descending into a conflict-free fantasy. The opposition, along with reactive training toward authoritarianism or Victorian morals, risks acting out these fantasies, which do not support protective growth nor organize the primary anxieties raised by identifications.

The insistence on positioning the debate between feminine and masculine as equally important does not mean the annulment of their uniqueness. In the same way, to read into that difference an assumption of power according to domination/submission logic detracts and, in this way, wraps the problem around incessant repetition. Let us not take away from the feminine that which confers identity. In the black continent, the feminine evokes the return to the maternal, a dizzying and fusional matrix, but to give support and show the way. That feminine, continent, bodily, concave, subjective, fertile, vital, receptive, mysterious, powerful, creative, and organized through primary and secondary identifications resides inside us. Representing the link, the mentioned separation. Once welcomed, recognized, esteemed, activated, and integrated, combined with a masculine fruit of these syntheses and struggles, it establishes the conditions to be the matrix of infinite possibilities that could enlighten new parts of our minds.

Combined and creatively integrated, the feminine and the masculine generate life, culture, and humor. Psychic bisexuality seems to ultimately represent a wish to consolidate the representation of these qualitative elements as an enabler of the progressive movement, in which the internal child is nourished by the possibility of access to the masculine in the maternal continent and where identifications with the feminine persist as a source of sensitivity that humanizes us to ourselves and others beyond fear of confusion.

References

Almeida, C. T. (2019). Da redoma de vidro aos telhados de vidro: Considerações sobre o feminino e a fragilidade. Comment on Virginia Ungar's From the glass slipper to the glass ceiling. Conference held in ISPA, Lisbon, October 2019.

Faimberg, H. (2005). *The telescoping of generations: Listening to the narcissistic links between generations.* Routledge.

Faimberg, H. (2013). *Transmission de la vie psychique entre générations.* Dunod.

Ferenczi, S. ([1933] 1992). Confusão de línguas entre os adultos e a criança. In *Obras completas – Psicanálise IV* (pp. 97–106). Martins Fontes.

Ferro, A. (2009). *Campo analítico. Um conceito clínico.* Artmed.

Freud, S. ([1905] 1955). Three essays on the theory of sexuality. In *The Standard Edition of the Complete Psychological Works of Sigmund Freud, Volume II* (pp. 123–246). Hogarth Press.

Freud, S. ([1912] 1998). La dynamique du transfert. In *Œuvres complètes, tome 11. Bibliothèque Sigmund Freud* (pp. 107–116). Presses Universitaires de France.

Green, A. (1993). *Le travail du négatif.* Les Édition de Minuit.

Guignard, F. (1996). *Au vif de l'infantile.* Delachaux et Niestlé.

Klein, M. ([1952] 1980). Quelques conclusions théoriques au sujet de la vie émotionnelle des bébés. In *Développements de la psychanalyse* (pp. 187–222). Presses Universitaires de France.

Ogden, T. (1992). *The primitive edge of experience.* Karnac Books.

Ungar, V. (2019). From the glass slipper to the glass ceiling. Conference held in ISPA, Lisbon, October 2019.

Chapter 3

Psychic bisexuality in the construction of subjectivity

Claudia Aparecida Carneiro and Eliana Rigotto Lazzarini

Considering the Freudian premise that psychic bisexuality inhabits us (Freud, [1905] 2016, [1930] 2010b), we seek to return to the originality of this notion, which contributed to the construction of the theory of sexuality, but focus on its impact on the constitution of subjectivity. We propose to think about what constitutes the human being as a singular subject, in which the processes of subjectivation would have the participation of psychic bisexuality as a mediator of these movements, along with other multiple variables at play in the psychic constitution.

The study of psychic bisexuality sheds light on the relationships established from the origins of psychic life and mark the subject's identificatory destinies. We understand that bisexuality participates in the construction of psychic space as an integration work imposed on the mind. In other words, in the processes of identification between the baby and his primary objects (represented by the figures of mother, father, or substitutes), psychic bisexuality would be embedded in a complex network of elaboration of these primary identifications, fantasies, and object choices. The progressive internalization of primary objects, and their integration into the psyche, would lead the subject to a recognition of otherness and difference.

Thus, we defend the idea that bisexuality is inscribed in the original psyche through the action of the object and shapes the subject's destiny in the dynamics of their identifications, fantasies, and object choices (Carneiro & Lazzarini, 2018, 2020). The elaboration of psychic bisexuality would allow the small human being to maintain one and the other object (in their parental functions) coexisting in their infantile unconscious. The non-integration of bisexual desires would produce impasses in the acceptance of difference.

Although the notion of difference may include the classical notions of sexual difference and symbolic castration, which would direct the subject to choose between one sex or the other, by revisiting the notion of psychic bisexuality, we propose considering the meaning of symbolic difference, which entails the recognition of otherness in the construction of subjectivity.

This understanding aligns with the reflection proposed by Glocer Fiorini (2001, 2017) about the concepts of diversity and difference. By discussing

DOI: 10.4324/9781003584483-4

contemporary family configurations and parenthoods, and how phenomena of subjectivation are generated in the symbolic sense, the author establishes a distinction between the categories of diversity and difference.

Diversity refers to the plurality of subjective presentations and their variants linked to sexuality and gender. The concept of difference, in turn, refers to a symbolic dimension. Glocer Fiorini (2015b) redefines the concept of sexual difference postulating that the access to difference is sustained at different levels of significance – anatomical, gendered, psychosexual, imaginary and symbolic – difference being recognition of the other.

Glocer Fiorini highlights that sexual difference is not the only key to accessing the category of *difference*. The construction of subjectivity goes beyond the logic of sexual difference, although it includes it. That is, subjective processes imply the recognition of sexual difference, but a revision of the way the notions of femininity and masculinity are interpreted is necessary. We agree with Glocer Fiorini (2015a) in stating that "the most significant issue is that the recognition of otherness and difference is inscribed in the parents, even if they are of the same sex" (p. 488).

There is a complexity of variables involved in the construction of subjectivity that needs to be recognized. Following Glocer Fiorini's (2017) proposal based on Edgar Morin's (2006) hypercomplexity paradigm, we understand that subjectivation processes should be thought from a heterogeneous and complex order, although the masculine-feminine binarism remains impregnated in culture. The logic of complexity goes beyond the binary logic of the masculine-feminine pair. But, as the author suggests, that does not mean ignoring the binarisms culturally inscribed, but rather including them in a hypercomplex logic.

The Freudian construction of psychic bisexuality gains emphasis in psychoanalytic practice, in the multiple expressions of bisexuality in the person's identificatory conflicts and in relationships with the other, particularly in the obstacles to recognizing internal objects and otherness.

If we consider that bisexual yearnings disturb a person's relationships from the beginning of their existence, we must ask whether it is necessary to choose one object to the detriment of the other. Or even, if father and mother, beyond the Oedipal problematic, could not coexist in the unconscious. The psychic constitution involves the progressive introjection of sexual polarity and its multiple variables. In this sense, psychic bisexuality participates in the construction of internal space, in a dual reference to the psychic positions of the feminine and the masculine. These references occur in relationships with parental objects or those that represent them. Thus, the internalization of primary objects would result in the coexistence of two in the psyche, in their singular or plural configurations.

The idea of a bisexuality integrated into the psyche makes it possible to move from its origins to its destinies, suggesting that bisexuality is not confined to a constitutional issue, but inscribes itself in the origins of the psyche as a product of two (the object and the other of the object), forming a third (Carneiro & Lazzarini, 2018). The nascent subject, who is a product of the relationship with the other, follows their instinctual destinies.

We will develop these ideas based on the models of Bion and Green of psychic constitution and how they conceive the notion of object from the earliest traces of the psyche. These models, within the Freudian conception of the psychic apparatus, are taken as a basis to examine the forms of psychic bisexuality in psychosexual development and the destinies that shape psychic life. The reading of contemporary authors who revisit the notion of psychic bisexuality allows us to conjecture the primary forms of bisexuality in two stages, the pre-genital and the Oedipal crossing, before following its destinies in the adult genital stage.

The dawn of psychic life

The earliest traces of the psyche are marked by the incipient action of the adult on the baby. At the origins of this rudimentary mind, the object imposes its own psychic bisexuality. Miller (2002) states that in different models of mental functioning, the polarities of masculine and feminine and the notion of a primal scene are embedded, at a moment of psychosexual organization when representations of sexual difference have no meaning.

The models proposed by Bion and Green allow us to understand how the object appears and relates to a baby's rudimentary psyche, and how the primary forms of bisexuality have their effects on the construction of mental space. These models are based on Freud's assumption of the first occurrence of the object. Freud ([1900] 2019, [1923] 2011) always considered the existence of a psychic apparatus under the action of specific forces that impose a work demand on the mind.

Initially, Freud proposes the notion of object in its intrapsychic character and in relation to the drive. The child invests his own body through auto-erotism. In 1923, Freud discusses the individual's first identifications with their parents, not as a result of object investment, but as a "direct, immediate identification, older than any object investment" of the child (Freud, [1923] 2011, p. 39). At this point, Freud speaks of a mind in a primitive state in relation to the object of the drive (intrapsychic). However, as there is no baby without a mother, in the *Compendium* Freud ([1938] 2018) will emphasize the idea of the breast as the child's first erotic object, which they would not distinguish from their own body and would carry with them "as one 'object', a part of the original narcissistic libidinal cathexes" (p. 202). This first object will later be completed in the person of mother, giving her a unique importance, according to Freud, "as the first and strongest love object, prototype of all later love relationships, for both sexes" (p. 202).

But it is the absence of the object in the early times of psychic life that will definitively mark human sexuality. In "Formulations on the Two Principles of

Mental Functioning," Freud ([1911] 2010a) points out the absence of the object as the element that causes the emergence of desire, with the infantile psyche's attempt, ever since, to find it again.

Following Freudian ideas about the occurrence of the object, Bion and Green highlighted, with different approaches, the impact of the real object on the subject. The proposals of the two authors, however, converge in understanding how the object is present and absent in the origins of the psyche, considering its dual condition, both internal and external, of fantasy object and real object.

The child's first psychic representations will be marked by the function of the mother's and father's psyche, or the adult who cares for and invests libidinally this child and carries the other object within themselves. Bion ([1962] 2021) proposes the notion of the mother's *rêverie* as a fundamental function so that the baby can develop their psyche – in Bionian terms, develop their capacity to think. A mother with the capacity for *rêverie* would have an open mental state to give meaning to the baby's activity, being able to receive, decode, and signify infantile anxieties, and then return them with meaning.

The idea that the baby has an innate preconception of the breast, arriving in the world carrying a state of expectation of that breast, supports Bion's ([1962] 2021, [1963] 2004) proposition that there is an object relationship from the origins of the psyche. The baby would first seek the mother's mind, so that she could lead them to the breast, which provides physical and psychic nourishment to the infant. From there, the emotional experience lived by the mother and the baby, resulting from the action of one on the other, will guide psychic development.

The concepts of container and content have their theoretical basis there. Bion ([1962] 2021) uses them as "models of abstract representations of psychic achievements" (p. 124) and for this he uses symbols that would allow greater abstraction. He deliberately uses the symbols feminine ♀ and masculine ♂ to designate container and content and warns that this does not exclude other non-sexual implications (Bion, [1970] 2006). He suggests, for example, that these symbols can be applied to models of pleasure or pain, evacuating or retaining, and other inclusion and exclusion models.

Despite this, it is evident that when using these symbols Bion gives a sexual value to his mind model, linking it to representations of the feminine and the masculine. Miller (2002) observes that Bionian notation assigns a sexual valence to two psychic movements and the mode in relationship between them, referring to the difference between the sexes, even if the only difference that begins to establish in these early movements is that of self and non-self. The projected and intrusive element is linked to a masculine symbol and the receiving and containing element is linked to a feminine symbol.

The containing function of the primary object would provide the baby, in their psychic movements, with the introjection of the activity shared by two individuals, favoring the construction of the ♂♀ apparatus in their own mind

(Bion, [1962] 2021). The mouth-breast relationship, represented by container-contained, would be the prototype of psychic development. For Bion, what penetrates the elements and allows them to be joined or separated is emotion. In this sense, emotion is a variable that unites masculine and feminine elements ($\male$ and $\female$). According to Miller (2002), the psychic apparatus can change emotions, in its capacity for receptivity and penetrability. The author states that, depending on the importance, value, and quality of the relationship with primary objects, the subject will have greater or lesser psychic malleability to deal with the identificatory movements of their bisexuality.

Bion ([1962] 2021) warns about situations of fear and terror that the baby may experience. If in their psychic movements the baby finds an indifferent breast (or does not find it at all), they will have to deal with an anxiety that, according to Green (2000), is present in the deepest layers of the primordial mind. It is at this point that the action of the external object gains all importance. Green argues that the mother's capacity for *rêverie* represents "the useful intervention of the adult, a mature mind that can be introjected by the child to transform a destructive internal experience" (2000, p. 140).

The importance of the double status of the object, as fantasy and real, internal and external, is advocated by Green, highlighting the participation of the real object in the organization of the psyche and in external reality itself. With this, Green draws attention to the opposition between psychic reality and external reality to the psyche, which involves the subject's body, the other's psychic reality, and external reality. But where does Green's thought go?

Green argues that "there is something primitive in the mind, not fully explained by the early stages of object relations in the baby's development" (Green, 2000, p. 134). He states that, in the primordial mind, sensory experiences (the *beta* elements postulated by Bion) are unthinkable without another mind to transform them. They are close to external stimuli and unpleasant bodily impulses. The baby, faced with a bodily experience of pain, transforms it into a scream. It is there that the baby's excessive anxiety can be transformed into psychic content and gain meaning, through a response from the external object, the mother's *rêverie*.

The role of the object (in its dual status both internal and external) in psychic constitution is emphasized by Green (2008) to propose *thirdness* as a matrix for the emergence of the psychic apparatus. Green reserves the father's place in the mother-baby duo, as a figure of absence, of the negative, without which the foundation of the psyche cannot be conceived. Green hypothesizes a primitive triangulation from the first exchanges between mother and baby, indicating the father's place, the third, not as a distinct person, but because, in some dimension, he exists in the mother's psyche. For Green (2008), there are indeed three objects: two that are separate parts and the object that corresponds to the junction of the two.

The third and the figures of thirdness are established at this point. In the psychic origin, there are three elements, not two. For Green, the father is from the beginning in the mother-baby relationship as *the other of the object*. But the author considers that this third, occupying a place in the mother's mind and effecting the symbolic separation in the mother-child relationship, does not necessarily refer to the father of the Oedipal structure.

In his studies on the configurations of the third (thirdness), Green (2008) notes that in triangular relationships the third does not precisely represent the paternal function. However, he understands that it is important not to get caught up in the dual relationship. His proposal for thirdness was initially supported by what he called the *ternary structure*, comprising the subject, the object, and the other of the object (the third). This other object can be, for example, an object of the mother's desire, real or phantasmatic, or an object from the mother's own childhood (her mother, her father, or another person). The configurations here are multiple.

We understand that this comprehension brings the psychoanalytic discourse on subjectivation processes closer to the debate on contemporary parental configurations and *subjectivities in transition* (Glocer Fiorini, 2017), sexualities, and sexual difference. These processes can be thought of in terms of complexity. The discussion about maternal and paternal functions is whether they can be understood independently of the concepts of feminine and masculine, which are contentious in current debates on subjectivities and family configurations.

In this debate, Glocer Fiorini (2015a) proposes the *third function* as a solution to the designation of the *paternal function*. This would be impregnated in an androcentric culture and would hide the symbolic meaning of the function. Added to this problem is the fact that mother and father exist as primordial objects, as present or absent objects, in the baby's fantasy and in the mother's psyche, and mark a double reference in the child's first identifications.

In defense of her proposal for *a third function*, a symbolic function, which could be exercised by the father, the mother, or others, and pointing out the decline of the paternal function, Glocer Fiorini (2015a, p. 482) states that:

> It is necessary to distinguish between the real father, the symbolic functions that a father can eventually fulfill, and the multiple facets of the exercising fatherhood in the broad field of parenthood. If we now focus on the psychoanalytic point of view, it is necessary to analyze what elements on which the proposal of the need for a symbolic paternal function is based, in clinical practice and psychoanalytic theory, to explain a subject's access to a symbolic universe.

Green's notion of thirdness (Green, 2008) rejects the idea of a dual mother-baby relationship in the beginnings of the psyche to center on Oedipus, not as a complex, but as a model of triangulation – Green (2008) designated a theory from *generalized triangulation to a replaceable third*. This is not about the Oedipal structure, because in these triangular relationships the third does not represent the paternal function. It refers to the other of the object. Green's reference to the three, in the early moments of psychic life, proposes a new way of understanding the primal scene, with the excluded third being taken as the triangular matrix of the psyche.

In "The Neutral Gender," Green ([1973] 1988a) states that bisexuality is organized by the constitution of the fantasy of the other sex in the Oedipal triangle. Here it is also not a primitive Oedipus with the presence of the father. Instead, it refers to an absent father-object in the mother and child since origin. That is, *between* the mother and the child. These primitive forms of bisexuality are inscribed in the infantile psyche and intervene in the constitution of the subject at successive moments of development.

Bringing together contributions from contemporary authors who rescue bisexuality as a mediator of psychic processes in subjective construction, we will now describe how bisexuality presents itself in three periods of psychosexual development and how it shapes the subject's destinies.

Bisexuality and early identifications

The notion of a primary psychic bisexuality proposed by Haber (1997) is based on the narcissistic origins of psychosexuality. This would be a first period of bisexuality, linked to primary narcissism, and distinct from the secondary and transformed psychic bisexuality, which appears at the time of the Oedipus conflict. The first period is marked by the child's initial identifications and the early forms of pre-genital bisexuality.

Haber (1997) considers Freud's premise of a constitutional bisexual disposition and proposes that psychic bisexuality is constituted, in part, on a basal bisexuality, which makes up primary narcissism. In the early moments, therefore, bisexuality, of narcissistic essence, presents itself in its early forms and marks the psychic development alongside the child's initial identifications.

By suggesting as the first and most significant identification of the individual, in the primitive oral phase, Freud ([1923] 2011) infers that during that period object investment (the maternal breast) and identification (the father of prehistory) "probably do not distinguish from each other" (p. 35). He states that the constitutional bisexuality of the individual is responsible for part of the complexity of these relationships.

Schaeffer (2002) points out Freud's ambiguity and his theoretical embarrassment when supposing that the object investment in the maternal breast as a prototype of the mother and identification with the prehistoric father are not distinguished. Post-Freudian authors highlighted, in this early period, the child's primary identification with the mother. Winnicott ([1951] 1975a) described the initially undifferentiated environment between baby and mother. Bion and Green highlighted the third object in the origins of psychic life, more precisely in the mother's psyche. Green (1997) emphasizes that this third object was intuited by Winnicott when defining the transitional object as a non-self possession, distinct from the primary object.

This is a primary oral-cannibalistic mode of identification, which in Schaeffer's (2002) description is a first movement of internalization of what was transmitted to the baby by the mother's psyche. It is an experience of fusion and undifferentiation. A psychic sexual indetermination, in which the child identifies with the mother as being one with her (*I am the breast*). According to the author, the fantasy of a two-person pre-genital bisexuality is created. For Haber (1997), the psychic dimension is directly intricate not only to the body, but also with the mother's and father's libidinal and narcissistic investments (conscious and unconscious). The child is also confronted with the mother's and father's psychic bisexuality.

These theoretical proposals follow what was advocated by Freud when considering original bisexuality: the existence of an active, instinctual baby participating in exchanges with their objects, without being subjected to them. Because it is based on the individual's narcissistic bases, primary bisexuality is active in the origins of psychic life and does not dissolve. Thus, it continues to shape the subject's psychic movements and, according to this theoretical understanding, can resurface in the adult's contemporary life in different psychic mobilities.

A second moment of pre-genital bisexuality occurs, succeeding the baby's most primitive identifications. The description of this new moment relies on Winnicott's ideas about the mirror relationship between the baby and the mother: the baby gradually leaves the state of undifferentiation and gradually assimilates the mother as a separate object. There is a modification of psychic bisexuality (Haber, 1997). Winnicott ([1967] 1975b) proposes that in primitive emotional development, if it is satisfactory, *the precursor of the mirror is the mother's face.* By looking at the mother's face, the baby sees themself. As such, the baby sees themself as another and, through the mother/mirror, has a sense of existence, the experience of self as subject and object. Ogden (1994) defined this situation as an experience of *relative similarity and relative difference.*

This moment of the child is marked by identifications in which bisexuality is dominated by primary homosexuality (Haber, 1997). In this phase, the baby will introject the figure of the same sex, in an identification with the mother's sex, which applies to both girls and boys. Also in this period, autoerotism develops through exchanges linked to primary homosexuality, a necessary passage for experiencing the erotic phase of sexuality.

Roussillon (2004) developed the notion of primary homosexuality in double. An experience of primitive satisfaction and preparation of the fantasy of the primal scene, where one has the *double of oneself.* As a double is another subject referred to oneself, it distinguishes itself from a state of undifferentiation and mother-baby fusion. Roussillon's hypothesis of a *primitive homosexual relationship in double* foresees that the primordial other is initially perceived as similar, with the same states of being and perceived in the subject's mirroring. Thus, the other functions as a double, but it is not an entirely accurate mirror. This relationship accommodates the intersubjectivity between mother and baby (Ogden, 1994; Roussillon, 2004).

Schaeffer (2002) emphasizes that this moment of the mother's erotic investment, that seduces and maintains the first love exchanges with her baby, the period of primary homosexuality, imprints the original maternal feminine mark on the child's psyche on both sexes. We know that it is necessary to experience the illusion to later go through disillusionment. Relying on Winnicott and Green's ideas, what follows is the establishment of the first observable triangulation in the human being: the primary place of absence, of the negative, of reciprocal abandonment. It is the time of the establishment of the loss of the primary object.

If primary homosexuality persists and creates difficulties for the child's psyche to differentiate themself from parental *imagos*, according to Schaeffer (2002), an archaic bisexual maternal imago will predominate, threatening to contaminate all subsequent relationships with femininity and the feminine in both sexes. In turn, the original maternal feminine mark, inscribed in the individual's psyche, leads us to think that the baby's feeling of being part of the mother reveals in them the feeling of femininity. In this situation, Haber (1997) presupposes the baby's bisexuality having a dominant feminine pole, which in no way restricts primary homosexuality to the girl. Depending on the intensity with which the mother allows her baby to separate, the boy will have more difficulty detaching from the early feminine mark and will be more vulnerable to it.

At this point we call upon Green to think about the figure of the father and how he participates in the configurations of pre-genital bisexuality, first of primary homosexuality and the original feminine mark in the infant psyche. Green ([1980] 1988b, 2008) emphasizes that the father is there from the origin, in the mother's psyche, as the other of the object, inscribed as a figure of absence and one of the primary sources of the negative. The father as a function (including here the third function, the mother's invested object), as the other of the object, will allow the inaugural inscription of the primal scene. In it lies the primary form of bisexuality.

The fantasy of the primitive scene mobilizes desires and contradictory identifications. It imposes a new organizational work on the child's psyche. Roussillon (2004) states that the child must initially be invested in and feel included, to then tolerate being excluded. It is necessary to experience pleasure to later better endure pain, noted the writer Bartolomeu Campos de Queirós (2011). Roussillon adds that, initially, the child does not recognize his sexual and generational difference from the parents, and the primal scene sets in as an organizing force of the psyche. It inscribes the child in an original triangulation, he/she perceives himself/herself as excluded from the parental couple's relationship, and, depending on the investment made by the object, the child may then tolerate this exclusion.

The psychic work of differentiation of the subject will operate gradually, with the relative distancing of the mother and the father, or the other-of-the-mother object (third object), participating in the negative, as a figure of absence. The figure of the father or the third is included in the problematic of pre-genital bisexuality. The primal scene is, therefore, the matrix of unconscious movements that provides the encounter of the parental couple (object and the other) and imprints conflicting representations in the infant psyche.

Miller (2002) suggests that, if we understand the Bionian container-contained relationship at the basis of the construction of the psyche, imprinting the masculine-feminine sign in the original relationship of the baby with the object, the polarities of the masculine and the feminine will come into play in the fantasy of the primal scene and will act as references.

It is worth considering the relative strength of the representations of the masculine and the feminine, marked by as many subjectivities as possible participating in the fantasy of the primal scene in the infant psyche. Miller (2002) points out that a dynamic of exchanges and infinite possibilities of combination links these two poles of psychic bisexuality. With the establishment of the fantasy of the primal scene, Oedipal identifications, and the child's erotic investments enter the scene, inaugurating the second time of psychic bisexuality, the Oedipal phase.

Mediation of bisexuality during the Oedipal phase

The fantasy of the primal scene triggers a new moment for bisexual desires, as the encounter with parental objects brings into play new identifications, intertwined with the child's desires and fantasies. This new psychic moment gives rise to a depressive position: the relationship with their objects places the child within a plot of identifications and Oedipal conflicts, which is not limited to the enigma of sexual difference but does include it. In this way, we can understand the castration complex as the psychic experience of lack and incompleteness, in which the child may find themselves having to choose one object or the other. The construction of subjectivity entails recognizing the other, accepting incompleteness, and assimilating difference. This is the symbolic meaning of castration, which goes beyond the imaginary aspect of distinct experiences for the two sexes.

Representations of the masculine and feminine are present in the Oedipal narrative in a profoundly intricate manner, signaling the mediating and connective function of psychic bisexuality (David, 1992). Freud ([1923] 2011) referred to the organizing force of bisexuality in the Oedipus complex, which would result in dual masculine and feminine identification. At this point, he began to consider the complete Oedipus, yet maintained the masculine-feminine dichotomy, asserting that the child's identifications are neither symmetrical nor equally strong; one will dominate the other.

These crossed identifications would enable the child to deal with the ambivalence of their loving and hostile impulses, present since the phase of primary identifications. In a reinterpretation of Freud's proposition, Chabert (2016) argues that the references to the masculine and the feminine should not be conflated with man and woman, much less with activity and passivity. Each sexual object will mobilize the child, and its traces will remain in the common representations of the masculine and the feminine.

The notion of a complete Oedipus broadens the horizons of subjective constitution. However, contemporary proposals to revise the classical theory seek to address the clinical impasses that the theory fails to encompass, when confronted with sexual and gender diversities and new family configurations and parenthoods. Along the lines of the *transfamilial* Oedipus proposed by Deleuze (Deleuze & Guattari [1972] 1973), which transcends the universe of the nuclear family (mother-father-child), Glocer Fiorini (2017) suggests considering the expanded Oedipus. This allows for addressing the blind spots of Freudian theory and considering the processes of sexed subjectivation in a triadic manner, beyond the restrictive binarism of positive and negative Oedipus. In other words, it involves including the role of bodies, identifications (including gender), and drive and desire.

Psychoanalytic authors who engage in dialogue with feminist and *queer* theories, to listen to a kind of psychic suffering present in the clinical practice, criticize the sexual difference based on binarism, anatomy, and the primacy of the phallus, as well as the hierarchy between sexes and the place occupied by women and the feminine in classical theory, particularly in Freud and Lacan.

Pombo (2018) emphasizes that the Oedipus complex also becomes a structural condition with Lacan, where the phallus and the "Name-of-the-Father" hold strategic positions. She states that, in both Freudian and Lacanian theory, the Oedipus is transformed into a rule of subjectivation and a condition for the transition from nature to culture. Alonso and Fuks (2014) assert the need for a critical reading of these binary and hierarchical references, as in the prevailing cultural norms, sexual difference maintains the masculine as the model and the feminine as negative and lacking.

Rodrigues (2023) draws attention to contemporary phenomena of childhood transgenderism and sexual and gender non-binarity. The term *non-binary* refers to people who do not identify fully or exclusively as feminine or masculine gender and/or whose expressions of desire are independent of gender or sex/body. The author highlights that these transgender expressions in childhood and adolescence require an analytical listening with openness and distanced from the classical interpretation of castration denial.

For Preciado (2020), who proposes a radical epistemological revision of psychoanalysis, gender transition and the affirmation of a non-binary gender challenge the normative notions of masculinity and femininity, as well as the categories of heterosexuality and homosexuality. He states: "In the coming years, we will need to collectively develop an epistemology capable of addressing the radical multiplicity of the living and that does not reduce the body to its heterosexual reproductive force" (p. 47).

Sigal (2017) argues that psychoanalysis, to remain alive, must think of new ways of producing knowledge, striving to incorporate the new and reorganize what is already known. She emphasizes that theory is not a dead body and can and must advance, even though there may be fears and confusion about how to integrate new knowledge. She believes that "rethinking psychoanalysis is a way of doing justice to the Freudian text" (p. 44).

The authors cited in theoretical articulations regarding the paths of psychic bisexuality highlight sexual difference as a route for identificatory movements and object choices, which are subject to the tensions and influence of bisexuality. In our view, this perspective does not exclude the proposal to consider an expanded concept of difference, as we understand that in subjective and intersubjective processes, sexual difference refers to the elaboration of symbolic difference, which translates into the recognition of otherness and difference in its broad sense.

The notion of sexual difference supports the idea of the existence and recognition of primary internal objects, active in movements of sexual choice. But this sexual and generational difference is not accepted peacefully, without conflict. Chabert (2016) argues that the intertwining of these two great references, masculine and feminine, configures the Oedipal complex under the sign of ambivalence, and follows the traces of a constantly active bisexuality.

In its narcissistic origins, bisexuality can remain attached to the early stages of psychosexual development, linked to the same object. But it also participates in the dynamics of identifications and relationships with objects in the Oedipal complex and is shaped by the work of elaboration and recognition of difference. This can also be included in the parents' psyche, in their multiple subjective configurations, and beyond the orientation of desire.

On the way to recognizing otherness

Bisexual desires, during psychosexual development, confront the fantasy of castration and the tension triggered by the mourning work forced by the renunciation of the object. This is how psychic bisexuality can follow the path of differentiation, toward a genital organization. We understand that bisexuality works *toward* its integration into the psyche, with the progressive introjection of sexual polarities; and in the process of recognition and integration of one and another object, the subject welcomes the difference. In the phase of the adult genitality, the equivalence of feminine-passive and masculine-active, recurrent in Freud, does not hold. As he himself highlighted, there are passive drive aims that are actively pursued. The idea of passivity and activity in a reciprocal relationship is extensively explored. As Chabert (2016) states, being passive means accepting to be excited, to be mobilized by the sexual other.

The psychic work of bisexuality in the construction of subjectivity can lead to a more harmonious integration of the emotions arising from the Oedipal experience marked by conflict. If this occurs, the psychic bisexuality of an adult subject can more easily dialogue with multiple instances of psychic functioning, in a free expression of their psychic qualities that can slide through the references of the masculine and the feminine and sustain their own singularity. Bokanowski (1997) observes that the work of the psyche, in its genital expression, uses the resources of bisexuality for defense and satisfaction. He adds that these movements can alternate reciprocally in favor of a more malleable and autonomous psyche.

The theoretical proposals presented here reinforce the irrefutable mark of the primordial other in the original psyche. This mark will be the trace of a constantly active psychic bisexuality, which redefines itself throughout the person's subjectivation process. The inscription of an inaugural primal scene paves the way for the organization of bisexuality at the various levels of psychosexual development, favoring greater freedom and more peaceful coexistence with difference in the adult subject (Carneiro & Lazzarini, 2018).

However, the pre-genital forms of bisexuality can remain linked to a conflicted relationship with primary objects, in the subject's inability to peacefully gather and integrate these objects into one's internal world. When this occurs, primary bisexual dispositions hinder the necessary flexibility for the subject's identificatory movements in the adult genital phase. The non-integration of bisexual desires triggers symptoms and inhibitions in adult life.

The usefulness of the notion of psychic bisexuality for thinking about new subjectivities, family configurations, and parenthoods comes across the difficulties that its semantic meaning imposes on the subject and assumes in Freudian theory. By bringing together feminine and masculine dispositions in its definition, psychic bisexuality receives the criticism addressed to binary and dualistic Freudian model, for the insufficiency of the binary and hierarchical model of sexual difference – if this is understood in its narrow form and outside the complexity paradigm.

For psychoanalytic authors who study sexual and gender diversities, in dialogue with feminist theories and queer studies, the concept of sexual difference does not account for the understanding and acceptance of contemporary subjectivities and identities. Pombo (2017) suggests that a review of binarism is necessary for psychoanalysis to account for the complexity and diversities of current forms of subjectivation. On the other hand, Ayouch (2015), who also proposes an epistemological rupture in psychoanalytic discourse, recalls that in Freudian work the separations between masculine and feminine are not reducible to a binary sexual difference, but are often related to an overlap within the same sex. He emphasizes that psychic bisexuality allowed Freud to deconstruct any essentialization of the masculine and the feminine.

According to Glocer Fiorini (2017), if we take the category of difference in the broadest sense, it could even be included in the parents' psyche, beyond their sexual orientation. The author states that, in this line, "both the recognition of sexual and gender diversity and the ability to generate symbolic differences demand the establishment of a relationship between both notions" (p. 96). The author goes on to say that this relationship can be one of agreement or disagreement, harmony or conflict.

These questions point to the relevance of understanding psychic bisexuality and its activity in psychic life circumscribed to the field of subjective constitution. Psychoanalysis should think about the impact of this activity on the constitution of the psychic subject, considering that in its references to objects (one and the other), bisexuality can be understood as mediating internal processes that translate into various possibilities of gender identifications and expressions of sexuality, opening to freer and more peaceful experience of the subject with their uniqueness and difference.

References

Alonso, S., & Fuks, M. (2014). A construção da masculinidade e a histeria nos homens na contemporaneidade. In P. Ambra & N. Silva Jr. (Eds.), *Histeria e gênero* (pp. 239–265). nVersos.

Ayouch, T. (2015). Da transexualidade às transidentidades: Psicanálise e gêneros plurais. *Percurso*, 54, 23–32.

Bion, W. ([1962] 2021). *Aprender com a experiência.* Blucher.

Bion, W. ([1963] 2004). *Elementos de psicanálise.* Blucher.

Bion, W. ([1970] 2006). *Atenção e interpretação.* Imago.

Bokanowski, T. (1997). La bisexualité en travail dans la cure (A propos du "féminin" chez l'homme). In A. Fine, D. Le Bouef, & A. Le Guen (Eds.), *Bisexualité* (pp. 111–130). Presses Universitaires de France. doi:10.3917/puf.finea.1997.01.0111.

Carneiro, C. A., & Lazzarini, E. R. (2018). A bissexualidade psíquica na constituição do sujeito: Sobre suas origens e destinos identitários. *Revista de Psicanálise da SPPA*, 25 (3), 585–612.

Carneiro, C. A., & Lazzarini, E. R. (2020). Acolher a diferença: A função da bissexualidade psíquica na construção da subjetividade. *Tempo Psicanalítico*, 52 (1), 155–186.

Chabert, C. (2016). Dis-moi qui tu préfères? *Le Carnet PSY*, 196 (2), 20–24. doi:10.3917/lcp.196.0020.

David, C. (1992). *La bisexualité psychique.* Éditions Payot.

Deleuze, G., & Guattari, F. ([1972] 1973). *El Anti Edipo.* Barral.

Freud, S. ([1900] 2019). A interpretação dos sonhos. In S. Freud, *Obras completas, Volume 4* (pp. 13–675). Companhia das Letras.

Freud, S. ([1905] 2016). Três ensaios sobre a teoria da sexualidade. In S. Freud, *Obras completas, Volume 6* (pp. 13–154). Companhia das Letras.

Freud, S. ([1911] 2010a). Formulações sobre os dois princípios do funcionamento psíquico. In S. Freud, *Obras completas, Volume 10* (pp. 108–121). Companhia das Letras.

Freud, S. ([1923] 2011). O eu e o id. In S. Freud, *Obras completas, Volume 16* (pp. 13–74). Companhia das Letras.

Freud, S. ([1930] 2010b). O mal-estar na civilização. In S. Freud, *Obras completas, Volume 18* (pp. 13–122). Companhia das Letras.

Freud, S. ([1938] 2018). Compêndio de psicanálise. In S. Freud, *Obras completas, Volume 19* (pp. 189–273). Companhia das Letras.

Glocer Fiorini, L. (2001). *Lo femenino y el pensamiento complejo*. Lugar Editorial.

Glocer Fiorini, L. (2015a). Desconstruindo o conceito de função paterna: Um paradigma interpelado. *Revista de Psicanálise da SPPA*, 22 (2), 479–491.

Glocer Fiorini, L. (2015b). *La diferencia sexual en debate: Cuerpos, deseos y ficciones*. Lugar Editorial.

Glocer Fiorini, L. (2017). Subjetividades em transição, parentalidades contemporâneas: Diversidade e diferença. *Revista Brasileira de Psicanálise*, 51 (2), 91–102.

Green, A. ([1973] 1988a). O gênero neutro. In A. Green, *Narcisismo de vida, narcisismo de morte* (pp. 223–237). Escuta.

Green, A. ([1980] 1988b). A mãe morta. In A. Green, *Narcisismo de vida, narcisismo de morte*. Escuta.

Green, A. (1997). A intuição do negativo em O brincar e a realidade. *Livro Anual de Psicanálise*, 13, 239–251.

Green, A. (2000). A mente primordial e o trabalho do negativo. *Livro Anual de Psicanálise*, 14, 133–148.

Green, A. (2008). *Orientações para uma psicanálise contemporânea*. Imago.

Haber, M. (1997). Identité, bisexualité psychique et narcissisme. In A. Fine, D. Le Bouef, & A. Le Guen (Eds.), *Bisexualité* (pp. 49–68). Presses Universitaires de France.

Miller, P. (2002). Formes élémentaires de la bisexualité psychique. *Topique*, 78, 7–19.

Morin, E. (2006). *Introdução ao pensamento complexo*. Sulina.

Ogden, T. H. (1994). The analytic third: Working with intersubjective clinical facts. *The International Journal of Psychoanalysis*, 75, 3–19.

Pombo, M. F. (2017). Desconstruindo e subvertendo o binarismo sexual e de gênero: Apostas feministas e queer. *Periódicus*, 7 (1), 388–404.

Pombo, M. F. (2018). Diferença sexual, psicanálise e contemporaneidade: Novos dispositivos e apostas teóricas. *Revista Latinoamericana de Psicopatologia Fundamental*, 21 (3), 545–567.

Preciado, P. B. (2020). *Je suis um monstre qui vous parle*. Grasset.

Queirós, B. C. (2011). *Vermelho amargo*. Cosac Naify.

Rodrigues, A. C. C. (2023). Diversidade e dissidências sexuais e de gênero: Desafios para a psicanálise na contemporaneidade. *Calibán RLP*, 21 (1), 154–156.

Roussillon, R. (2004). La dépendance primitive et l'homosexualité primaire "en double". *Revue française de psychanalyse*, 68 (2), 421–439.

Schaeffer, J. (2002). Bisexualité et différence des sexes dans la cure. *Topique*, 78 (1), 21–32. doi:10.3917/top.078.0021.

Sigal, A. M. (2017). Ainda a psicanálise no campo da sexuação. *Estudos de Psicanálise*, 47, 35–46.

Winnicott, D. W. ([1951] 1975a). Objetos transicionais e fenômenos transicionais. In D. Winnicott, *O brincar e a realidade* (pp. 13–44). Imago.

Winnicott, D. W. ([1967] 1975b). O papel do espelho da mãe e da família no desenvolvimento infantil. In D. Winnicott, *O brincar e a realidade* (pp. 153–162). Imago.

Chapter 4

The feminine side of the force

The elaboration of the feminine identity

Ana Teresa Vale

Becoming a woman

A woman's identity has several foundations, all contributing to a very personal and unique construction. Among the elements that are part of this construction, we find the categories of masculine and feminine and how they are unconsciously represented by the individual, which make part of the rhizomatic construction of gender, as Amir (2022) puts it. In this conceptualization, there is an unsaturated part of the unconscious representation of being a woman that comes from very subtle experiences, fleeting feelings, transient fantasies, building blocks for fragmented representations that have a great potential for change and can be integrated, or not, in more solid constructions. Alongside this unsaturated part, there is a saturated aspect that is more easily accessible which comes from the oedipal identifications.

Dana Amir draws from Adrienne Harris' writings, who in 2000 had already postulated the idea of gender as a non-rigid construction, a soft assembly, highly variable among individuals and in the history line of the same individual, comprising saturated and unsaturated aspects, the first being more stable and the latter more fluid. Change and development are not linear nor predictable, since gender construction is influenced by many different factors.

To begin with, the construction of the masculine/feminine categories is influenced by transgenerational heritage because parents and other family members convey messages to children concerning these issues. These messages will be both conscious and unconscious, but psychoanalysis has shown that the unconscious messages being enigmatic and needing interpretation (as Laplanche described in 1987) will have a greater and deeper impact on the individual than what is conveyed consciously.

Moreover, from the birth on, all the sensory experiences the baby has in the relationship with the parents or caregivers also plays a part in this construction, since men and women relate differently to baby girls and baby boys. Later, physical contact and relationships with siblings and other children and other emotionally significant adults also form part of the large amount of information the child gathers concerning these categories (Cournut-Janin, 2018).

DOI: 10.4324/9781003584483-5

This myriad of experiences and the unconscious meaning the child will give to them will contribute to the rhizomatic construction of gender. These experiences often involve the body, including very early sensory experiences in the relationship with significant others, the exploration of one's female body during childhood and adolescence, bodily transformation – as it happens in menstruation, pregnancy, menopause – the experience of sexual intercourse, all play a crucial part in the construction of the feminine identity (Balsam, 2003; Zhilka, 2018). Another important process in this construction is the emotional separation between mother and daughter, which is a very difficult task to accomplish and in a way is never complete (Perelberg, 2017).

The relationship between masculine and feminine also calls forth the representation of the primal scene (Perelberg, 2018), therefore sexuality is an intrinsic part of this process. Either in sexuality or in the construction of the personality, identifications to both feminine and masculine elements form part of what we call psychic bisexuality. In positive outcomes, bisexuality is "a silent structuring and organizing" building block of identity and sexuality; in more negative outcomes, we will find "a fragmented, split or inoperative psychic bisexuality" (Zilkha, 2018, p. 151).

Psychic bisexuality

The primary bisexual disposition we find in humans is a fundamental brick in the construction of the feminine, the masculine, and the subject's identity. As Richard (2019) puts it, bisexuality is at first built to contain and hide a chaotic, incestual primitive world where both the omnipotent mother and the grandiose father ask for exclusive love and threaten the subject's life and capacity for growth.

Afterward, we will find a secondary elaboration of bisexuality comprising oedipal identifications that restructure narcissistic foundations and orient desire to a certain kind of object with specific characteristics.

In the analytic process, the psychoanalyst oscillates between different forms of thinking and feeling, of holding the patient in her mind, of reacting to the transference movements and of elaborating her countertransference. These reactions are felt either as masculine or feminine, creating the feeling of an internal alterity. At the same time, the analyst listens to different aspects of the patient that are recognized as feminine or masculine as well. But of course, what is represented as feminine by a man is quite distinct from what is represented by a woman; and the other way around also holds true (Richard, 2019).

Therefore, the representation of the feminine, of the masculine, and of the relationship between both, is an essential part of becoming a subject and building a separate identity. According to Richard (2019), an eclipsed primary object remains in the unconscious, always drawing the subject to a passive baby-like position. In fact, the primary identifications are never totally relinquished and the figures of the omnipotent mother and grandiose father, with their very archaic sexuality, are always present in the unconscious mind.

Godfrind (2018) postulates that there is a primary core in the organization of bisexuality in women. In her conceptualization, alongside with oedipal love, the identification with the father – or, more exactly, with the masculine elements of the significant others – also allows for a way out of the primary homosexuality that threatens to engulf the girl forbidding separation from the maternal object. But for the masculine to be strong enough to compete with this archaic mother, it needs to be idealized and omnipotent, to be attractive enough to make the girl turn away from this powerful mother. In this point, Godfrind's and Richard's points of view overlap – both in their different ways of thinking, suggesting that in the primitive mind we find omnipotent idealized objects being either maternal or paternal and that bisexuality is a way out of this primitive world.

If this identification to the father provokes too much conflict or is in some way made impossible in the unconscious fantasy, the girl has the feeling that she has to steal the father's penis in order to survive the omnipotent archaic mother. Envy of the omnipotent penis will be, according to Godfrind, the substructure of penis envy. Also Harris (2000) highlights the complex relationship women have with the idea of the "masculine" either in themselves, as a part of their identity, or in relation to men or to the masculine part of others.

In Harris' conceptualization, women's identity may have enough fluidity to allow for growth and transformation, or may on the contrary rigidify and freeze. The analytic process may then lead to the possibility of less conflicted identifications and a better integration between masculine and feminine elements.

The concept of bisexuality brings light to certain aspects of the mind, while leaving many others in the shadows (Levy, 2019). As said before, psychic bisexuality will come into conflict with prohibitions, internal censorship, hindrances of different sorts that have to be negotiated, and will create problems to be solved, all throughout life. That is why human sexuality is intrinsically traumatic, because it forces the subject to let go of the infantile omnipotence, to recognize the existence of the other and the sexual and generational difference, and to acknowledge the incompleteness inherent to the human condition (Mcdougall, 1996).

Zilhka (2018) talks about a feminine in abeyance where bisexuality is fragmented or in clusters. In such cases, women may exhibit symptoms that have the function of obliterating the body, as if the feminine body did not exist, and of denying temporality. The author links these situations to problems of separation from the maternal object that have profound roots within the mind. Fascinated by the mother's body (and the analyst's body in the transference), these women tend to forget their own body or entertain the fantasy that their body and their mother's body are one. Identification to masculine aspects is thus kept in clusters that escape this engulfing quality of the maternal object not integrated in the personality as a whole.

Therefore, if bisexuality as a state of being is part of the human condition and inherent to human sexuality (Mitchel, 2018), it may be more, or less, integrated leading to more, or less, conflict. On one hand, conflict and frustration give rise to the capacity to think; but, on the other hand, if they are too intense for the mind to handle, they may create several hindrances in the process of a person's development.

In fact, the masculine and feminine representations, which in the primitive mind clash with each other in a violent and destructive primal scene, have to be transformed by benevolent good-enough objects and experiences in order to give rise to secondary identifications to a creative affectionate parental couple. In this latter case, masculine and feminine end up by being seen as complementary and so the process of de-idealization of both mother and father is possible together with the reparation of the narcissistic wound this process entails (Godfrind, 2018). When it is not the case, the patient is left with a terrifying primal scene where masculine and feminine compete for power and survival (Richard, 2019).

This scenario could happen in a family where the parental figures are too narcissistic to take into account the needs of the child; in that case, the maternal and paternal object will be too close to the primitive archaic representations, and the subject will be constantly threatened by their destructivity, which renders impossible the process of a healthy identification. Or it can come from non-elaborated transgenerational trauma, in which case the parents convey not only enigmatic messages but messages about sexuality and about the masculine/feminine categories that are interpreted by the child as violent and destructive. It may also happen in families afflicted by tragedy, where painful affects are overwhelming and destroy the family fabric – as it was the case of Adriana.

Adriana – strength and vulnerability

Adriana came to analysis in her early twenties after breaking up with her boyfriend. Throughout the first years of analysis we came to identify how she represented in a quite caricatural way the masculine and the feminine – masculine being equated to strength and feminine to weakness. The only solution she found to that conundrum was to base her identity on an unconscious bisexual fantasy, as if she could be both male and female at the same time. This led to several disturbances in her relationship to men, in her sexuality, and in her experience of being a woman.

Her analysis was mostly based on the elaboration of her childhood and family history, and the fantasies she had built around it, working through that eventually allowed her to let go of her infantile omnipotence, which crystalized in the unconscious belief that she could be both woman and man. That work led to more gratifying sexual and emotional relationships. At the end of analysis, she became pregnant and had a child, which also allowed us to go back to working on her femininity.

Her family had gone through difficult emotional experiences. Her father had two children from a previous marriage, and one of these children died following a tragic accident when Adriana was a small child. Consequently, her father was severely depressed, could not work, and sat on the couch all day, absent-minded, and refusing any kind of help. Eventually, after years fighting the father's depression, her mother decided to get a divorce, coinciding with Adriana's puberty.

When she was a teenager, one of her siblings struggled with an addiction and another developed an eating disorder. She witnessed her mother always fighting to find solutions for the family's problems and at the same time keeping her highly demanding job where the livelihood of the family came from.

Although her mother was a very emphatic and understanding person, in the midst of all this turmoil she did not always have the availability Adriana needed. The mother's unavailability reactivated in my patient this terrible experience of abrupt separation and loss when her father had come home after the death of her sibling and demanded all the mother's attention when she herself was just a toddler.

During her childhood she remembered her father calling her by a boy's name (his own name, in fact) because he saw so much of himself in her. Adriana remembered her wish to be a boy – she insisted on urinating standing up as boys do – and during adolescence she was a tomboy: short hair, masculine clothing, avoiding what she saw as female activities or girl talk, but at the same time always secretly falling in love with boys – secretly because she felt that being in love was something shameful.

Nonetheless, she could not trust any boy to protect her – she felt she had to protect herself and be the one to protect and save other people. In her dreams, there were a lot of war/conflict scenarios or dangerous situations where she tried to save others from harm. We focused on her feeling of omnipotence emerging in her dreams – she felt nothing was impossible. She had to have the sword in her hand so she would not find herself in need. As Gallop (1982) would put it, Adriana needed to have the phallus in order not to give anything up – that way, she could be both man and woman.

In her dreams the encounter between the masculine and the feminine was a violent and deadly clash. An example of this was a dream where there was a terrible fight between a man and a woman. The woman threw an oven to the feet of the man, and this caused a fire that burned down all the trees in the forest killing all the animals that lived in those trees. She was shocked, saddened, and tried desperately to save the animals, but when she was able to get to them, they were already dead.

As the analytic work progressed, she became more capable of being in a vulnerable position toward her boyfriend and let go of the need to be the one in charge all the time. But this brought to her a very difficult question – if she was not the "man" in the relationship, how could she occupy the place of the woman? Being a woman necessarily meant to her being fragile, dependent, and impotent. But in the relationship with her analyst, she began to realize that being a woman could be different from what she had envisioned, when she discovered I had knowledge about things she thought a woman would not know of or appreciate, and that I could navigate between different positions or ways of being in the relationship to her without losing touch with my identity as a woman.

At a certain point in the transference, she started to see me as her father, and it became clear that in her childhood the explanation she gave to the fact that her father did not take care of her was that he had wanted a son and not a daughter. So unconsciously she was always trying to be the son she imagined her father had wanted (or the patient she imagined the analyst wanted to have on her couch), and if she was able to accomplish that, she could save the father from his depression (and perhaps avoid all the family tragedies).

We worked a lot around the issue of power and fragility, what it meant to be powerful and strong. But she found these topics dangerous because, unconsciously, she thought the analyst was asking her to let go of her strength. She was not keen to do it, because she felt that if she relinquished her position of power, she would lose the armor that had been her protection since she was a teenager. But by not recognizing herself as a woman, she remained haunted by the feeling that she was being constantly undervalued because she was a woman.

After five years of analytic work, she finally started to get in touch with the profound sadness she had been avoiding up until then. She started to recognize in herself deep feelings of longing, emptiness, and vulnerability, namely in the transference relationship. At this point, Adriana struggled to accept the tragedies her family had gone through and the lasting consequences they had had; she also struggled to understand what it meant to be a woman and how she could start to feel at ease with her female identity without losing her strength. The sessions were filled with a palpable pain, which was very difficult to bear for both of us. Her attachment to the analyst was strong and her feelings of sadness for having to part from me during holiday breaks were poignant.

At this point she had a dream about a baby where we could see very clearly the confusion between herself as a baby, her dead sibling, and her father. She thus started to understand how she had confused her identity with her helpless sibling and her fragile father unable to deal with his emotions – and the armor she once needed was a result of this confusion. This dream inaugurated another period where the question of her feelings about being a woman and her relationship to her female body were the center of analytic work.

When analysis was coming close to termination, she became pregnant (consciously, by chance; unconsciously, it was a very desired child and symbolized the analytic baby). Since it was not planned, at first she was anxious and a bit lost, but during our sessions she began to understand that she so much desired this child that was also the child of the man she loved deeply and with whom she wanted to spend her life. The pregnancy went smoothly;

but as she discovered that her baby was a girl, all her anxieties about her female identity came to the fore again, allowing us to work them through one more time. In her words, "it took me so much time to understand what it is like for me to be a woman, will I be able to teach her how to be at ease with being a girl? I don't want her to suffer, and I don't want her to feel the need to wear an armor!"

The third trimester of pregnancy forced her to confront some physical limitations, which, at first, she experienced as a great frustration. At this point, she had to let go momentarily of all the things that had made her feel strong before (her success at work, her being in charge around the house), and so she found herself confronted with the question – what is the female side of the force? (An obvious reference to the *Star Wars* saga, of which she was a great fan). Carrying a child in her womb, delivering a baby into the world, and taking good care of a family also demanded a great amount of strength, she discovered.

Concluding remarks

The elaboration of bisexuality is crucial in the construction of one's identity in order to feel at ease with one's body and with the strength and vulnerability that comes with being human. As we can see in Adriana's analysis the holding on to the unconscious fantasy of being both man and woman was a defense against a profound pain coming from the terrible experiences her family had gone through during her upbringing.

Adriana illustrates very well what Harris (2000) describes in her work about tomboys – her masculine identification comprised at the same time her fascination for the masculine, her rivalry with men, and her fear of intimacy with them, in addition to being a defense against trauma. Her identity as a tomboy was built through her identification with the vital and competent parts of her parental figures, mostly her mother's – aspects that in her unconscious representation were identified as masculine.

Adriana's analysis showed clearly how in the unconscious profound layers of the mind we found a primitive scenario containing the figure of an idealized powerful father with which she felt the need to identify. This unconscious powerful father, far away from the conscious image she had of her real father, was needed for several reasons. First, it was an attempt to survive the abrupt separation she felt from her mother that left her helpless and lonely. This separation was understood by Adriana to mean that her mother would rather take care of her father – a man – than her – a little, powerless, girl. Simultaneously, being the boy she imagined her father had wanted her to be, she was attempting to get his love and attention while trying to repair the huge wound the separation to the mother had left inside her.

Moreover, other elements of her and her family's history reinforced the splitting between the powerful strong man and the fragile helpless woman, so she felt forced to run away from the female position that she considered belittling.

At the same time, stuck with this omnipotent figure that she could not transform, she was threatened by a violent primal scene where destruction was always imminent; so, for her, sexuality was a dangerous affair, and therefore she unconsciously chose to be in an active, penetrating role, rather than a receptive one that she associated with fragility and death.

Paradoxically, she unconsciously associated strength with maleness and vulnerability with femaleness. But in fact, in her family her mother was the one who assured the livelihood of the family, kept the family going, was able to work through emotional experiences, and find solutions to the problems her family faced. Her father, on the other hand, was submerged by depression, unable to mourn and emotionally invest in his living children and wife.

Adriana recognized her mother's strength in herself, but she unconsciously attributed it to the masculine in her mother; and she also recognized her identification to her father's depression (from the start, she had a conscious fear of falling into depression and ending up like her father), but, unconsciously, she associated this vulnerability with femininity. Avoiding a female identity was therefore a way of avoiding depression. Of course, the social fabric we live in facilitates this splitting. But there were also more elements to this that came from the circumstances around her sibling's death and from transgenerational heritages.

This splitting was an attempt to explain the unexplainable – why her sibling had to die, for example. It was more reassuring to have an explanation, even if it was one that caused her many hindrances, than to face the fact that sometimes certain things remain unexplainable and we have to keep on living without knowing the answers.

Alongside this identification to the powerful grandiose father that she used as armor against depression and vulnerability, she hid from everyone a very strong identification with a maternal object, empathic, loving, and caring. But she could seldom show this to anyone as this part of her made her feel ashamed. During analysis, as we worked through all these features of her internal world, she would observe how the analyst could navigate between different states of mind and different identifications inside herself allowing for the patient to witness how the analyst made use of her own psychic bisexuality. This feminine identification, with its difficulties but also with its strengths – what we ended up calling the feminine side of the force – came slowly to the fore and as time went by it was more and more possible for her to use it in her relationship to others and to herself.

The pregnancy at the end of analysis, and the way she experienced it, were clear signs of how these identifications had been transformed. We could also think that getting pregnant when the analysis was ending was a way to avoid the emptiness of separation when the analysis would be over. After termination, she would not be alone without the analyst but with her baby girl and the family she had built. If it was a way out of the separation issues she had had with her mother, it was certainly a healthier way than the one she had prior to analysis.

At the end of analysis, her psychic bisexuality was much more fluid, integrated, and useful, inevitably causing conflict (as it does in all of us) but without leaving her stuck in an insoluble conundrum. She was now able to represent a creative and loving primal scene, therefore death and danger were no longer at the center of her preoccupations; and life could take hold.

References

Amir, D. (2022). Boys don't cry: On the radical unsaturation of gender dichotomy. *The Psychoanalytic Review*, 3, 333–343.

Balsam, R. (2003). The vanished pregnant body in psychoanalytic female developmental theory. *Journal of the American Psychoanalytical Association*, 51, 1153–1179.

Cournut-Janin, M. (2018). The origin of psychoanalysis between bisexuality and transference. In R. Perelberg (Ed.), *Psychic bisexuality: A British-French dialogue* (pp. 90–102). Routledge.

Gallop, J. (1982). *Feminism and psychoanalysis: The daughter's seduction.* Macmillan.

Godfrind, J. (2018). From bisexuality to the feminine. In R. Perelberg (Ed.), *Psychic bisexuality: A British-French dialogue* (pp. 122–132). Routledge.

Harris, A. (2000) Gender as a soft assembly: Tomboys' stories. *Studies in Gender and Sexuality*, 1, 223–250.

Laplanche, J. (1987). *Nouveaux fondements pour la psychanalyse.* Presses Universitaires de France.

Lévy, J. (2019). Ombres et lumières de la bisexualité. *Revue française de psychanalyse*, 83, 1421–1476.

Mcdougall, J. (1996). *Eros aux mille et un visages.* Gallimard.

Mitchel, J. (2018). Foreword. In R. Perelberg (Ed.), *Psychic bisexuality: A British-French dialogue* (pp. xvi–xxiii). Routledge.

Perelberg, R. (2017). Love and melancholia in the analysis of women by women. *International Journal of Psychoanalysis*, 98: 1533–1549.

Perelberg, R. (2018). Introduction. In R. Perelberg (Ed.), *Psychic bisexuality: A British-French dialogue* (pp. 1–57). Routledge.

Richard, F. (2019). La bisexualité, l'inceste et la mort. *Revue française de psychanalyse*, 83, 1347–1408.

Zilhka, N. (2018). Stumbling blocks of the feminine, stumbling blocks of psychic bisexuality. In R. Perelberg (Ed.), *Psychic bisexuality: A British-French dialogue* (pp. 151–169). Routledge.

Chapter 5

Bisexuality

Freud and Woolf meet

Barbara Stimmel

In asking gay friends – and lesbians, bisexuals, trans folks and closeted people – about their similar experiences with this exhaustion and coy, post-out closeted-ness, a recurring frustration was that as soon as queer life is broached, straight people often act entitled to ask personal questions. Are you a top or a bottom? Are you postoperative? Do you have a penis? Which do you like more, men or women? There is a tyranny there that conscripts queer people as servants to straight awareness, paid intermittently in the minimum wage of tolerance. Queer people would never do this to straight people; we're not allowed.

My essence is that I am a riddle even to myself. I identify as unknowable, and I'm not sorry about it. Isn't that the beautiful Mandelbrot of mystery we call the human condition? Outness doesn't end mystery any more than a bar mitzvah or a quinceañera ends immaturity.

(Morgan, 2019)

Without taking bisexuality into account I think it would scarcely be possible to arrive at an understanding of the sexual manifestations that are actually to be observed in men and women.

(Freud, [1905] 1955, p. 220)

At first, it may appear strange to juxtapose two such apparently different aspects of the same construct, written 107 years apart! What I am calling the same construct is the ineffable, unrealizable comprehension of human sexu-ality. And, as Morgan implies, it is always a personal mystery that no one should have to explain to anyone else, ever. Yet here we are trying to discuss bisexuality, an intrinsic part of the lesbian, gay, bisexual, transgender, and queer or questioning (LGBTQ) community while at the same time a con-ceptual mainstay of psychoanalytic theory on human sexuality. Among the most complicated psychic/behavioral tangles psychoanalytic theory continues to grapple with is the differences between the sexes – concrete and abstract. Bisexual cohesion is a universal fantasy that, in part, helps people contend with these differences. By this I do not mean "simply" the wish for a penis in women or the wish to have a baby in men, but rather the more fundamental shared wish men and women have to possess both female and male genitals.

DOI: 10.4324/9781003584483-6

In other words, to be both. Intuitively, the wish/fantasy of bisexual completeness also has an important meaning for creativity of any kind.

Returning to the epigraphs above, and given the theme of this book, it is important that we consider the complicated, often vexing, interface between analytic theory and cultural concerns. The reason to do so is self-evident. Psychoanalytic thinking always seeps into various levels of its surrounding intellectual/political universe; it has from its origins until today and that because it is constantly focused on the Mandelbrot (or conundrum) of mystery we call the human condition.

This chapter invites the reader to consider that such an intense focus perforce crosses borders of lived experience simultaneously affecting multiple social/cultural institutions (hospitals, schools, arts, etc.); psychoanalytic theory is reciprocally affected and thus a significant back-and-forth ensues. My point is not that psychoanalysis has the last or always correct word on things. Just, and powerfully, that it has an impact that should not be ignored.

Before entering into the interesting juxtaposition of Freud and Woolf, even if inadvertent, let us take a quick look at the impact both have had on "feminism." This is a concept that needs to be within quotation marks since it is such an extraordinarily broad, poorly defined, overly used and misused, unfortunate shorthand for the complexity of human relations and, for the purposes of this paper – an unfortunate weapon. It was hurled at Freud and sometimes even at Woolf.

Both were intellectual, social, and psychological representatives of time and place. Both were gifted observers of human sexuality, and neither was afraid to address it head-on. Freud was often misunderstood, even as he at times misunderstood all that one wishes he had considered in his theorizing about female sexuality. And Woolf, who understood a great deal about female sexuality, beginning at least on paper with *A Room of One's Own*, also renounced her "feminism" as she posited that one need not be one or the other: why not both?

Yet, as is often the case, mistakes that are mistaken as prejudice can lead to great breakthroughs in understanding that do not necessarily refute mistakes but incorporate them into broader and more complete ways of understanding a concept. Female sexuality, actually human sexuality, is one of these multifaceted, unbelievably complex subjects about which there will always be new and more things to say. As a matter of fact, for Woolf, her feminism was mostly at the fore in the concepts of warfare and government. And for Freud, his feminism was most powerfully at the fore when he "liberated" female sexuality from its repressed background of women's existence.

Now, and first, let us return to the main topic at hand – bisexuality – as we reflect upon cultural expectations, misapprehensions, general attitudes, and biases in particular of, about, and toward bisexuality – behavior, object choice, and its place in the LGBTQ community. Then we will look closely at classical analytic theory regarding psychic bisexuality as we attempt to see how each is germane to the other. This all in the expectation that increased understanding of bisexuality within a theory of the mind enhances its acceptance, understanding, and, ironically, its ordinariness in human existence.

Given that myths are projections, it is worth considering that the Judeo-Christian origin myth is but one of many. Woman created from Man's body is as absurd as its opposite, as found in Mesopotamian, Egyptian, Chinese, and certainly Greek explanations of the creation of humankind. Probably the most familiar is that of Plato who proposed three original sexes: female, male, androgyne. There are different versions of why these prototypes were split in half – from the retribution of the gods in response to human defiance to its opposite, namely, the protection of the human race from hurtling toward destruction. Interestingly, the Greek gods themselves were spontaneously male and female although created from the union of Chaos and Gaea, both female versions of earth and sky. But returning to the split humans, their destiny was to seek their other halves, continuously. Only the androgyne speaks to heterosexuality while split females/males drawn to versions of themselves in seeking unity describes homosexuality. Where and how does bisexuality arise and fit in? The continuum between heterosexuality and homosexuality is a cultural construct as represented in philosophy and religion. Placing bisexuality within this model makes a kind of sense but not necessarily for those sometimes choosing sexual partners among those with the same morphology and at other times those whose bodies are differently constructed.

Focusing on Virginia Woolf is logical for several reasons, not least because she was an apt resourceful thinker to Freud, as we shall see. But first, Woolf was one of many who was seriously and unwaveringly opposed to considering bisexuality a defining term. Woolf's assertion was simple yet profound: all women (at least) naturally desire other women at times. She averred that desire was the leading aspect of human sexuality in that it transcends specific object choice and is rather a state of sexual longing that has a certain indiscriminateness. Although just one voice, her reach was wide and long-lasting; she was an avatar, a kind of sublime teacher. In this sense, she was not telling us something that she alone knew, rather, she had the ability to describe this to multitudes, influencing culture along the way.

She was a married woman devoted to her husband, Leonard, while at the same time she had a longstanding sexual affair with Vita Sackville-West, another married woman in the Bloomsbury circle. The men who dominated their group spent much time philosophizing/musing on male homosexuality, a preferred form of sexual gratification among them. They did not seem to trouble themselves with their apparent bisexual behaviors while some women in their circle definitely did. Thus, Vita described herself as a bisexual woman, while Virginia adamantly disagreed. She was a woman, plain and simple. She protested strongly that bisexuality is not a gender identity, rather it is an ordinary and expected aspect of sexual longing among women, and, most likely, men. Her preferred way of conceptualizing human sexuality was as androgynous – neither one nor the other, rather the entwinement of both female and male sexuality.

Leonard Woolf, a great admirer of Freud, famously published his collected works at Hogarth Press. *The Standard Edition*, as it is known, was the first and, for more than a century, the definitive version of Freud. Virginia's brother and his wife were in psychoanalysis for years and the philosophically sophisticated, highly educated "Bloomsberries" were very knowledgeable about this Viennese doctor and his extraordinary impact. However, Virginia, placing herself in opposition to Freud, believed firmly that not only was his thinking antithetical to creativity, literature, art, and almost everything reflecting the human condition, but also that he did not especially understand female sexuality. Of course, she was/is not alone in that! And perhaps even more to the point, Woolf's criticism of Freud was indirectly expressed by an unidentified character in her last novel, *Between the Acts*. "But why always drag in sex?" Freud answered this question constantly throughout his work.

Yet Virginia had not read Freud until soon after meeting him for tea in 1939 when he emigrated to London. They spoke apparently only about responsibility and guilt with regard to Hitler and The Great War. Two years later she drowned herself. But in that short period Virginia read him apparently ravenously and found herself with a transformed understanding of his understanding of those things she most prized. And while she never formally specifically addressed his theorizing about human sexuality, it seems their overlaps, while subtle, are significant. Because Freud, too, did not see bisexuality as an object choice per se but rather as a fundamental of the human condition and as a substrate in all human sexual exchange. Therefore, it is interesting to consider how strongly Woolf argued for leaving bisexuality out of any taxonomy of gender identity. Her thinking was a harbinger of current debates; she was prescient while at the same time reflecting, indirectly, another contemporary mindset – the Freudian proposition of psychic bisexuality.

Thinking upon Freud, we know that his aims included erecting a theoretical scaffold of a general psychology; its positive impact was powerful, deep, and pervasive. Yet so too was the pushback over time, particularly from women both in and out of the profession. The term "dark continent" captures Freud's ignorance and unfortunate mistakes in theory and treatment. However, basic concepts allow for revision and refinement of theory while recognizing transcendent truths. Too often psychoanalysis is polemical, proselytizing, and pernicious in its prescriptions of "normal" human development and behavior. Nonetheless, the best of psychoanalysis is flexible, fluid, and fair to all-comers, given its interest in understanding, not prescribing, human behavior. In the end, dialogue and discussion, hopefully, help us transcend problems while availing ourselves of strengths in the ongoing study of people, sexual beings that we are.

It is not digressive to spend a moment noting that it has been acceptable, even applauded, to look at Freud's personal psychology and life to explain basic tenets of his theory. Here, is one example:

> The greater acceptance of non-normative sexualities and genders is reshaping the discourse on bisexuality and gender in many corners of our profession, yet, ... that evolution is far from universal. A strain of unquestioned heteronormativity and cisgenderism (...) has roots (...) in Freud's unresolved mourning of his inchoate homosexual self.
>
> (Gulati & Pauley, 2019, p. 78)

To my mind, this is as shortsighted as it is futile. Futile because we can never know actual motivation in understanding products of the mind unless perhaps amid an in-depth treatment process; shortsighted because inevitable overlaps between an individual's psychology and their thought products only matter if the ideas themselves are without stand-alone merit. And, in the end, no matter to whom we apply "wild" psychoanalysis, the result is shallow and unfair moralizing. We continue from the fallacy of *ad hominem* reasoning, which distracts from powerful ideas that can modify misunderstanding, to a review of Freud's actual ideas. This gives us the opportunity to think for ourselves about the validity of his propositions regarding bisexuality.

> In psycho-analytic treatment it is very important to be prepared for a symptom's having a bisexual meaning ... The bisexual nature of hysterical symptoms, which can in any event be demonstrated in numerous cases, is an interesting confirmation of my view that the postulated existence of an innate bisexual disposition in man is especially clearly visible in the analysis of psychoneurotics.
>
> (Freud, [1908] 1955, p. 165)

I start here because this is so often misread to mean that for Freud bisexuality is neurotic, when what he specifically means is that, first, those in analysis allow for the discovery of all things human and, second, that neurosis develops when aims and objects become subjected to guilt, revenge, and repression. In other words, ordinary predictable states and fantasies such as, but not only, psychic bisexuality, can become inveigled in neurotic compromise. The wish for everything (for bisexual completeness) is not in itself a problem; rather it is the disruption of bisexual symbolization that follows the guilty disavowal of such a wish. This disruption is at least one possible determinant of neurotic inhibitions of intellect and creativity. We can expect that its inverse, the unconflicted unconscious self-representation of possessing both male and female genitalia, most likely lends itself to productive and pleasurable intellectual and artistic endeavors. Let us look behind these assertions.

One partial answer to the philosophical conundrum "how does matter (or, in our case, the mind) know itself?" might be found by reflecting on the facility of the mind to fashion itself after parts of its own extension in space, the body. These extensions represent one possible version of the mind that, in turn, then knows itself by assessing the body. The psychic and cognitive feats of displacement and metaphor are central to this question of knowing, a logical assertion is that one way that children come to know the world and themselves is through their anatomy. Reciprocally, they make sense of their anatomy in part by observing the opposite sex as well as the same sex. As we shall see, bisexual fantasies are an intrinsic part of that developing self-knowledge. Conceptualizing the mind as a mirror of genital anatomy, though, tends to obscure the power of the idea of the mind as an organized reflection of the self. Theories of the self, sense of self, and self-representation offer a complex array of possible frameworks from which to think about how the child comes to know their sexual self.

The developmental march through various erotogenic zones – the pleasures, fantasies, and dangers inherent in all of them – implies that at each stage the child will know herself, her mind, and her world in part as she knows her own body. This self-knowledge continues to transform so as to include the most recently interesting part of the body, which will also be a palimpsest of all that had been traversed before. Yet we also know that in normal development the genitals are the ultimate in the line of the child's (proprioceptive and exteroceptive) sensory and (conscious or unconscious) fantasy fascination and preoccupation with parts of his or her body. And we know that children are fascinated with the genitals of the opposite sex as well. In this way, one's identity depends on an experience of extension in space, namely the body, with the resulting implication that the mutuality of mind and body requires that each of them help define the other. These definitions are not bound by the limitations of language and metaphor. Rather, they are ways of knowing, of experiencing. They are phenomenologically real in that they allow for the use of the body to make sense of the mind, of the self.

There is a long theoretical line, going back to Horney and Jones and continuing to the present, which states that physiology and psychology come together in gender formation so that girls experience primary femininity and, by implication, boys primary masculinity. Ironically, one can argue from within psychoanalytic theory itself there is no concept of the primary – and therefore no primary femininity or masculinity. Regardless of the basic or derivative level on which one believes gender enters identity formation, it is not conceivable that either boy or girl could escape the pull of bisexual aims amid biparental object ties. The combination of a universal wish with increasingly complex object identification becomes the mechanism of imbricating in the sense of self, in the experience of the mind, a multifaceted body representation with the genitals at center stage.

Psychic realities thus blur the edges of anatomy, which has us all deal with the same few body parts, each in his or her own creative way. It is the integration between feminine/masculine – passive/active – that helps account for unconflicted expressions of creativity. It is the unconflicted (to the extent this is truly possible) integration of these multiple anatomical and psychic identifications that allows for the fullest use and enjoyment of ego capacities, such as intellect and creativity. Women have to be able to bring their ideas forward, into space, and men must be able to nurture their thoughts and bring them to fruition.

Neurotic compromises occur when there are guilt and shame about the need and wish to combine. And it is here that we see the complexity of bisexuality as a wish-fulfilling fantasy. It gratifies the narcissistic longing for completeness and freedom from need of the object. At the same time, contradictory as it may seem, the necessary internal presence of the object, the other, is the closest we ever come to having everything. "Anatomy is destiny" perhaps means that the mind is the sum of all that is part of the human body, male and female. And in this centrally profound way, bisexuality is not a choice, not an identity, but an essential aspect of all human experience.

We return to Virginia Woolf and those who maintain that bisexuality is not a type of identity but rather an intrinsic aspect of sexual desire. I, a Freudian psychoanalyst, would agree even while accepting that most people neither gratify nor consciously acknowledge such desires. But Woolf did, and that gave her the motivation to explain to others one basic aspect of the phenomenology of desire, decoupling it from gender identity. And Freud did the same thing in the language of psychic choice. Together, they are a formidable team.

References

Freud, S. ([1905] 1955). Three essays on the theory of sexuality. In *The Standard Edition of the Complete Psychological Works of Sigmund Freud, Volume 7* (pp. 125–243). Hogarth Press.

Freud, S. ([1908] 1955). Hysterical fantasies and their relation to bisexuality. In *The Standard Edition of the Complete Psychological Works of Sigmund Freud, Volume 9* (pp. 155–166). Hogarth Press.

Gulati, R. & Pauley, D. (2019) The half embrace of psychic bisexuality. *Journal of the American Psychoanalytic Association*, 67, 97–121.

Morgan, S. (2019). Coming out used to be about freeing yourself. Now it's about placating everyone else. *The Washington Post*, October 11, 38–39.

Chapter 6

Passion and melancholia, red and black

The vicissitudes of the sexual in an analytic process[1]

Rosine Jozef Perelberg

Your hair was not your own. It was mine, the work of twenty years of care and attention. You have disposed of a precious trust that I confided in you.

(Letter to Colette by Sido: Colette, 1953, p. 13)

Beauty, my mother would call me, and "Jewel-of-pure-gold"; then she would let me go, watching her creation – her masterpiece, as she said – grow smaller as I ran down the slope.

(Colette, 1953, p. 147)

Introduction

"Now Dr B.'s child is coming" (letter from Sigmund Freud to Stefan Zweig, 2 June 1932, in E. L. Freud, 1960, p. 413), exclaimed Anna at the end of her last session with Breuer – at which Breuer took flight. At that moment, with that phantasmatic pregnancy, psychoanalysis was inaugurated with the *force* of a dramatization of an incestuous heterosexual phantasy, leading to the first phantasmatic baby of psychoanalysis.[2]

Many years after Anna O's analysis, Freud was to say in a letter to Stefan Zweig on 2 June 1932, that "At this moment he [Breuer] held in his hand the key that would have opened the doors to the 'Mothers', but he let it drop" (E. L. Freud, 1960, p. 413). The reference to the "Mothers" is an allusion to Faust's mysterious research in Goethe's *Faust* (Part II, Act 1). The mysterious mothers are goddesses who dwell below, in an internal *void, without space, place or time* (Pollock, 1968; Perelberg, 1999). The 1932 letter to Zweig was written subsequent to Freud's discovery of the pre-oedipal relationship to the mother, the powerful, phallic, maternal imago for children of both sexes. The mother had, however, already appeared as the first seductress in several other papers, such as *The Interpretation of Dreams* (Freud, 1900) and *Leonardo Da Vinci* (Freud, 1910). In those texts Freud described that first passionate relationship, the prototype of all future love relationships.

DOI: 10.4324/9781003584483-7

With his reflections on Anna O's treatment, Freud established the link between symptoms, bisexuality, and excess: the force of the drives that seek representation in the psychoanalytic endeavor. If, on the one hand, the drive is conceived of as having the same peremptory quality as a bodily need, the concept of *Trieb* distinguishes itself from an animal instinct because

> it is a wandering force which searches without knowing exactly what it is searching for. It finds it almost without having searched for it, or it gives the impression of having obscurely searched for something else, and *retroactively* discovers the meaning of its lack of satisfaction.
>
> (Green, 1987, p. 163)

In psychoanalysis, sexuality refers to unconscious phantasies and infantile sexuality, defined by transgression and incestuous desires that are repressed and repudiated, defying the possibility of ever being fully known (Kohon, 1999, 2017; Perelberg, 2017b). From his "Project" (Freud, 1895), written in 1895 but published after his death, to the *Outline of Psychoanalysis* (Freud, 1940), Freud attempted to explore the relationship between the drives and their representations, the somatic and the psychic, positing a discontinuity between the two. Already, in *Studies on Hysteria* (Freud & Breuer, 1895), sexuality is conceived of as traumatic because of its excessive nature. Freud points out the way in which what is traumatic is un-absorbable by representation and inaccessible to symbolization. Corporeal experiences are at the very origin of the constitution of the psyche, and it is only progressively and *incompletely* that they become constituted as psychic reality.

In 1920, Freud postulated the existence of a drive that does not correspond to any representation but is expressed though the repetition compulsion (Freud, 1920). The structural model of the mind instituted a close relationship between the id and the soma. The id is described as "chaos, a cauldron full of seething excitations" (Freud, 1933, p. 73). Psychoanalytic work becomes concerned with the way the experience of an infantile traumatic past in its unmetabolizable aspects may present itself in the consulting room. If the drives are at the root of psychic activity, this "implies that something is basically *in excess*, an overload charge on the mind, linked with the bodily exigencies of the drives whose derivatives have to be sent back to the unconscious because their free expression forbids psychic organisation" (Green, 1998, p. 660; Perelberg, 2003, 2015b).

This will be Laplanche's point of departure for his theory of generalized seduction, whereby "an adult, may proffer to a child verbal, non-verbal and even behavioural signifiers which are pregnant with unconscious sexual significations" (1987, p. 126). Laplanche highlights what he calls "'the enigmatic signifiers' … transmitted via parental messages to the other as a key element in the creation of the unconscious." In Laplanche's words, "the *enigma* is in itself a *seduction* and its mechanisms are unconscious" (1987, p. 126). What makes the message into an enigma is that the messages are unconscious to the emitting adults themselves. The infant is a receptor of a sexual message that has not reached awareness in the consciousness of the adults. These enigmatic messages then become "unmetabolizable foreign bodies" – the alien in one-self, as we will see later.

Laplanche has coined the term *"le sexual"* – by definition multiple and polymorphous – which refers to infantile, perverse sexuality. He stresses that the *"sexual"* is the psychoanalytic object:

> The infantile "sexuel," the "sexual," is the very object of psychoanalysis. A matter of drives and not instinct, functioning according to a specific economic system that is the seeking of tension and not the seeking of tension reduction, having at its origin the fantasmatic object, at its origin and not at its outcome, hence reversing the "object relation," it comes to take up all the room by trying to organize itself in a way that is always precarious, until the upheaval of puberty when the instinctive genital will have to come to terms with it.
>
> (Laplanche, 2007, p. 218)

These ideas establish a link between sexuality and temporality, capturing the inherent diphasic nature of human sexuality. Infantile experiences will only reach meaning in *après-coup*. The notion of *après-coup* institutes a separation between the moment of the experience and its understanding, which can only be reached retrospectively (Perelberg, 2006).

Madeleine

A young and attractive woman, Madeleine, came to see me many years ago because of profound episodes of depression that left her incapacitated and unable to function. For some time she had also become stuck in her work as a sculptress. She had no idea what this was connected to. She would feel as if she was disappearing, or disintegrating – a sense of void and emptiness. She felt suicidal at times; at other times she felt as if she was already dead.

It was somewhat difficult to match this account with the smiling, tall, slim young woman who entered my consulting room. Her long blond hair seemed to float around her, framing a beautiful, vivacious face, with large, intelligent green eyes. She exuded a sensuality that was there, apparently visible to be appreciated – and yet, nevertheless, I experienced a sense of absence in her, as if she was not totally there. It would take a few years for me to understand the hidden element of shame in her sensual presentation. Madeleine came from a large, very successful professional family; she was the youngest of five siblings. She described having had, as a child, an adoring relationship with her mother, who was the centre of her life. Throughout the first year of her analysis she talked about her experience of closeness to her mother as a young girl, describing her mother's voice, her laughter, her skin, her clothes, make-up, and perfume. They often slept in the same bed while the father was tra-velling abroad on business. Hand-in-hand, naked, they would spend hours talking about the many aspects of life together. The house where they lived had a huge garden, and Madeleine remembers sitting with her mother on a double rocking chair on long summer afternoons, when the scent of flowers would fill the air and there was no sense of time.

The father was described as absent – a silent presence when at home, involved with his reading and papers. He was experienced as gentle and kind. The other four siblings, all boys, were much older, so that in many ways Madeleine had the experience of being an only child.

In the first few months of her analysis, the transference conveyed very powerfully a sensorial aspect of her relationship to her mother. This would be expressed by Madeleine's minute attentiveness to and descriptions of the light, scent, flowers, and trees as she came down the street on the way to my con-sulting room, as well as her experience of lying on the couch and being in the room with me. In the sessions themselves she produced thoughts, dreams, associations. She responded to my interpretations with further associations, and there was a sense of a strong alliance and intense work taking place. The very way in which she immersed herself in our work became the live experi-ence of a very seductive and erotic childhood relationship with her mother. Once she said to me: "Each session feels like a jewel, something magical happens. Nothing dramatic; but you surprise me with what you say to me, the way you talk to me." And another time: "Sometimes I just like lying here in silence, taking in everything about this room. It feels to me so feminine."

Progressively, however, another aspect of her mother emerged: a dominant and powerful figure in her life, who would define her and tell her who she was. Perhaps their relationship changed with the approach of adolescence. I noticed how reluctant and even frightened Madeleine seemed to be when telling me about these experiences. In many ways they did not seem real to her. Or was it the other idealized aspect that was not real? Throughout her childhood her mother had made decisions about Madeleine's hair and clothes, and about the way she should speak, especially to the many visitors in their house.

For as long as Madeleine could remember, she had believed that her mother was having an affair with a man, as she disappeared during certain holidays each year. She would look for clues, listen to her phone calls, try to imagine where she went when she was out of the house. It was a secret that no one dared to talk about. The siblings had never discussed this with each other. She had no idea whether her father knew, and she felt somewhat sorry for him. In the course of the relationship to me in the transference it emerged that she felt betrayed at the thought of the mother having (another) lover. She experienced that she and her mother formed the couple in the family.

Madeleine seemed to have negotiated the various challenges of adolescence: she was intelligent, did well at school, and entered a prestigious university. She had a few boyfriends and had her first sexual experience aged 18. She had had two long-term relationships since then, which included what she said was "a good enough sexual life," but she felt that she could not fully engage with sex. Something prevented her from being able to be "fully there."

As Madeleine entered my consulting room one Thursday morning, some two years into her analysis, she said that she had been invaded by an inexplicable fear. She had a sense of foreboding, a reluctance to come in, as she commented on the perfume coming from the winter jasmine in my front garden. Immersed in looking at the tall bushes surrounding the white flowers, she had a physical sensation of panic and wanted to leave. As she crossed the threshold of my consulting room, she thought that she was entering "*a no man's land.*" This expression was said in English, although the language of her analysis with me was French.

During the previous weeks she had spent quite a long time talking about her relationship to her elder brother. This idealized brother, who is a well-known artist, had come across in the previous sessions as cruel and attacking, often humiliating or mocking her. This picture emerged through her telling me, for the first time, the cruel words that he used to say to her when she was a child. He still says cruel things to her, but she had never fully registered this, as she felt that she needed him so much. As she had entered adolescence and her relationship with her mother had become more complicated, she found solace in her relationship with this brother. We had in recent weeks examined the way in which at times the aggression was couched as humor, and the only response available to her was to laugh. My spelling out his aggression to her felt to her like a revelation.

So, on this Thursday, as she communicated her thought about entering a "no man's land" I wondered with her whether this followed the sequence of sessions when she had progressively discovered her brother's cruelty. Would she now be left just with me, in a world with women only, a "no man's land"?

She says that my comment makes her think of the Amazons – a tribe of fierce and violent women who did not need any men. They were composed entirely of women. I comment that this sounds pertinent, as she knows I am Brazilian, so an Amazon. She is stunned, as she has not consciously made the link. Crying, she says that she is afraid of becoming a woman who despises men.

Then she talks about the fact that among her group of friends, women who are single tend not to be invited to parties or dinners, as they are now all in couples. Single women become a "dangerous matter," she says. I indicate that the danger has become myself in the analysis, a fear that I would want her all to myself, on my couch, in a world without men. She takes a deep breath and says that this is exactly her experience with her mother. As she became an adolescent, her mother grew very critical of her: what she wore, the way she looked, the way she did her hair. She would also not let her have any friends, especially male friends. She would not bring them home, as her mother would flirt with them and want to show how interesting she was.

A silence and then Madeleine adds:

> In the last two weeks I have not wanted to come. It is as if I had lost trust in you. It's a special refusal to trust you, of putting myself in your hands. I have really had the experience of danger. Yet, I have been so happy for quite some time. The sessions used to leave me with a sentiment of lightness, happiness, and freedom. This has all changed recently. Perhaps, indeed, the reluctance to talk about my relationship to my brother.

I say that she has experienced herself as being with me in this *"no man's land,"* and this has left her very anguished. She cries. There is a silence, during which she calms down. Then, it is time.

At the following session she tells me how much she has been thinking about yesterday's session. There is a long narrative about her mother's constant interest in her male friends, flirting with them, being so seductive with them. Her mother had never been interested in her female friends and had always been proud of being able to seduce any man. She believes that this is a curse that follows her. When being with her male friends, she thinks of her mother.

I comment that perhaps she is afraid of her mother's presence inside her. Is she betraying her mother when she goes out with her male friends? She responds that this is exactly the case. There is a long pause.

She continues. It reminds her of the film *Alien*, as if her mother were trapped inside her. As if she inhabited her. She does not know how to get rid of her. She sobs.

After a while, I say that perhaps there is a paradox: is it her mother who cannot let her go, or is it that she herself cannot let her mother go? Madeleine remains quiet, reflective. She is much calmer as she leaves.

It took two years of analysis before Madeleine's ambivalent relationship with her mother was revealed in the context of the transference. Her mother's presence inside her – as she describes it – is a reminder of Freud's "Mourning and Melancholia" (1917), and his description of the shadow of the object: an object-loss is transformed into an ego-loss that alters and impoverishes the ego through identification.

The particular aspect that led me to write about Madeleine, however, was the pathway through which the unconscious material made its way into the session and the transference. The "no man's land" expression came *at the threshold of my consulting room, as she was entering it*, first through the scent of the jasmine and the bushes, the sensorial pathway that enabled the repetition of a past experience in the here-and-now of the transference situation, which was then put into words. The scent of the flowers and the description of the tall bushes brought forth a phantasy of a phallic world, which refers to the pre-oedipal domain containing the overwhelming presence of a powerful maternal imago. Then, the foreign language, which is not the usual language in which analyst and patient engage with each other in this analysis, enabled the negative of what was until then more on the surface – the negative transference – to make its way into the consulting room. *No man's land* appeared at the crossroad between past and present: a childhood experience, not fully understood and which provoked anxiety, made its way *après-coup* into the here-and-now of the transference.

Green suggests the idea of a *"multilocular structure"* (1977, p. 136) in order to capture the heterogeneity of elements present in a psychoanalytic process.[3], [4] In this example the *multilocular* structure included sensorial experiences and images, unspoken phantasies that belonged to the pre-oedipal domain, now expressed through the repetition compulsion, all inserted into a complex temporal model under the dominance of the *après-coup*.

The foreign language that erupted in the session was the marker of anxiety. In "The 'Uncanny'," Freud (1919) sought the translation of the word "uncanny" in many languages: unfamiliar, familiar, strange, mysterious, sinister, disgusting, surprising, ghostly, frightening. In looking at the meaning of the term in other languages, was Freud attempting to master the foreignness of the uncanny? I am reminded of the various moments in his work when Freud appeals to a language other than the one in which he is writing. In the case of Dora, he says that *"J'appelle un chat un chat,"* when referring to Dora's genitals (Freud, 1905a, p. 48); in his letter of 3 October 1897 to Fliess, when he refers to the episode when he saw his mother naked, he refers to her as *"matrem"* and her nakedness as *"nudam"* – the foreign language perhaps expressing an attempt to mitigate his incestuous desires (in Masson, 1985, p. 268). Is the search for the meaning of the word "uncanny" in a foreign language already evoking the anxiety connected to the phenomenon Freud is attempting to understand?

Freud understands that the uncanny is the recurrence of the same thing – he explored *unheimlich* in relation to the maternal body:

> [...] whenever a man dreams of a place or a country and says to himself, whilst he is still dreaming: "this place is familiar to me, I've been here before," we may interpret the place as being his mother's genitals or her body. In this case too, then, the *unheimlich* is what was once *heimisch*, familiar; the prefix *"un"* ["un"-] is the token of repression.
>
> (Freud, 1919, p. 245)

Every individual has passed through their mother's genitals. How can one deal with this homosexual/heterosexual incestuous beginning?

One cannot, certainly, remember one's own birth: the experience of coming out of one's mother's body. The work of culture imposes a general repression and specifically the repression of that which Cabrol has called *primordial incest*. The erotic maternal and primal seduction is at the foundation of psychic reality (Cabrol, 2011). Cabrol suggests that the birth trauma might be understood as a traumatic experience of primordial mother-child incest that is rejected by culture and also remains hidden from psychoanalytic theory. Might the analytic treatment, with its promise of rebirth and the prohibition of touching, reactualize this primordial incestuous phantasy (Perelberg, 2019)? Would it be speculating too much to say that the white jasmine surrounded by the tall bushes evoked an incestuous anxiety about the maternal body as Madeleine was about to enter my room?

How to think about the bisexuality that permeates this phantasy? The baby/girl as a penis that comes out of her mother's body, does this not characterize the bisexuality of all human beings from this very beginning?

In previous work (Perelberg, 2015a, 2015b, 2019), I linked the uncanny to the question of what happens at night between a child's parents. There is an important reference to the sexual father. The text on "The Uncanny," therefore, raises questions about the maternal and the paternal, the sexuality of the feminine and the masculine, and the puzzle about the question of what happens at night between the parents. It provokes curiosity and refers to incestuous desires that are frightening, forbidden, and disgusting. Is it that the act of sex is, by definition, uncanny because of the experience that "one has, therefore, been there before"? Is incest at the core of the riddle of anxiety?

One is navigating the realm of unconscious phantasies, of infantile sexuality, defined by transgression and incestuous desires, which are repressed, repudiated, and experienced as the stranger in ourselves (Kristeva, 1991). The uncanny is thus profoundly likened to the object of psychoanalytic investigation, the unconscious, by definition familiar and unfamiliar, never fully knowable.

It took quite a few years of analysis before Madeleine was able to tell me, very hesitantly, about a comment her mother had made to her once, when she was 9 or 10 years old. She could not remember what she had said properly, but it was a comment about her vagina. Madeleine had not understood what she meant, but this comment had stayed with her. From then on she had often examined her vagina to identify what was wrong with it. It made her feel awkward when with her boyfriends. She had never been able to share this with anyone else and had never again let anyone else see her vagina.

Is it that the mother's comment about her vagina was experienced as her mother taking possession of it, in a way that prevented her from being available to anyone else? Was it an unconscious message about a vagina being, by definition, wrong, wounded, castrated? Was this the experience of a "no man's land," the stamp of the "*mère*-version" (as a transformation of perversion) (Kristeva, 2002, p. 27)?

Green has suggested the distinction between the red and the black. The red is the signifier of the wound, castration, the violence of the division between the sexes. The black is the expression of depression, severe depression, or states of emptiness (Green, 1986). The hatred is the consequence of a loss experienced at a narcissistic level, which has led Madeleine to seek treatment. Green suggests that in relation to the dead mother complex, behind the experience of mourning and depression, one catches glimpses of the "mad" passion for the mother.[5]

The sexual and the melancholic are intertwined in this analysis without any chronological sequence. They are woven together in a complex structure. One is referring to the processes of transformations, extensions, fixations, regressions binding and unbinding the libidinal drives (Green, 1997; Perelberg, 2017a, 2017b). This perspective emphasizes the movements in the psychic apparatus that defy any linearity.

On that Thursday session, as Madeleine arrived for her session, she was in a profound state of anxiety: whether to leave her mother/analyst, whose love and protection she sought, or to remain as an object of her phallic narcissistic desire for ever.[6]

Bisexuality, compulsion to repeat, death drive, sexuality

> Although, for psychoanalysis, difference is sexual, the question of bisexuality is related to psychoanalytic theory as a whole, said Andre Green in his paper "The Neuter Gender."
>
> (Perelberg, 2018)

Freud was to use the term "bisexuality" 44 times throughout his work. In the initial phase, at the time of his correspondence with Fliess, Freud was still concerned with matching his ideas on bisexuality to the anatomical-biological substratum proposed by Fliess, to whom he attributed the discovery of bisexuality. It is only progressively that bisexuality acquired a more fundamental psychological meaning in his work. In time Freud was to regard bisexuality as an inherent characteristic of all human beings.

Hysteria and bisexuality have an essential link for Freud, who suggested that hysterical attacks express an experience of rape in which the hysteric plays both roles. It was in the discussion of the case of Katharina in 1896 that Freud himself first related hysteria with the primal scene (Letter 52, in Freud, [1896] 1950). Freud mentioned at least three further cases linking anxiety to the primal scene – in a letter to Fliess, in his paper on anxiety neurosis (Freud, 1895), and in his analysis of Dora (Freud, 1905a) – although throughout his work he oscillated between regarding this as a "real event" and a "phantasy":

> I maintained years ago that the dyspnoea and palpitations that occur in hysteria and anxiety neurosis are only detached fragments of the act of copulation.
>
> (Freud, 1905a, p. 80)

The interplay of masculine and feminine identifications in relation to the primal scene is implicit or explicit in each of Freud's case studies, from Dora

(Freud, 1905a) to Little Hans (Freud, 1909a), the Rat Man (Freud, 1909b), Schreber (Freud, 1911), the Wolf Man (Freud, 1918), and "The Psychogenesis of a Case of Homosexuality in a Woman" (Freud, 1920). The contrasts between passivity/activity, femininity/masculinity, and sadism/masochism are indeed central to Freud's understanding of the structuring of psychic reality in each individual, male or female. They are the axes around which Freud thought about most of his patients, whether hysterics, obsessional neurotics, perverse or psychotic, and, I suggest, are present in any analysis.

The compulsion to repeat, death drive, sexuality

The profound link that is progressively established between the repetition compulsion and sexuality gains its full force with the introduction of the structural model of the mind. In 1920, the notion of sexuality changed from being associated with love to becoming demonic and unbound, linked to the death drives. "Beyond the Pleasure Principle" (Freud, 1920) brought forward a conception of infantile sexuality, which is not that of the "Three Essays" (Freud, 1905b). Rolland (1997) has suggested that it is a conceptualization of infantile sexuality that is "specifically analytical." It is recognizable in the analytic process, through the analysis of the transference, of its pressure to repeat. It also highlights the "tragic, traumatic and painful" aspect of this infantile sexuality (Green, 1997, p. 164).

"An Outline of Psycho-Analysis" (Freud, 1940a, p. 147) summarizes the dual characteristic of the drives: "Though they are the ultimate cause of all activity, they are of conservative nature." According to Green,

> They are therefore necessarily involved in the broadening of mental life and its diversification by their ability to change their aim and object, but at the same time prove resistant to changes and developments which would be excessively at variance with their fundamental demands.
>
> (1987, p. 167)

One is pointing out the paradoxical nature of the drives. If, on the one hand, they resist representation, in that there is something always in excess; on the other hand, they also seek representation. In the felicitous formulation of Jean Claude Rolland (1997), there is a compulsion to represent. The object becomes, in the final analysis, the revealing agent of the drives.

It is the force of the repetition compulsion that enables repressed infantile bisexuality to find its way in the transference so that it can be named, in its contradictory and opposing forces – red and black – for the first time.

Notes

1 This article was previously published in *The International Journal of Psychoanalysis, 100* (6): 1237–1247.

2 Appignanesi and Forrester (1992) have suggested that this baby was psychoanalysis itself.
3 This term is derived from Freud. In 1923 Freud states: "Internal perceptions yield sensations of processes arising in the most diverse and certainly also in the deepest strata of the mental apparatus. Very little is known about these sensations and feelings; those belonging to the pleasure-unpleasure series may still be regarded as the best examples of them. They are more primordial, more elementary, than perceptions arising externally and they can come about even when consciousness is clouded. I have elsewhere expressed my views about their greater economic significance and the metapsychological reasons for this. These sensations are multilocular, like external perceptions; they may come from different places simultaneously and may thus have different or even opposite qualities" (Freud, 1923, pp. 21–22, emphasis added).
4 In his letter to Fliess of 2 May 1897, Freud states: "the psychic structures which, in hysteria, are affected by repression are not in reality memories – since no one indulges in memory activity without a motive – but impulses [drives] that derive from primal scenes" (in Masson, 1985, p. 239).
5 One is here reminded of Lacan's formulations in that the I and the body image are accomplished in an alienating process that takes place through the mediation of the other. It is the mother who indicates to the child that what she sees in the mirror is herself. "There, this is you," she will say when the child is looking at herself in the mirror. In this process, her own unconscious relationship to her own body and sexuality will have an impact on her child, as discussed by many French analysts (Lacan, 1973; Braunschweig & Fain, 1975; Laplanche, 1987). The child's body image is rooted in the way it is seen and invested by the demand of the Other. When thinking about this process, one can reflect on the impact of mother's comment on Madeleine's sense of her female body.
6 One is also reminded of Freud's statement about melancholia: "when the ego finds itself in an excessive real danger which it believes itself unable to overcome by its own strength, it is bound to draw the same conclusion. It sees itself deserted by all protective forces and lets itself die" (Freud, 1923, p. 58).

References

Appignanesi, L., & Forrester, J. (1992). *Freud's women*. Weidenfeld & Nicolson.
Braunschweig, D., & Fain, M. (1975). *La nuit, le jour. Essai psychanalytique sur le fonctionnement mental*. Presses Universitaires de France.
Cabrol, G. (2011). Le refoulement de l'inceste primordial. *Revue Française de Psychanalyse*, 75, 1583–1587.
Colette, S. G. ([1953] 1966). *My mother's house and Sido*. Penguin.
Freud, E. L. (Ed.) (1960). *Letters of Sigmund Freud*. Basic Books.
Freud, S. (1895). Project for a scientific psychology. In *The Standard Edition of the Complete Psychological Works of Sigmund Freud, Volume 1* (pp. 281–391). Hogarth Press.
Freud, S. ([1896] 1950) Letter 52 from Extracts from the Fliess Papers. In *The Standard Edition of the Complete Psychological Works of Sigmund Freud, Volume 1* (pp. 233–239). Hogarth Press.
Freud, S. (1900). The interpretation of dreams. In *The Standard Edition of the Complete Psychological Works of Sigmund Freud, Volumes 4 and 5*. Hogarth Press.

Freud, S. (1905a). Fragment of an analysis of a case of hysteria. In *The Standard Edition of the Complete Psychological Works of Sigmund Freud, Volume 7* (pp. 1–122). Hogarth Press.

Freud, S. (1905b). Three essays on the theory of sexuality. In *The Standard Edition of the Complete Psychological Works of Sigmund Freud, Volume 7* (pp. 123–245). Hogarth Press.

Freud, S. ([1909a] 1955). Analysis of a phobia in a five-year-old boy. In *The Standard Edition of the Complete Psychological Works of Sigmund Freud, Volume 10* (pp. 5–148). Hogarth Press.

Freud, S. ([1909b] 1955). Notes upon a case of obsessional neurosis. In *The Standard Edition of the Complete Psychological Works of Sigmund Freud, Volume 10* (pp. 155–251). Hogarth Press.

Freud, S. (1910). Leonardo Da Vinci and a memory of his childhood. In *The Standard Edition of the Complete Psychological Works of Sigmund Freud, Volume 11* (pp. 63–138). Hogarth Press.

Freud, S. ([1911] 1958). Psychoanalytic notes on an auto-biographical account of a case of paranoia. In *The Standard Edition of the Complete Psychological Works of Sigmund Freud, Volume 12* (pp. 9–80). Hogarth Press.

Freud, S. (1917). Mourning and melancholia. In *The Standard Edition of the Complete Psychological Works of Sigmund Freud, Volume 14* (pp. 243–258). Hogarth Press.

Freud, S. ([1918] 1955) From the history of an infantile neurosis. In *The Standard Edition of the Complete Psychological Works of Sigmund Freud, Volume 17* (pp. 7–104). Hogarth Press.

Freud, S. (1919). The "uncanny." In *The Standard Edition of the Complete Psychological Works of Sigmund Freud, Volume 17* (217–256). Hogarth Press.

Freud, S. (1920). Beyond the Pleasure Principle. In *The Standard Edition of the Complete Psychological Works of Sigmund Freud, Volume 18* (pp. 7–64). Hogarth Press.

Freud, S. ([1920] 1957). The psychogenesis of a case of homosexuality in a woman. In *The Standard Edition of the Complete Psychological Works of Sigmund Freud, Volume 18* (pp. 147–172). Hogarth Press.

Freud, S. (1923). The ego and the id. In *The Standard Edition of the Complete Psychological Works of Sigmund Freud, Volume 19* (pp. 1–66). Hogarth Press.

Freud, S. (1933). New introductory lectures on psychoanalysis. In *The Standard Edition of the Complete Psychological Works of Sigmund Freud, Volume 22* (pp. 1–182). Hogarth Press.

Freud, S. (1940). An outline of psycho-analysis. In *The Standard Edition of the Complete Psychological Works of Sigmund Freud, Volume 23* (pp. 139–208). Hogarth Press.

Freud, S. & Breuer, J. (1895). Studies on hysteria. In *The Standard Edition of the Complete Psychological Works of Sigmund Freud, Volume 2* (pp. 155–166). Hogarth Press.

Green, A. (1977). Conceptions of affect. *International Journal of Psychoanalysis, 58,* 129–156.

Green, A. (1986). The dead mother. In *On private madness* (pp. 142–173). Hogarth Press & The Institute of Psychoanalysis.

Green, A. (1987). Instinct in the late works of Freud. In J. Sandler (Ed.), *On Freud's analysis terminable and interminable* (pp. 149–170). International Psychoanalytical Association.

Green, A. (1997). *Les chaines d'Éros. Actualité du sexuel.* Éditions Odile Jacob.

Green, A. (1998). The primordial mind and the work of the negative. *International Journal of Psychoanalysis*, 79, 649–665.

Kohon, G. (1999). *No lost certainties to be recovered.* Karnac Books.

Kohon, G. (2017). Bye-bye sexuality. In R. Perelberg (Ed.), *Psychic bisexuality: A British- French dialogue* (pp. 258–276). Routledge.

Kristeva, J. (1991). *Strangers to ourselves.* Columbia University Press.

Kristeva, J. (2002). *Le génie féminin. Colette.* Folio.

Lacan, J. (1973). *Le séminaire, Livre XI. Les quatre concepts fondamentaux de la psychanalyse.* Éditions du Seuil.

Laplanche, J. (1987). *New foundations for psychoanalysis.* Basil Blackwell.

Laplanche, J. (2007). Gender, sex, and the sexual. *Studies in Gender and Sexuality*, 8, 201–219.

Masson, J. M. (Ed.). (1985). *The complete letters of Sigmund Freud to Wilhelm Fliess, 1887–1904.* Belknap Press.

Perelberg, R. J. (1999). The interplay of identifications: Violence, hysteria and the repudiation of femininity. In G. Kohon (Ed.), *The dead mother: The work of André Green* (pp. 173–192). Routledge.

Perelberg, R. J. (2003). Full and empty spaces in the analytic process. *International Journal of Psychoanalysis*, 84: 579–592.

Perelberg, R. J. (2006). *The controversial discussions and après-coup. International Journal of Psychoanalysis*, 87(5): 1199–1220.

Perelberg, R. J. (2015a). *Murdered father, dead father: Revisiting the Oedipus complex.* Routledge.

Perelberg, R. J. (2015b). On excess, trauma and helplessness: Repetition and transformations. *International Journal of Psychoanalysis*, 96: 1453–1476.

Perelberg, R. J. (2017a). Love and melancholia in the analysis of women by women. *International Journal of Psycho-Analysis*, 98 (6), 1533–1549.

Perelberg, R. J. (2017b). *Psychic bisexuality: A British–French dialogue.* Routledge.

Perelberg, R. J. (2019). *Sexuality, excess and representation.* Routledge.

Pollock, G. H. (1968). The possible significance of childhood object loss in the Josef Breuer – Bertha Pappenheim (Anna O.) – Sigmund Freud relationship. *Journal of the American Psychoanalytic Association*, 16, 711–739.

Rolland, J. C. (1997). Le rythme et la raison. *Revue Française de Psychanalyse*, 61 (5), 1589–1651.

Part II

Challenges in the construction of a gender and sexual identity

Chapter 7

Crossing borders

Persona, mask, who am I?

Mona Chahoury Charabaty

Introduction

We do not choose the circumstances of our birth – our parents, our neigh-borhood, our country, or the community to which our family belongs, what-ever its nature. These are the circumstances into which we are thrust, the foundations upon which our lives are built, often without our consent. Yet, it is within these very circumstances that we must navigate the complexities of identity, belonging, and self-determination.

Borders to cross

I was born in a Middle Eastern country, a land as diverse and multifaceted as the region itself. Like many nations in the area, it is a mosaic of religious, ethnic, and cultural communities, each with its own distinct traditions, beliefs, and ways of life. This heterogeneity, while a source of richness, has also been a source of tension.

Over time, I witnessed how the nation – much like some of its neighbors – began to fracture along these lines of difference. What emerged in my country was a patchwork of mini-governances, unofficial systems of control that operated outside the bounds of the law and the constitution. There is a clear division between "us" and "them." These groups, often referred to as mino-rities, are intricately connected to larger populations beyond their immediate surroundings, with whom they share deep ties of identity and allegiance. They are bound by shared social, religious, cultural, and political commitments so deeply ingrained that they often border on indoctrination. The norms impose significant pressure regarding the status of women and their sexuality. The more cohesive these groups become, the greater the pressure they exert on individuals and families to conform. Uniformity is prized, while individuation is stifled. The construction of one's subjective identity is confined within a rigid framework, leaving little room for personal exploration or deviation.

Yet, human beings are not static entities. A tree, rooted in place, cannot move. An animal, driven by instinct, acts primarily for survival. But humans

DOI: 10.4324/9781003584483-9

possess a unique duality: we have roots – a place of birth, a sense of belonging, a context that shapes us – yet we also have the capacity to transcend these roots. Our psychobiological constitution is malleable, allowing us to question the forces that determine us, to challenge the narratives imposed upon us, and to redefine ourselves. The masks we wear to conform or to hide are not made of iron; they can be removed, reshaped, or discarded altogether. The evolving subject, the individual in pursuit of self-awareness and autonomy, can cross the boundaries placed on their path, reimagine their identity, and forge a new sense of self. The ambition of psychoanalysis, since the clinical and theoretical path of its founder, is to bring about this possibility of subjectivities.

But is it always so? Is the journey toward self-determination as straightforward as it seems? Or are there invisible chains – cultural, societal, and psychological – that bind us more tightly than we realize?

Crossing the borders?

Broadly speaking, crossing borders often refers to passing through geographical borders. Sociologists tend to think in terms of religious, ethnic, socioeconomic, and political factors, among others; whereas psychoanalysts know that "the" frontier has been already crossed straight to one's shadow zone. They are aware that being always ready to overcome obstacles cannot be avoided, that conquering the resistances that pose opposition, barriers, limits, or traps often faced is inescapable, whether during one's inner journey or that carried out by patients who are willing to go through this risk with them.

And yet, poets, artists, musicians, dancers, painters, choreographers, and filmmakers are all capable of crossing such borders as they are not encumbered by their persona, not intrinsically attached to their mask, feeling that they should remain chained to their "social self." Their unconscious is ready to be open, in an alert state. This allows them to express themselves and their creativity through various universal mediators that are available to them. The artist's and creator's freedom is unique and incomparable. Can we say the same about the psychoanalyst?

According to Freud ([1908] 1953), the writer and the artist possess an intuitive understanding of unconscious processes. The writer is someone who unconsciously and unknowingly expresses repressed, infantile truths. Freud suggests that the writer learns from within themself what others might learn from external sources (Freud, [1907] 1953), accessing universal themes through a process that is both cathartic and heuristic. Writers and artists help us cross the boundaries between topics, the conscious and the unconscious, and the limits of space and time. Note that at Freud's death, his library contained more than 2,000 volumes.

Winnicott ([1951] 2016, [1971] 1991) evokes and develops the concepts of false and true self. In the best-case scenarios, the false self can be a kind of socially concealing self, protecting but not hiding or repressing the true self. When a person's adaptive self is heavily loaded, opaque, or submitted to trendy images, it leads one to wonder whether it can feature some transparency for reflecting an individual's true self. For instance, feminine models often set a "cliché stereotype" through media and social platforms, namely through promoting the ideals of eternal youth, body shapes, and dress codes that often become fashion standards, thus concealing and hindering women's original and personalized expression of the feminine appearance.

This said, veils and *burqas* serve as examples of uniforms, like religious and professional uniforms (nurses, doctors, pilots). They are distinctive, referring to belonging. Yet, fashion and display forms, often, impose restrictions, signaling also social status.

Are analysts really protected by the frame-setting?

In terms of analytic practice, we often find ourselves committed, as of the moment when we schedule a first appointment made through direct requests or referrals, even throughout one session, in a relationship whose beginning, course, and end are unknown. We may have gained a sufficient understanding of the relevant theoretical knowledge, armed with experience and goodwill; however, every first appointment with a patient remains a ready-to-open Pandora's box, an unpredictable adventure yet to be discovered.

My office is on the border between two distinct areas. On one side, there is a region controlled by heavily armed political religious parties and, on the other, a peaceful bourgeois neighborhood, housing a diverse population, including mixed couples, both interfaith and same sex. The first neighborhood has expanded, fueled by an unparalleled demographic boom.

In this respect, I will share the adventure of a unique session I engaged in. Given its intensity and the rapid crossing journeys gone through by the patient, myself, and the framework, it seems that this analytical experience required major efforts and availability. It serves as an example, illustrating what personas and masks can hide and, paradoxically at the same time, allow to reveal behind it a heavy content of inner conflicts, avatars, failures, and distortions, imposing themselves on the feminine personality and psychic bisexuality, and the desperate attempt to cross boundaries.

The doorbell rings. I was startled, although I was notified of the appointment taken by a woman via WhatsApp where she asked to see me urgently. She was referred to me by one of my well-known acquaintances, a journalist who works for a TV channel on which I have participated in many interviews on mental health and parental guidance. All female journalists working for this channel were veiled and I would be asked to wear a scarf to cover my neck and shoulders if I was wearing a sleeveless dress. The TV crew were all very respectful toward me, although they were well aware that I did not necessarily share their viewpoints. However, upon arriving in the neighborhood where the TV channel premises were located, I always had the impression that I was entering into a world that was not even remotely connected with the rest of the city, whether in terms of the street odors, the cars and motorcycles, the movements, sounds, colors, and even clothing … It always seemed to me that the world I was entering was one where masculine domination was widespread and concealed a discreet, almost secret, feminine presence. It always felt like I was crossing borders, blindly trusting the driver assigned with taking me from the location where I had my car parked to the destination. The studio was located in the basement. Hence, arriving there, instantaneously turned me into Jules Vernes, discovering what was hidden beneath the surface while being led by my guide through mazes.

Recalling this may lead one to wonder: why did I even agree to go on such adventures, especially as, three days after I participated in a TV show broadcast by this channel, their premises were bombed?

Crossing borders

Significant childhood memories would offer a better insight. When I was three years old, I held the hand of my cousin who was two years older than me and took him to explore the fields located beyond the village where our families were spending summer vacation. I was constantly seeking to escape the confines of the house after the birth of my sister, whom I felt had taken over the entire physical and emotional space of the family home.

Years later, as young newlyweds, when civil war broke out in our country we were repeatedly forced out of the places we called home. The first triggering incident occurred on the edge of the neighborhood where we lived. The war lasted 15 years, during which we had children and raised them like nomads, moving them within the same country and sometimes abroad. Frequently, we had to "cross a border" to escape to safer regions, passing through battlefields or snipers' zones. Our workplaces changed according to the rhythm of the fighting. The country became a mosaic of communities engaged in absurd fratricidal wars against each other. We were in a floating space-time, navigating through non-places, seeking refuge in homes that did not belong to us.

Yet those years were not all about facing dangers, they also had a silver lining. It was then that I was surprised to receive an offer of a scholarship from the French embassy for pursuing my postgraduate education in Paris. I grasped the opportunity to undergo analytic training and personal analysis. In Paris I was not alone as members of my family were already there, including my mother who was a naturalized French citizen, a perquisite of my father who, at the time, was working for the French as a military man and a translator. In addition to Greek and Latin, my father knew three other languages. He was capable of crossing linguistic borders! That said, is such intergenerational transmission reflected in our desires and passions? And what exactly does it transmit to us: greater empathy, flexibility, or tolerance? On the other hand, escaping or changing our place of residence, as well as the environment and culture to which we are exposed, disrupts our habits and enhances our ability to embrace the differences and alterity.

Let's go back to our appointment. The profile photo on WhatsApp featured a verse from the religious book of the person who contacted me.

Where I live, having an insightful conversation over the phone is always preferable before agreeing to an appointment. It helps identify if a psychosis has been left untreated and provides us with preventive measures and information.

On the phone, the patient's voice was not gendered, it sounded asexual. It could have been a man's voice.

The doorbell rang ceaselessly. I looked through the peephole where I could see two long silhouettes standing, one wearing all black and the other fully dressed in white. I was expecting a woman. I hesitated for a moment before opening the door. Were they two men, or a couple? At the time, the cleaning lady was in the kitchen. I asked her to remain alert should I call her to warn a neighbor of a danger I might be in. For some reason, I was scared out of my wits and felt the need for a third party to rescue me if necessary. It all seemed irrational, yet perhaps it wasn't. The city had been quite eventful lately: tensions were escalating, assassinations were occurring here and there, and explosions were erupting right on the streets and in crowded neighborhoods. The environment was highly paranoid – and I was immersed in it myself.

I had no choice but to open the door. The couple introduced themselves: a sheik and his wife. Being aware of customs and traditions I did not shake the sheik's hand. His wife was entirely covered with black. Only her eyes were showing. Yet even those were covered with glasses. She was wearing men's shoes, and her hands were covered with black gloves. As a matter of fact, *burqas* were not that common in my country. They were only worn by some tourists.

Psychoanalysts are often confronted with an unusual situation, a situation they are unfamiliar with.

Once I had confirmed that the consultation was for the woman and not for the couple, I admitted her into my office while her husband waited in the reception area. Zeina began expressing her suffering, starting with the present, and then visiting her past where she described herself as a child who was martyred by her brothers. Her family treated her as Cinderella and addressed her in aggressive and disrespectful manners. She was born in a neighboring country to a large family where she always felt different. This made me think of the "Ugly Duckling." I realized I was connecting her situation to tales and stories I had read as a child. Was it an attempt to connect with her? To translate her situation? Or to dampen emotional overwhelm?

Her words were choked by the thick fabric covering her face. They were barely passing through this veil, which served as a filter for their ferocity although the hatred for her family and the world was often expressed through resorting to raw and violent terms.

I listened without having the possibility of intervening in her flow of anger, envy, hatred, doubt, and rage, and I could not help but think of her husband: I wondered how he was able to take all these negative feelings and keep his composure, even maintain his calmness. It was as if he was coming straight out of another world: He was tall, white, thin, blue-eyed, and resembling Nordic people. He looked different. The only thing she found to complain about when it came to him was his sexual demands. She was reluctant about sexual intimacy with him, yet she felt forced to oblige.

Based on a call made by a cousin, this man crossed the borders along with his family to propose to his now-wife. They got married a few weeks later although they barely had the time to get well acquainted before marriage. In some conservative areas of the region, it remains common for a man to ask a woman for marriage without getting to know her. And it is for the males of the family whether father or older brothers to decide for women.

I had mixed feelings during the appointment. At times I felt sorry, a kind of empathy for all the injustice this woman had gone through. At others, I felt unease, sometimes annoyed and even angry especially when she attempted to block the only visible part of her face, her eyes hidden behind the glasses, by lowering the veil covering her head and raising the lower veil so as to hide the already barely visible area that gave me access to her gaze and expression.

The psychoanalyst is confronted with the mystery of the other's desire, and the obstacle of reading it during the session, even if the other's speech is expansive and flowing. The *burqa* is the metaphor.

Was Zeina viewing me as an aggressor who intended to penetrate her body's space?

On the other hand, I could not refrain, against all evidence during the entire session, from asking myself whether she was a man or a woman: she was tall, thin, all covered in black, and standing just like the trunk of a palm tree.

While listening to her, memories were flashing in my head of my last meeting with my paternal aunt, which made me think of André Green (2012). The analytic situation can be seen as a return to oneself through the similarities with the other and I might even add "to that of strangers" too. The free association in our mind would then play out between otherness and sameness.

I often had terrifying encounters with this aunt. She was always wearing a long black dress which made it look as if she was mourning endlessly. Tall, thin, and in a straight posture, she was always capable of petrifying her interlocutor through her sharp tongue, ironic attacks, and accusations. She was a self-proclaimed dictator, granting herself unlimited power, and supported by her four sons, obedient soldiers.

And yet, these cousins, much older than me, all of them colossi, awakened within me from an early age a perplexing fascination with men. They were all handsome yet guarded by this ruthless castrator who established herself as the guardian of women's virtue. The youngest among them, who had offered to comfort me in the aftermath of a particularly painful scene, was not spared from her wrath.

Was it then a woman wearing a *burqa* or my aunt who had returned to haunt me in this office that now looked too narrow to fit both of us? What was it that was making me so powerless and terrorized, reminding me of my teenage years when I found myself, upon the death of my father, having to represent my family regarding heritage matters? She was practically yelling at me: "Do you think you are a man?" She was reminding me that I was *only* a "female" unable to face her, who had proclaimed herself as the man of the family, supported by five male subjects whose power had been reduced to a secondary position.

The surprise at the end of the session came after an attack on the framework under the aegis of the good cause. Zeina's cell phone alarm went off, interrupting the flow of her speech. "It's time to pray," she said. As astounded as I was, she announced that she was going to accomplish her duty, got up, turned toward Mecca, and discreetly recited her prayer.

This was unexpected. My office was turned into another place. I left it and closed the door behind me. I walked past the reception area where her husband was also praying. For a moment, there I felt like a stranger in his place. I went back to my office, and I resumed listening to the speech of hatred and guilt before announcing that only five minutes were left of the session. She stood up, looked me in the eye, intensely excited and enraged, and just like someone who is taken by the dream of imminent revenge, said: "I asked God to grant me another life upon my death, a life where I will be a man, so I can 'fuck' all women."

Zeina chose a stranger to her, to her country, and even to her sociocultural environment, to express her anger and hatred. She confided in me to express a burning desire and the failure that she felt she was for being born a woman, her dream of a paradise where she would be a man, a paradise she would enjoy, and endlessly allow all the women of the universe to feel a sense of pleasure, and enjoy an endless orgasm, the heavenly one that she was unable to reach with a man. She wanted the paradise of pleasure promised to men, her brothers, her father, and her husband.

How to manage these paradoxes that she was experiencing, and that touched me, confusing me in my countertransference and my desire to help her? What to do with these contradictions between her total submission to traditions and cults on the one hand, and her revolt against the customs imposed on her condition as a woman on the other hand? How to untangle them?

Zeina crossed the limits and barriers of language. She crossed the borders that were restricting her to a situation she had never accepted, that of a woman who is subject to traditions, who is enslaved to a frozen social structure that is resistant to transformation, change, self-discovery, and self-expression. She overcame the sociocultural hindering wall upon which her desire was stumbling.

Choosing a therapist from the same community probably meant her risking being subject to prejudices related to the desire to explore oneself and understand predetermined factors that are decided by God and accepted by believers. It meant attacking and criticizing one's parents, which is already forbidden by the religious books whereby they shall be respected regardless of who they are.

Feminine sexuality, environment and analytical process

I have tackled this topic and elaborated upon this clinical vignette because it reflects crossing limits on the one hand, and on the other reflects the avatars of the development of a blossoming feminine, an idea often rejected by the archaic social consensus. The evolution of affect and desire finds itself hindered from the very beginning of such a process. This leaves such evolution to the only freedom possible: fantasy, in which women live in the greatest secrecy (Assoun, 2003).

Doesn't this also apply to homophobia and racism in hostile repressive families as well as in many social enclaves or communities?

When a woman's multidimensional being is reduced and limited to her sexual or servant role, she can become inclined to reject her biological gender (and that of her daughter), as a "weaker limited sacrificial" gender, and consider her son to be a substitute, mending the psychological gaps and frustrations through fantasies of phallic redemption and empowerment.

Hence, "penis envy" would be deactivated or reduced, to say the least. However, when society is devoted to hegemonic masculinity often associated with the affirmation of virility, deconstructing gender polarities becomes almost impossible and the entanglement of bisexuality turns into a hard task, a disaster even.

The case of Zeina is a proper illustration of Freud's affirmation ([1905] 1953): the rejection of femininity often arises for the woman as "penis envy." Whereas such a concept is associated with the oedipal register, thus to men, fathers, and male offspring, such envy becomes a "desire of" the penis. Whereby both genders agree on the refusal of the feminine when assimilated to the danger of passivity. Penis envy in this woman has prevented access to the experience of Oedipal castration. The social mandate imposing a drastic division between the sexes has set a non-negotiable limit on the evolution toward an Oedipal configuration where the possibility of loving investment in the father is possible. Accepting castration offers the little girl the possibility to compete with the mother, receive the father's love, and bear him a child. This desire to appropriate the male attribute when exacerbated and pushed to its extreme, would lead to the failure of the feminine among women. Finding herself neither a transsexual, nor homosexual, nor even a woman, Zeina is then reduced to a negative version of her sexual being, a failure of her bisexuality's conjugation.

Hence, Zeina, first a victim of her childhood, was not able to combine her inner destructivity with her life's driving force. Rather, she takes her revenge by chastising her husband with her frigidity and hatred of the "real" penis while simultaneously dreaming of appropriating it.

After having vomited her anger, she prays, perhaps in an attempt to be forgiven, before further diving into her identity paradox, thus transforming her defeat into victory with the help of God, who will grant her what her mother, who brought boys into the world, has deprived her of.

It is worth noting that countertransference and analyst transference dispositions assume an essential role in this respect. However, in examining countertransference shall we refer to Freud or Ferenczi ([1924] 1989)? Shall we become aware of it and get rid of it, thus becoming more neutral or shall we feel it, live it, experience it, and invest it within the analytical field as a spur to our listening and a guide to our interventions and positioning?

> Acknowledging one's anger, rejection, annoyance, and curiosity, even tolerating these emergencies without, however, blaming oneself, and abiding by strict yet absurd benevolent neutrality is essential for ensuring the authenticity of our intervention.
>
> (Khoury, 2018)

Furthermore, the process requires clearing one's mind of one's own prejudice, being aware of the links with one's history, and letting oneself be guided by what emerges from one's unconscious mind. The result surely is satisfying as it translates into a conquest of oneself and the opportunity for growth and for crossing one's limits, thus fostering fluidity and creativity. It is not about preventing oneself from being overwhelmed by strong emotions as a result of a patient's experience. Rather, it is about "processing" such emotions, thus representing processable "affects."

Strangers and psychotics (Lacan, [1955] 1993) often cause the therapist to find themself in the same situation where they are forced to explore their archaic enclaves, their "black holes," and their powerlessness. They often shake their narcissistic roots, even expanding to their psychic integrity, their "psychic home" (Kennedy, 2014). They push the therapist to their limits and pierce the protective layers they envelope themself with. The analyst working with a patient from a different culture is compelled to perform a "tour de force," to move out of their familiar zone and welcome material that is difficult to assimilate. They must acquire the ability to grasp and integrate codes, norms, beliefs, and life criteria that are opposed to or different from those of their own culture. This is to create the possibility of establishing a transitional space where creativity is stimulated by the curiosity to discover the stranger.

Massoud Khan (1963) explored the concept of cumulative trauma that impacts the individual psyche. It can lead to significant psychological disturbances, but it can also shape the individual's ability to adapt and navigate different cultural, social, and psychological environments.

Borders again?

On the patient's side, the ego is threatened by its inability to seize, apply, and integrate codes and norms, including linguistic, belief, and lifestyle criteria when they are different, even as opposed to one's group of belonging, one's community. That is why being cautious and prudent in the context of our intervention should be of the utmost importance while considering the sub-mission of the patient to the intransigent superego of the "collective body" (Emile Durkheim, [1893] 1964) as it is often compliant with non-negotiable life rules and beliefs that are reinforced by the familial culture. In a con-ference (Charabaty, 2021) I developed the concept of a "collective psychic envelope" ("*collective moi-peau*"). The environment of a small or large group can provide an envelope conducive to the development and protection of an individual psychic ego. However, it can also, through its failures and rigidity, lead to a regression that exposes its vulnerabilities.

Freud was interested in how the collective and the individual interpenetrate in the link between the interpersonal and the intrapsychic. In "Totem and Taboo" ([1913] 1953), Freud not only shifts the analyst's focus from the indi-vidual to the social group but also introduces a whole new set of issues. In "Moses and Monotheism" ([1939] 1953), Freud notes that the content of the unconscious is a collective effect, a general property of the human being. He places the group of murderous brothers of the primitive horde at the source of social organizations, moral restrictions, and religions. The group is thus situ-ated between the horde and the state.

In "Group Psychology and the Analysis of the Ego," Freud ([1921] 1953) relies on Gustave Le Bon's book, *The Crowd: A Study of the Popular Mind*, which explores group phenomena such as suggestion and contagion. When individuals merge into an ideologically driven crowd, they substitute their own identity to that of the ideal ego represented by the leader's persona. A psychologically isolated individual does not exist. It is impossible to construct oneself without a group, without others.

As a matter of fact, to leave one's "collective body," to think differently, to dress differently, is to betray it, to expose oneself to guilt, even to shame, and in any case to the fear of being condemned by the community, left alone in a world that is strange to the individual, a bosom that has not nourished and carried the subject and whose codes have not been tamed. The West, upon completing its conquest of individuality and subjectivity, by secular laws that feature no reli-gious aspects, no longer accepts these codes and beliefs and no longer accepts returning to a time when kings' powers represented non-negotiable divine wills.

Sharing with colleagues who face similar issues and concerns

Reading, participating in conferences, in think-tanks on a given topic, discussing with colleagues who have worked within the frames of different sociocultural norms and challenges, all allow analysts to step out of the solitude of their offices and comfort zone and share and understand diverse experiences.

This is why I sought out analytical writings focused on the theoretical and clinical work of analysts practicing in countries and environments where insular communities enforce rigid codes of belonging. These norms often prohibit deviations and impose non-negotiable pressures, primarily on women, while men take the role of guarantors of these systems.

Julia Kristeva (1991) explores identity, otherness, and the role of the foreigner-concepts that are essential when engaging with clinical material from culturally "othered" contexts.

As for Gohar Homayounpour (2012), an Iranian psychoanalyst, she focused her work on how cultural and religious factors influence the psyche; she explored how crossing cultural boundaries impacts identity and self-perception. She advocated for a psychoanalysis that encounters cultural specificity, a culturally sensitive approach that respects patients' backgrounds and experiences.

Sudhir Kakar (1995), an Indian psychoanalyst, emphasizes in his work the necessity for psychoanalysis to incorporate cultural and religious dimensions, recognizing their profound impact on the inner world and the individual's concept of self.

Amrita Narayan (2023), an Indian psychoanalyst and writer, examines how cultural taboos and societal pressures influence an individual's sense of self and sexuality. She emphasizes the importance of creating a safe and non-judgmental space in psychoanalysis where individuals can explore and reconcile conflicting aspects of their identity, particularly about cultural and sexual norms.

Rachel Blass (2003), in her article, "On Ethical Issues at the Foundation of the Debate over the Goals of Psychoanalysis," discusses how cultural factors influence the objectives and practices of psychoanalysis. But she argues that while cultural contexts shape the therapeutic process, the fundamental aim of psychoanalysis – to uncover unconscious truths – should remain constant.

Concluding remarks

Toward this end, maybe we should refrain from considering our tool – psychoanalysis – as used for liberating individuals from their sociocultural chains but rather from their internal prisons, whereby the transformation of internal objects from threatening persecutors to tolerant and negotiable objects of love is in itself a success of the intervention.

Furthermore, establishing alignment and rhythm with the patient and accompanying them step by step, carefully and respectfully, is based upon the good conjugation of the analyst's psychic bisexuality. Hence, the analyst's containment and interventions play at the double maternal and paternal register, thus helping individuals to mend wide rifts and addressing unhealthy projections.

In short, a good entanglement in the analyst's mind of life and death drives and supporting such a process with tolerant and negotiable internal objects enables them to hold out. The analyst's skills lie upon experiencing their internal migrations, their psychic mobility, as allowed by a good Eros/Thanatos coupling, a good masculine/feminine and maternal/paternal coupling and containment. This will contribute to the creation of an environment where transitional spaces can be established and blossom thus liberating and engaging psychic creativity.

However, the hardest task remains to facilitate the passage of the patient from an archaic, non-negotiable superego to an oedipal superego, that can certainly be exposed to the risk of being dimmed, but that most surely refers to a third party that extends beyond biological parents and religious or political icons.

Experiencing conflicts related to the omnipresent family path and leading their journey, unveiling their desires, and anchoring their milestones at the levels of new objects they can identify with, the individual can select their own developmental path. It means risking making a radical change in terms of the originally idealized objects.

The aforementioned, however, begs the question, how many youngsters will be able to engage in adequate and suitable projects while ensuring their constant development through feeding on the already familiar maternal environment and nurturing? Durkheim ([1893] 1964), exploring the concept of "collective conscience," refers to the shared beliefs, values, and norms that unify members of society, contributing to social cohesion and order.

Adolescence, taking advantage of the Oedipal third-party approach, offers the chance for questioning, distancing, and freeing oneself from the influence of the collective consciousness. If the adventure is failed, the mold locks the individual into deadly repetition, which freezes and blocks creativity and originality. To break free from the mold, one has to accept breaking from familiar belongings – and dare to do it. Usually, women pay a higher price.

It is clear that Zeina could have visited another colleague from her community, yet she had knowingly chosen me. However, should she have engaged in a session with another colleague, one who's immersed and familiarized with her community, would she then have been able to express her suffering as a little girl among her family? As an unhappy wife of a Sheik boasting a good reputation and enjoying, to some extent, the respect of the environment they live in? Would she be able to let out her cry of rage and desire just like she did at the end of our session? Would she be able to say: "In another life, I want to be a man"? To violently declare one's truth is, in itself, a protest whose traces must be erased.

She did not ask for another appointment. She went, and did not come back.

References

Assoun, P. (2003). *Freud et la femme.* Payot.
Blass, R. B. (2003). On ethical issues at the foundation of the debate over the goals of psychoanalysis. *International Journal of Psychoanalysis*, 84, 929–943.

Charabaty, M., & Debbas, Y. (2021). Déchirures du Moi-peau collectif, mise en danger de l'enveloppe individuelle. Lebanese Association for the Development of Psychoanalysis, Beirut, June 10, 2021.

Durkheim, E. ([1893] 1964). *The division of labor in society.* Free Press.

Ferenczi, S. ([1924] 1989). *Thalassa: A theory of genitality.* Routledge.

Freud, S. ([1905] 1953). Three essays on the theory of sexuality. In *The Standard Edition of the Complete Psychological Works of Sigmund Freud, Volume 7* (pp. 123–246). Hogarth Press.

Freud, S. ([1907] 1953) Delusions and dreams in Jensen's Gradiva. In *The Standard Edition of the Complete Psychological Works of Sigmund Freud, Volume 9* (pp. 1–96). Hogarth Press.

Freud, S. ([1908] 1953) Creative writers and day-dreaming. In *The Standard Edition of the Complete Psychological Works of Sigmund Freud, Volume 9* (pp. 141–154). Hogarth Press.

Freud, S. ([1913] 1953). Totem and taboo. In *The Standard Edition of the Complete Psychological Works of Sigmund Freud, Volume 13* (pp. 1–162). Hogarth Press.

Freud, S. ([1921] 1953). Group psychology and the analysis of the ego. In *The Standard Edition of the Complete Psychological Works of Sigmund Freud, Volume 18* (pp. 65–144). Hogarth Press.

Freud, S. ([1939] 1953). Moses and monotheism. In *The Standard Edition of the Complete Psychological Works of Sigmund Freud, Volume 23* (pp. 3–205). Hogarth Press.

Green, A. (2012). Interview of André Green by Catherine Clément (recorded in 1992). *Le Magazine Littéraire*, published on 26 January.

Homayounpour, G. (2012). *Doing psychoanalysis in Tehran.* MIT Press.

Kakar, S. (1995). *The colours of violence: Cultural identities, religion, and conflict.* University of Chicago Press.

Kennedy, R. (2014). *The psychic home: Psychoanalysis, consciousness and the human soul.* Routledge.

Khan, M. R. (1963) The concept of cumulative trauma. *Psychoanalytic Study of the Child,* 18, 286–306.

Khoury, M. (2018). The desire of the analyst and counter-transference: From the mirroring analyst to the desiring analyst. In L. Bailly, D. Nobus, & S. Bailly (Eds.), *The Lacan tradition* (pp. 189–206). Routledge.

Kristeva, J (1991). *Stranger to ourselves.* Colombia University Press.

Lacan, J. ([1955] 1993). *The Seminars of Jacques Lacan, Book 3: The Psychoses.* W. W. Norton.

Le Bon, G. ([1895] 2011). *The crowd: A study of the popular mind.* Filiquarian Publishing.

Narayan, A. (2023). *Women's sexuality and modern India: In a rapture of distress.* Oxford University Press.

Winnicott, D. ([1951] 2016). Transitional objects and transitional phenomena. In *Collected Works of Donald Winnicott, Volume 4.* Oxford University Press.

Winnicott, D. ([1971] 1991). *Playing and reality.* Routledge.

Chapter 8

Integration of the feminine and the masculine in the analysis of a woman

Ester Palerm Mari

Introduction

From the earliest stages of life, the baby establishes its initial identifications through bonds with parental figures, in both their maternal and paternal roles. Freud, throughout his work ([1914] 1953, [1923] 1953, [1940] 1955), describes how these early identifications, along with those developed throughout life, shape the individual's internal dynamics and influence the formation and interaction between the Id, the Ego, and the Superego.

Melanie Klein ([1920] 2017, 1932, [1946] 1975, 1957) expands on this perspective by emphasizing the importance of early identifications with maternal and paternal figures as pillars of the child's emotional development. These identifications are fundamental, as they foster the capacity to repair, love, and resolve internal conflicts.

Various contributions, primarily by women, have explored psychic bisexuality in women, considering it not only from the perspective of opposition, renunciation, or conflict, but also from that of integration. In this regard, authors like Balsam (2001) analyze how masculine and feminine elements intertwine in each individual, with varying degrees of integration, thereby promoting a deeper and more complex understanding of female identity.

Mariam Alizade (2016) introduces the concept of the "fourth complementary series" to highlight the influence of social, cultural, historical, and political contexts on the structuring of the psyche. These factors play a crucial role in the integration or dissociation of masculine and feminine aspects, affecting the quality of interpersonal relationships. In some cultures or social sectors, when identifications with masculinity and femininity are excessively rigid, they can reinforce hierarchical dynamics. These dynamics generate feelings of superiority and promote the idealization or normalization of certain relational patterns, such as women's passivity and submission. This rigid approach not only reinforces inequalities but also limits the development of more flexible and balanced identities.

When differences are not structured hierarchically, new possibilities for identification emerge, transforming the perception of the self and the object.

DOI: 10.4324/9781003584483-10

This fosters a greater capacity for emotional containment and a greater discernment of what one is receptive to. In this sense, identifications with masculinity and femininity should complement each other to encourage flexible identifications that allow individuals to face life's challenges with greater balance.

Technological advances have opened up new possibilities for relating with others in the current cultural and social context. Nevertheless, the use of these technologies is conditioned by the way in which one perceives oneself, and the quality of the relationships one forms. Therefore, understanding how these technologies are used will allow us to observe the interaction of identifications and the degree of integration or dissociation of masculinity or femininity.

In order to reflect upon some of these questions, I will use the clinical material of a patient in analysis, initially four sessions a week, later increasing to five sessions a week. I will present five clinical vignettes in chronological order, which show different moments of the analytical process. I will explore the patient's evolution over a five-year period, centered on the parallel development of three aspects: the analytical relationship, how she uses social networks to find a partner, and how this partner is chosen.

Dating apps and their uses

The last few decades have witnessed a skyrocketing in the use of the internet, encompassing broad sectors of society. A variety of reasons has undoubtedly contributed to the current situation: easy access, the huge diversity of informational content, as well as a multitude of apps to interact with other users, many of them in real time.

Certain features of these apps, depending on how they are used, can become addictive: on the one hand, due to the immediate satisfaction that comes from being able to make contact with a great number of people simultaneously; and on the other hand, because frustration – in the case of an unsatisfactory experience – is quickly compensated by creating new contacts. At times, this virtual world can give rise to varying degrees of withdrawal from external reality, in such a way that the problems of real life are substituted by the complacencies of a virtual world. In some pathological organizations, it becomes a psychic retreat from anxiety and suffering (Steiner, 1993).

As analysts, we must understand these new forms of relationships. Various questions arise about the kind of link these foster, including whether they encourage relationships based on narcissistic reaffirmation, or the search for an ideal object, or, in contrast, whether they encourage a creative bond, fostering mutual development for both partners.

The beginning of treatment

Maria consulted me because she was concerned about her emotional state, which was dependent upon her relationship with her partner at the time. It oscillated between being very gratifying at times and very bad at other times.

She was very pleased to have a partner, and she wanted to get married and have children. Her partner, in contrast, was resisting the idea because she had previously had relationships with other men, which caused him to be deeply mistrusting and controlling of her. Nonetheless, Maria was very fearful that he would leave her and, at the same time, she also feared not being competent enough professionally, although her job was clearly very inferior to her level of education.

When she spoke about the relationship between her parents, she did not communicate any information regarding emotions, but rather how the relationship functioned: her father made the decisions, and her mother was happy to delegate these to him. Her family had faced certain difficulties, as one of her siblings was born handicapped.

Regarding her childhood, she said that she had been a happy child. She was well behaved and did everything that was expected of her. She later adds that she was very shy and lacked confidence, and from an early age she was afraid of being alone. Since childhood, she had always had boyfriends, although she did not have sexual relationships until she was 17. She never took the initiative to choose boyfriends, so consequently she was always the one being chosen, not the one making the choice.

Once the analysis began, the patient complied scrupulously with the setting. She always arrived on time and engaged well. She would communicate her distress, which was always linked to her external reality in a very concrete way, with few nuances, oscillating between feeling good, feeling bad, or feeling anxious/nervous. In spite of her difficulties in associating and connecting with her emotions, from the start her dreams greatly helped the analytic work.

She often arrived at her sessions anxious to talk about what had been happening to her, and seemed genuinely relieved simply to be listened to. This was most evident at the first session of the week. She felt the need to explain everything that had happened since the last session, and if she did not have enough time, she would pick up at the next session where she had left off.

Maria always paid close attention to my interventions to see if what I was saying implied any kind of indication or hint concerning what she should do or not do. If my interpretations contributed to an insight, she experienced this as her own failing, feeling stupid for not being able to figure it out by herself. She feared, being so inept, that I would get fed up with her and end the treatment. In Maria's eyes, I was the one who knew how things should be, and she was convinced that if her behavior met my standards, her analytic space would be assured.

A few months after beginning analysis, Maria's boyfriend decided to break off the relationship, and she felt it was her fault for not having done better and not being able to avoid the break-up. After this point, she began to contact different men via social media apps.

Clinical Vignette 1: To be herself or to adhere to the other

One day, I opened the office door to let a patient out, and Maria was there, standing on the landing. She began that session telling me that she was used to waiting outside and not ringing the doorbell, so as not to bother me. She asked me what she should do if she arrived early to her session. Should she wait or ring the bell?

My first impulse was to answer her directly, but almost immediately recognized my desire to alleviate her anxiety so I contained myself. I pointed out that she knew that there was a waiting room, but at the same time she felt she could not use it so as not to bother me; she therefore had neither physical nor mental space for herself, so she had to adapt to me and ring the bell right on time.

She responded by saying that it had not even occurred to her to think that the analyst should have to adapt to her. She only saw it from her point of view: *"Not bothering anyone was better than intentionally being a nuisance."* In this way she enacted her fear of causing situations that created problems, such as the analyst having to be attentive to the doorbell and in consequence losing concentration with the patient she was with. It made her anxious to think that she was asking too much, so she had not even asked me about it before.

She also spoke to me about the difficulties she had in her job. If she did not know how to do something, it was difficult for her to ask for help. In such situations, she would spend a lot of time wondering whether what she wanted to ask made sense or whether it was important enough to justify interrupting her colleagues.

At first, Maria's question as to whether she should ring the doorbell might be regarded as an identification with her mother, who delegated the decision-making to the father-analyst. However, Maria took some time to ask this, and mentioned her fear of upsetting the analyst, and of this being a motive for rejection. This anxiety was evident both in her relationship with the analyst, as well as in her external world.

Within this context, my first countertransference reaction was to respond to her directly, rather than analyse the situation. Thus, the analyst became aware of the identification with a part of the patient, who, like her, had to appease any tension by becoming a good object that did not frustrate, because of the risk of being rejected. In order for this threat not to become a reality, Maria had to take precautions not to upset the analyst. This was likely the reason for her not being able to make use of the things the analyst offered her, such as the waiting room, and needing reassurance on what she should do. This situation seemed an inversion of the container/contained relationship (Bion,

1962), which occurs when the containing function, performed by the mother or other caregiver, cannot receive the experiences of the baby/child and projects her anxieties onto the infant. In other words, not only the infant/child does not feel contained, but he/she is exposed to the experience of being used as a receptacle for the massive projections of the mother or caregiver (Williams, [1977] 2018).

For this reason, Maria was extremely attentive to my answers and careful to deduce whether they might indicate what she should do or whether her behavior was appropriate. In such a way, she safeguarded her acceptance by me and ensured that I did not become a persecutory object. Thus, she avoided jeopardizing the continuity of treatment. Furthermore, the idea that I knew everything was likely a defensive idealization that enabled Maria to trust me, her analyst. In other words, she sought a containing object that would accept her and serve as a guide to help her to grow. In this way, she experienced the hopelessness of not knowing what to do, but hoping that her analyst would, and could help her. Klein ([1952] 1992) notes that idealization, being a defensive function, is also essential to the development of the Self, in the sense that it alleviates the persecutory anxieties of the infant.

Maria, in reference to her feeling of insecurity, achieved a fragile sense of trust by adhering to the other person. In this way, she felt that by adapting to the other she became somebody, as well as avoiding the threat of not being valued, being able, at the same time, to turn the object into a protector. This mode of functioning has parallels with the concept of adhesive identification, developed by Bick (1968) and Meltzer (1975), which arises when there has been insufficient identification with a containing object, thus the sensory qualities of the object predominate over its capacity to generate thought.

So as not to feel the lack of a containing object, Maria would adhere to the object and therefore avoid any difference, simultaneously avoiding being used as a receptacle for the other's projections by presenting herself as an inadequate object.

This search for a containing object explained her very evident anxiety to tell me everything that had happened to her in the first session of the week. I believe it was not so much due to the separation *per se*, but to the lack of containment caused by her not having her sessions. She needed analysis to talk about what had happened to her. She was quite simply relieved just to be able to talk and have someone listen to her, rather than through any desire to understand. That way there would be no risk of being invaded by the analyst's projections, which might make her feel dreadful. In any case, she needed to protect the analyst and direct all her aggression and guilt at herself for not having done better.

Thus, Maria needed to feel that the analyst was able to offer her a receptive and containing mental space. However, for the analytic relationship to be a fertile and creative exchange, she needed to develop a capacity for receptivity and containment concerning the analyst's interventions.

Clinical Vignette 2: Developing a containment capacity

Maria always said yes to men whenever they asked her out. She met them initially through dating apps and the frequency of their encounters was sporadic. She would wait for a message from them, and would answer straight away, always available to meet up with the person who had messaged her. She was also always afraid that they would not contact her anymore and leave her.

In one session, Maria told me that she had received a message from a man who had not been in touch with her for several days. On this occasion, instead of immediately answering him, as she usually did, she answered his message later on. Even she was astonished that she had been able to put off answering him, feeling surprisingly calm doing so.

That same day, another man also messaged her asking if they could meet up as he was in the area where she lived. She was able to refuse and to acknowledge that she did not feel like meeting him, because this particular man's way of living was to not worry about anything and live in the moment. Furthermore, he had told her that she overthought everything, and that she should think less and live like him.

Maria explained that not answering him immediately gave her satisfaction. However, shortly afterward, she had the feeling she was not doing the right thing – not answering felt like attacking someone who was important to her. She was also worried that this man would become angry with her, and she did not know how to defend herself. She added:

> If he gets angry with me, I don't know how I would react. It's as if other people have a lion in them and I can't defend myself against the lion – I can only try to run away from it. So, it's just better to pet the lion as if it were a kitty cat, so as not to provoke it by poking it in the mouth or the eye.

I interpreted that she was quite satisfied with herself in that she had been able to assert herself, to recognize and tolerate her anger, however this feeling did not last long because she became fearful of being attacked for being different, by having her own criteria. As such, both her analyst and her friend became lions that she would have to tame. Maria answered that perhaps this was true because her friends used to tell her that they had never seen her angry.

In this vignette, we see that the patient no longer needs to adhere to the other to feel secure. Fear of abandonment does not predominate so much as fear of being different from the object and, in consequence, fear of the object's aggression and being unable to defend herself.

Therefore, at this point, Maria had already developed a certain capacity to contain her anger, to *not* feel the need to calm herself down immediately, and to tolerate anxiety and waiting. Moreover, Maria felt satisfaction at this accomplishment of hers, despite not yet possessing the necessary strength to sustain the risks of having her own identity.

In fact, having her own identity is felt as "poking the lion in the eye" and, in order to avoid this, she tries to pet the lion. However, this strategy carries the risk of establishing relationships with men who base their identity on a phallic, omnipotent masculinity, eager to control and dominate women. These are relationships in which the needs and desires of the other are not recognized, nor are differences valued; in this case, Maria's way of being, including her femininity. In contrast, mature sexuality involves acknowledgement of difference and, at the same time, recognition of incompleteness and the need of the object.

On the other hand, neither was Maria receptive to the other. Rather, as Williams ([1997] 2018) states, she was a receptacle for the other. In this sense, receptivity does not imply passivity, i.e., accepting the unfiltered projections of the other. Rather, receptivity is dynamic, in that it requires the containment of the receptive attitude, an attribute more associated with women. However, it also requires an attitude of strength and capacity, which are attributes more associated with men. And yet, in both women and men, both attitudes are necessary to perceive one's own value and limitations, as well as those of the other, and to accommodate differences. In other words, in both women and men, the creative relationship requires a receptive attitude, particularly to the thoughts of others, through the ability to receive and contain projections; at the same time, allowing oneself time to process and assess how to manage them.

Along these lines, Steiner (2018) points out that receptivity is important for exchange, and yet, at the same time, an awareness of vulnerability is required. This enables us to assess which objects can be trusted to be receptive. It is therefore understood that awareness of vulnerability should go hand-in-hand with the ability to recognize one's own capacities to preserve one's identity.

Some authors suggest that containment is a maternal function, whereas for Birksted-Breen (1996, pp. 652) containment involves both the maternal function of being with and the paternal function of observing and linking: "To contain her infant, a mother (and an analyst) has to receive the projections with empathy (the maternal function) and also take a perspective on this (paternal function)."

Clinical Vignette 3: Curiosity and the integration of the internal world

Maria began the session by telling me about a dream she had had the previous night that left her feeling off. In the dream, there was a little girl and a little boy of around ten years old dressed as bride and groom. It was as if their parents had arranged the marriage, and the church was crowded. As the couple entered the church, the boy was very happy, but the girl was crying. The boy thought that all life's problems were behind him as now he had someone to be with. Meanwhile, the little girl was crying profusely because this was not the wedding she would have wanted, and she didn't feel ready to get married.

Shortly after telling me about the dream, Maria told me that she had met up with a man, and after some time to gather courage, she had asked him if he had been seeing other women. He replied that it was none of her business and that she should not be asking him questions like that. When Maria told her female friends, they also berated her for asking those kinds of questions, because they made it obvious that she was too keen on marrying and having children. Maria complained, in the session, that she had no right to do anything, not even ask, let alone complain or get angry.

In this session, the dream about two children who get married evokes the primal scene, which, as Freud ([1905] 1953) said, is linked with infantile curiosity. Klein ([1928] 1992) related this to the desire to know about the contents of the mother's body. Later, Bion (1959, 1962) showed that the desire to know requires an emotional experience with a containing object. In the case of Maria, her lack of curiosity suggests deficiencies in the object's containing function, rather than a defense erected against bonding with the other.

In the dream, the parents arrange the marriage, which is far from an adult relationship between a man and a woman. The dream represents the dissociation between the more regressive aspects and those that need help to mature. Thus, a part of her, like the little boy in the dream, believes that all her problems will be solved if she gets married, regardless of the qualities of the object. So, she lives the illusion of feeling safe when she is fused with the other. Thus, there is no room for separation and, therefore, the complexity of living with difference does not appear.

This aspect, represented by the boy, comes into conflict with the girl, who does not feel ready to live as a couple. In this sense, we could understand her crying, not as something defensive in the sense of opposing growth and remaining as a little girl, but because she needs to be allowed enough time to be able to grow and mature.

This was in fact her internal struggle: to be like the boy and calm down her anxieties by adhering to the other, and as such feel protected, or to be like the girl, who is beginning to look at herself and feel curious about her internal world, and realize for herself when she will be ready. In this way, she needs first to become herself, by taking care of her own desires and needs, together with those of the other, and therefore learning to live with the differences the other brings, before she can establish a relationship with a man.

At the same time, she acknowledges her disappointment and a sense of grievance or injustice when her friends minimize her experiences. In the dream, this aspect may be reflected by internal parents who organize her marriage, without taking into account the girl's tears or wondering what may be the matter with her.

Clinical Vignette 4: Reactions to separation

In the first session after the summer break, Maria said that, together with another friend who also wanted to find a boyfriend, they discovered a new app that required two females and two males to set up a date, and that they had gone on various double dates. To this, she added: "This has turned into a bit of a circus because every time I met up with my friends, they would ask me who I had seen and how it had gone." Her friends said that they doubted they would go out looking for another partner again if they had to. That made Maria indignant, because these were friends who already had partners. In a protesting tone she said: "This is not how I am by choice. It wasn't my decision not to have a partner." After a short pause she continued:

> Today it was hard for me to come back and talk about these things. I have not been here for over a month. I didn't want to think about the holidays, as I was afraid of getting stuck in circles that I might not be able to get out of and not know what to do. Then I could start screaming like a mad person or run myself down to the point of exhaustion.

I had told her that during the summer break she would have to cope with the idea not only of not having a partner, but also of not having this space, in addition to tolerating her friends' lack of understanding. Perhaps, today, she was concerned about how the analyst was going to understand what it meant for her to endure this situation that she had not chosen – the break from analysis. Perhaps she feared that I would belittle all her efforts to face this separation and manage her fears without becoming overwhelmed.

Maria answered:

> Before the summer, I was very worried about your holidays and by the end I stopped worrying. I completely stopped worrying and I stopped trying to foresee everything. This was vacation time. Normally I would go round in circles in my head about what if this or that were to happen. This time, I was able not to do that for a month, but I do not know if I would be capable of continuing for much more.

At the end of the session, she was able to say in tears: "If there was something I felt this summer it was loneliness, but also incomprehension. We each have our own lives, but I have felt very lonely."

In the face of the impending separation, she had taken refuge in a world of stimuli. Meeting men was her way of defending herself from her feelings of loneliness and abandonment. As seen in this vignette, despite being able to share this experience with a girlfriend and put on a happy face, she herself recognized that deep down she knew she felt lonely and did what she could to cope with the situation. In other words, despite her manic defense, there was no longer a denial of her emotions. To achieve this, she had had to contain and acknowledge her emotions, in all their nuances – such as outrage, fear, loneliness, and dread of becoming overwhelmed.

It is also clear that at this point she was more able to contain her aggressive aspects without being horrified by them, and without them endangering her relationships. Another important aspect was her awareness of vulnerability, as she recognized that her defenses were temporary, and she would not have been able to hold on much longer.

Clinical Vignette 5: Looking at herself, looking at others, and being looked at

In the fourth year of analysis Maria spoke about talking with a man who, up to that point, she had hoped would become her partner. However, the last time they had seen each other, she said to herself:

> It's clear to me now that it's just an occasional relationship. I´m alone although I might occasionally meet someone who passes through my life from time to time and makes me feel accompanied, but the fact is I am not.

She also explained that for six months she had been in contact with a single man online. Although he insisted that they should meet, he never proposed a date. Finally, they had recently met, and the date went well. Even so, there were things about this man that she wanted to know more about, so she needed to take it slowly, because she did not know if he was trustworthy. She noticed some contradictions. About this, Maria added:

> it remains to be seen what the truth of all this is, because what he says and what he does don't match up. Everything he's telling me shows he's not at all trustworthy.

At this point, she recognized how much she wanted to be able to be sure about things, although she also told herself that nothing is certain; at the same time, when she had nothing, or nobody to meet up with, this triggered alarm bells in her head.

Near the end of the session, Maria expressed her reticence to speak about this relationship with her analyst because she was afraid that I would tell her that she was guileless, that she was day-dreaming or even that I would spoil her relationship in some way.

In this fifth vignette, Maria showed that she was now able to look at herself, and at the same time look at the other with greater depth. This enabled her to take a broader view. Thus, she wondered to what extent she could trust what she was being told or not; whether this concealed a masculinity in which narcissistic satisfaction and humiliation predominated, or a masculinity that could hold present the other. In this regard, the honesty of the man she was getting to know could be understood as a way of showing his most fragile feelings; namely, not feeling ready for a relationship, though not wanting to hurt her either.

At the same time, Maria acknowledged that she did not have the answer, she had to tolerate the uncertainty of not knowing and recognize the need for time to see how this interaction with the other person developed. Along these lines, Anne Álvarez (1992) points out that a caregiving object is necessary for the healthy emotional and cognitive development of the infant, one that possesses, among other qualities, willingness, constancy, coherence, and predictability. This facilitates the introjection of a caregiver object that cares about the child's wellbeing, and in whom the child can trust.

In this vignette, we see that she has already introjected an object (the analyst) with these functions and thus she has increased confidence in her capabilities, and less dependence on the external object; while another part of her expresses her state of alarm when she has nothing or nobody to be with.

It is noteworthy that Maria hesitated in telling the analyst that she was meeting another man. This may be understood at different levels, which are not necessarily mutually exclusive. A first aspect may be her fear that the analyst would not tolerate her growth and the consequent separation. In this sense, Maria's delay in telling her analyst could be related to avoiding the analyst's projections, avoiding the risk of feeling inadequate or naive for getting her hopes up.

A second aspect may be related to a decrease in splitting; in other words, when the good and bad aspects are not so clearly delineated, but she does not yet know how to manage a total object. Therefore, the analyst is no longer a persecutory object or, conversely, an omnipotent object that knows everything and that she can always trust in. Now new nuances emerge regarding how Maria perceives the analyst and how she feels looked at by her. Despite Maria now taking decisions, there is still suspicion and mistrust surrounding how they will be appraised by the analyst.

Maria was still not sufficiently confident that her hopes of having a partner were realistic or whether she had succumbed to omnipotent fantasies. It is likely that her silence on the matter was not intended to deceive the analyst, but related to her doubts as to whether she could trust herself.

By projecting her fears onto the analyst, Maria was able to preserve her hope for more satisfying relationships. In turn, her progress enabled her to integrate different aspects of herself, as well as to tolerate disappointment if she did not achieve her expectations. The fact that she could finally speak about this in analysis opened up the path to integrating both her fear of making a mistake and recognizing her progress. Thus, Maria was able to start taking responsibility for what took place in her life.

A third emerging aspect may be that Maria was beginning to recognize her progress, and becoming able to tolerate her anxiety or choose relationships that may be more satisfying. This augurs in a new stage, one where she can make herself more visible, or present, in her relationships. This entails the risk of awakening in others not only the recognition of her capabilities, but also of being envied by them (Steiner, 1993, 2006).

During the two years following this vignette, Maria's relationship increasingly strengthened, giving rise to the desire for a shared future. While not without its complexities, this shared goal would later be cemented with the conception of two children. As with all creative bonds, there were moments of achievement and moments of frustration, while tolerating the uncertainty of the future.

Concluding remarks

Identifications with parental figures – in both their maternal and paternal function – are the first to influence how the infant, the child, and later the adult, will identify with the masculine and feminine aspects of their personality. These identifications are also molded by the cultural and social context and are reflected in an unique way in every individual history.

I start with the premise that psychic bisexuality implies the presence of feminine and masculine aspects in every person throughout their life. This does not imply that both of these aspects are at odds with one another, but rather, that they are dynamic and complementary traits, susceptible to change depending on the different levels of psychic maturity. When they are experienced as superiority or inferiority of one over the other, it does not depend on each element's intrinsic nature, but rather the degree to which they are integrated with each other or not. This can either promote or hamper personal development.

In the case that I have presented to illustrate these ideas, Maria associated the masculine with a strong, dominant, active, and competent father at the start of her analysis. In contrast, she associated the feminine with a passive, weak, submissive mother, valued for her sacrifice in the caring of others. In this regard, the parental figures represent a model of rigid identification with the classical representations of the feminine and the masculine.

Throughout a long period of analysis, this relational pattern conditioned the analytic relationship. In this sense, Maria found herself at a crossroads, since she could not "use" the analyst in either the paternal or the maternal function, due to the qualities represented by being each one of them. Therefore, when the analyst within a fatherly transference showed her knowledge in order to care for her, she associated this with the masculine aspects of the father, experienced as castrating and devaluing.

In this context, to prevent the analyst-father from becoming a threat, Maria felt the need to care for me, although always fearful of not doing it well enough; but, as a consequence, the treatment would end. Her concern about the wellbeing of the analyst implied a pattern of submission and adaptation to the object's desires – in this case, her analyst. This preoccupation was far removed from her ability to think for herself.

On other occasions, omnipotent features were attributed to the analyst-father, because Maria was convinced of my wisdom. This dynamic led me to believe that she had experienced a lack of both feeling contained and feeling protected, suggesting that there had been flaws in both parental figures. Maria perceived the feminine figure as a receptacle lacking its own abilities, whereas the masculine figure appeared narcissistic. Moreover, her attempts at looking after herself were experienced as being aggressive.

At the same time, this pattern manifested in her use of dating apps: she was always checking to see if she had received any messages, and she would respond immediately to satisfy the other person's desire.

Maria reached a turning point when she managed to stop responding immediately to these messages. One could think of identification with aspects of maternal receptivity and contention. However, she could only maintain this ability for a short time, because her paternal identifications of self-assertion and anger did not represent protection for her, but rather her aggression toward the other person. Here again, the paternal function seemed incompatible with the ability to care for others. Nevertheless, in those moments the fear of arousing aggression in the object predominated in Maria, because she was different, only to then be unable to defend herself. Therefore, to avoid fleeing, she adopted a supposedly feminine attitude of "better to stroke the lion – as if she, Maria, were a kitten," to not provoke or anger it.

The dream of the boy and girl dressed as a groom and bride helps us understand her internal world. I believe that this dream is not directly connected to the biological sex, but instead with two of her attitudes that can manifested in both genders: the persistence on being cared for and the fear and desire to grow up and take on – in Maria's case – her feminine identity. One could argue that the dream represents her internal struggle: on the one hand, the dissociation between her masculine and feminine aspects to avoid growing up, represented by the boy; but on the other hand, the desire to be helped in order to grow and integrate both aspects, and so avoid repeating the relationship patterns that she sees in her parents' dynamic.

In the fourth vignette, after a lengthy holiday, Maria was able to voice her complaints about her friends, showing that she no longer identified with the girl who had previously fulfilled everyone's expectations and was afraid of ending up alone. Now she could assert herself without feeling so threatened or aggressive.

Maria was now in a different phase; she had internalized new, more flexible, identifications that integrated how differently she felt about her masculine and feminine aspects. They were not, however, sufficiently internalized to withstand a long wait. In this respect, she acknowledged having used the apps and her encounters with men to distract herself and help herself while awaiting her re-encounter with her analyst.

In the last vignette, the relationship between Maria and her analyst was intertwined with Maria's latest contact with a man via the dating apps. One can see a positive evolution in that Maria is able to integrate her fears, not only in relation to men, but also to her analyst. She voiced her reluctance to share certain things, such as the fact that she was getting to know another man. The figure of the analyst acquired new nuances as a castrating analyst-mother figure, envious of Maria's attributes as a woman who can attract men.

Maria wondered if she would know how to defend herself against this analyst or the man she has met, if needed, doubting the intentions of both of them. However, she felt better off by herself, with her thoughts and reflections, and recognizing her vulnerability. Another way of understanding her femininity emerged, and she recognized that her desire was to feel good in the company of others and not to please them out of fear, nor to renounce her desires as a woman.

This evolutionary process implied that new identifications, as well as disidentifications, helped Maria separate herself from the parental figures of her external reality. We can see the emergence of another way of feeling her femininity and sharing it with someone she decided is worthy of it. Although there was still a long way to go, she was then involved in a process of integration of her masculine and feminine qualities as a woman. This ongoing process needs to continue to evolve as she progresses through the different stages of her life.

References

Alizade, M. (2016). *Parentalidades y género: Su incidencia en la subjetividad*. Letra Viva.

Alvarez, A. (1992) *Live company: Psychoanalytic psychotherapy with autistic, borderline, deprived and abused children*. Routledge.

Balsam, R. (2001). Integrating male and female elements in a woman's gender identity. *Journal of the American Psychoanalytic Association*, 49(4), 1335–1360.

Bick, E. (1968). The experience of the skin in early object-relations. *International Journal of Psychoanalysis*, 49, 484–486.

Bion, W. R. (1959). Attacks on linking. *International Journal of Psychoanalysis*, 40, 308–315.

Bion, W. R. (1962). *Learning from experience*. Karnac Books.

Birksted-Breen, D. (1996) Phallus, penis and mental space. *International Journal of Psychoanalysis*, 77, 649–657.

Freud, S. ([1905] 1953) Three essays on the theory of sexuality. *The Standard Edition of the Complete Psychological Works of Sigmund Freud, Volume 7* (pp. 123–246). Hogarth Press.

Freud, S. ([1914] 1953). On narcissism: An introduction. *The Standard Edition of the Complete Psychological Works of Sigmund Freud, Volume 14* (pp. 67–102). Hogarth Press.

Freud, S. ([1923] 1953). The ego and the id. In *The Standard Edition of the Complete Psychological Works of Sigmund Freud, Volume 19* (pp. 1–66). Hogarth Press.

Freud, S. ([1940] 1955). An outline of psycho-analysis. In *The Standard Edition of the Complete Psychological Works of Sigmund Freud, Volume 23* (pp. 141–207). Hogarth Press.

Klein, M. ([1920] 2017). The development of a child. *The collected works of Melanie Klein. Volume 1* (pp. 1–53). Routledge.

Klein, M. ([1928] 1992). Early stages of the Oedipus conflict. *The writings of Melanie Klein, Volume 1* (pp. 186–198). Karnac Books.

Klein, M. (1932). *The psychoanalysis of children.* Hogarth Press.

Klein, M. ([1946] 1975). Notes on some schizoid mechanisms. In *The collected works of Melanie Klein,* Volume 3 (pp. 289–305). Hogarth Press.

Klein, M. ([1952] 1992). Some theoretical conclusions regarding the emotional life of the infant. *The writings of Melanie Klein, Volume 3* (pp. 61–93). Karnac Books.

Klein, M. (1957). *Envy and gratitude and other works.* Free Press.

Meltzer, D. (1975). Adhesive identification. *Contemporary psychoanalysis,* 11, 289–310.

Steiner, J. (1993) *Psychic retreats: Pathological organizations in psychotic, neurotic and borderline patients.* Routledge.

Steiner, J. (2006). Seeing and being seen: Narcissistic pride and narcissistic humiliation. *International Journal of Psychoanalysis,* 87, 939–951.

Steiner, J. (2018). Overcoming obstacles in analysis: Is it possible to relinquish omnipotence and accept receptive femininity?, *Psychoanalytic Quarterly,* 87, 1–20.

Williams, G. ([1997] 2018). *Internal landscapes and foreign bodies. Eating disorders and other pathologies.* Routledge.

Chapter 9

Masculinity as appearance

Silvia R. Acosta

Psychic bisexuality as a conceptual umbrella

The question of the modes of masculinity, its singular forms, has for some time been an issue that we have tried to understand in the light of the emergence of diversity in the expressions of sexuality and gender. Just as we psychoanalysts have been asking questions about femininity for decades, we have also been looking at masculinity.

What Freud ([1905] 1981) described as sexual polymorphism, a sexuality of diffuse onset that is poorly related to a univocal expression of the body-gender-sexuality relationship, also includes cisgender people of heterosexual orientation. The ways in which the subjects express their body and sexual orientation are not exempt from conflict and suffering. It is therefore an area of exploration and of clinical research for psychoanalysis.

Regarding psychic bisexuality and the ego and object drives in Freud's work, it is possible to understand those concepts as a complex net of relationships between different constitutive elements of the primary psychism. Considering some of Freud's concerns about psychic bisexuality it is possible to understand that psychic bisexuality is more than feminine and masculine positions. Freud does not displace its centrality by using the terms active and passive but, rather, is struggling for a more sophisticated definition. Returning to scattered remarks in his texts and those of early analysts, I argue that the active-passive binary is something separate from the masculine and feminine binary and suggests that there is a masculine and feminine position along both poles. Ultimately, Freud is describing different libidinal positions. They involve, in fact, object relationships and drives: masculine/active/penetrating and feminine/passive/receptive drives centered on the self-satisfaction or centered in the other's satisfaction.

Freud always emphasized the importance of bisexuality from the early stages of psychoanalysis to his final writings. In "Three Essays," he states that pure masculinity or femininity cannot be found in human beings, either psychologically or biologically. Instead, every individual exhibits a mixture of character traits from both their own sex and the opposite one, as well as a

DOI: 10.4324/9781003584483-11

combination of activity and passivity, whether or not these traits align with their biological sex (Freud, [1905] 1981).

In his later writings, Freud continued to uphold this idea, albeit with sometimes contradictory reflections. It became a general formula:

> We are accustomed to say that every human being displays both male and female instinctual impulses, needs, and attributes; but though anatomy, it is true, can point out the characteristics of maleness and femaleness, psychoanalysis cannot. For psychoanalysis, the contrast between the sexes fades away into one between activity and passivity.
>
> (Freud, [1930] 1981, p. 105)

This complexity is maintained by the various post-Freudian authors who have addressed the subject. Despite recognizing the importance of the meta-psychological positing of the integration of all these polarities, few have been able to describe the way in which psychic bisexuality contributes to thinking of an integrative, creative, and potentially elaborative psychism.

Psychic bisexuality thus involves an internal organization of the self around two positions, as described by Freud in terms of "masculine" and "feminine," although he acknowledged that these labels were flawed descriptors. Psychoanalysis focuses on psychosexuality, which is ultimately determined not only by one's physical sex, but also by unconscious fantasies uncovered by analyzing the complex interplay of identifications as they are manifested, are enacted, and are experienced within the transference and countertransference dynamics of the analytic encounter (Perelberg, 2018).

Following Hurwood's ideas (2009), Houzel's concept of "psychic bisexuality" and Birksted-Breen's "mental bisexuality" are distinguished as two distinct stages of development that facilitate the establishment of psychic space and thought. Psychic bisexuality refers to the structuring of the self and the development of inner space. Mental bisexuality refers to the functioning of the mind, with the development of space between internal objects, and between self and others.

Houzel (2005) focuses on the notion of psychic bisexuality within the framework of object relations theory, in particular Bion's model of the container/contained relationship. In Bion's developments of psychoanalytic ideas about autism, Houzel focuses on better understanding the role of psychic bisexuality from the beginning of psychic life. According to the author, this primitive bisexuality underlies the development of the Oedipal constellation through the processes of reparation and oscillation between the paranoid-schizoid and the depressive positions.

Understanding the underlying dynamics of these container-contained representations is important for the understanding of another of Houzel's concepts, that of the "structural stability" of the mind. She states that the container object is the structurally stable part of the dynamic system created by the containment relationship. The concept of structural stability is an integral part of the dynamical systems theory, and it denotes the ability of such a system to generate stable forms within itself despite the constant motion to which all its components are subjected. According to this, the maternal continent is a stable part of the dynamic relationship between her and her baby. However, this container is not only composed of maternal elements; it must also have paternal qualities that are intimately linked to the maternal ones. Without oversimplifying the complexity of these theorizations, Houzel, in line with Tustin, states that qualities such as receptivity and flexibility belong to the maternal-feminine side of the container, while others, such as consistency and orientation, belong to the paternal-masculine side. From the point of view of the mind, they correspond to the maternal and paternal identifications of the mother, united in a harmonious relationship. So, it is important to remember this double polarity; male or female, we all have maternal and paternal objects in our mind in a more or less harmonious relationship. So, the infant must first process the psychic bisexuality of the container; on this depends any possibility of integrating psychic bisexuality at the most primitive of levels.

On the other hand, Birksted-Breen theorizes the points of connection and disconnection between theory and practice, and the creative spaces that form between the analytic dyad. According to the author, penis and phallus are often confused: the former, an organ; the latter, a symbol of an ineffable notion of the self (Birksted-Breen, 1996; Pontalis, 1973). In this line, for the author, the distinction between the phallus, which is magical and possessed in fantasy by a male or a female, and the penis-as-a-link, allows us to articulate in a single unit what Birksted-Breen understands as "the reproductive capacity of the couple." The phallus is not an attribute of an individual, but a link that allows the creation of a generative plot where the integration of the two positions complements and elaborates the lack implicit in castration.

In her paper "Phallus, Penis and Mental Space," Birksted-Breen (1996) describes a phallic state of mind that, among other things, serves to repudiate the potential for a creative link between internal parental objects and the ability to think. In order to survive psychically, the patient on whom she based her theorizations frequently resorted to a phallic state of mind. That is, deficits of internal and external objects in that patient's psychic world meant that useful parental qualities, associated with the development of psychic bisexuality, were not available for introjection and identification, promoting splits, experiences of shame and humiliation, and feelings of inadequacy about oneself and present in countertransferential tension experienced by the psychotherapist, insofar as her own creative resources, based on her own internal objects, were unavailable, thus hindering her own ability to think.

In conclusion, to include the notion of psychic bisexuality in order to think about our clinical practice means to assume that, in each analytic trajectory, a series of conceptual elements that we know are always present are intertwined:

the drives, the primal scene, infantile sexuality, the archaic and the oedipal, the parental imagos, and primary homosexuality. Shifting identifications are enacted in the analytic couple in different ways throughout an analysis and within a session; psychic bisexuality is always at play in the transference-countertransference. The process of working through our contradictions, our conflicting identifications, to accept our psychic bisexuality while accepting sexual difference, is an ongoing, lifelong work. The way in which we unconsciously resolve these differences also has an impact on the relationship with our body as a vital support for our relationship with the external world and our sexuality.

The notion of psychic bisexuality is a theoretical model that is useful for understanding the dimensions of psychic conflict in the expression of sexuality at a singular level, and its extension to the concept of mental bisexuality allows us to think about the subject's capacity to incorporate otherness, to resolve his or her contradictory identifications.

Drawing on the ideas of Birksted-Breen (1996) and Houzel (2005), I use the concept of bisexuality to understand a way of expressing the traumatic. That is, since the psyche is bisexual and this is one of its structuring aspects, we can visualize the self as a result of this relationship between our internal objects, and between the self and others.

Following these ideas, I would like to present some segments of clinical material, in which the articulation of the notions of trauma, mourning, and body, from the perspective of psychic bisexuality, allows an analytical understanding of a conflictive and emotionally distressing manifestation related to the sexuality of a male, cisgender, and heterosexual patient.

The impact of transgenerational traumatic events

Trauma is the key concept and fundamental Freudian construct. It is located in the encounter between the external and the internal, with its dynamics of excess, rupture, loss; with its disarticulating power and its function of alarm, as well as protection (Gampel, 2006).

Although its power and source are often uncertain, it allows us to glimpse what can operate beyond pleasure. The hypothesis proposed by Freud (1917) suggests the image of a blackout that puts the traumatic scene in direct contact with an original time of individual experience, perhaps in a form of consciousness not yet known (Gampel, 2006), a dark side of consciousness (Lévinas, 1996), a foreign territory within oneself.

However, the place of the "historical reality" of the traumatic has been the subject of controversy since the beginnings of psychoanalysis and has made it possible to explore the effects of transgenerational trauma and its disruptive potential in the present. We now know that the subject is capable of endlessly repeating, through different expressions, a traumatic situation that is impossible to remember, unthinkable or unrepresentable, because it does not belong to their history, but precedes it.

Baranger, Baranger and Mom (1988) distinguish the external form of the "pure" and unassimilable trauma from the retroactively historicized forms, reintegrated into the vital passage of time that we achieve through analytical work.

What is traumatic is at the same time a disarticulation of the former self, and a form of exit toward survival, which implies psychic consequences for the subject with a costly and often incomprehensible legacy that can affect, as in this case, the modalities of affective and sexual life.

Mourning in the body

Since 1917, mourning has been understood in the psychoanalytic model as a process of identification, catechization, and decatechization due to the loss of a love object, the search for the precipitate of abandoned object-cathexes and their vicissitudes (Freud, [1917] 1981). This model was important in identifying the characteristics of both normal and pathological grief. Today we know that this frozen grief, silenced in the past, is validated and reactivated in the present, seeking its resolution and inclusion in the vital line of each of us.

The body is our body, an exercise of responsibility, a terrain of recognition of the self and one's life. If there is a break, a rupture, a non-recognition, the duality soma/psyche is produced (Bion, 1962). Embodying this more or less harmonious or painful relationship is a way of resolving those incommunicable and private messages transmitted to us in the first stages of life by the parental couple through their caring functions (Laplanche, [1987] 1992). What we construct as subjects in response implies a way out of this soma/psyche duality.

The primary functions that create life and its consciousness – sensation, breathing, movement, desire, fear – are the roots and models upon which representations of the self and the world are organized. Freud states that

> the ego is primarily a bodily self and not merely a superficial being, but the ego is also a superficial projection. [...] The ego is ultimately derived from bodily sensations, especially those that come from the surface of the body. The ego may be regarded as a mental projection of the surface of the body, and furthermore [...] represents the surface of the mental apparatus.
>
> (Freud, [1923] 1981, p. 26)

This includes the singular modes of sexual pleasure – the erotic surface potentially available to the subject depends to a large extent on the impact of these contradictory representations on the body surface itself.

Articulating these concepts, we can therefore observe the impact of different traumatic situations (present and past), understood as frozen grief, in the crystallization of contradictory identifications that leave their mark on the body, its sexual positioning, and its modes of sexual satisfaction.

The concept of bisexuality thus makes it possible to create a psychic territory in which singular experiences belonging to the context of the primary relationship are expressed, modeled by unrepresented disruptive situations resulting from grief or traumas of the previous generation, which co-exist in the psychic life of the subject in a divided way and with conflicting goals, affecting one's passionate life, relational capacity, and sexuality.

A parallel life

Mariano consults for the first time at 40 years old and is referred by a Colombian colleague who helped him find a Spanish-speaking analyst who worked online. Mariano is Venezuelan and was living in Germany for ten years. He was married to a German woman and they had a seven-year-old daughter. The couple had married when they discovered they were going to be parents.

In the first interview, Mariano says that he needs therapy because he is in crisis with his partner, that he fantasizes about leaving her, but that it scares him a lot, it worries him; he adds that he is afraid of being alone, but he is also afraid that his separation will affect his immigration status. In time we will see that this is a fantasy, but at the beginning of the interview it was a powerful fear that prevented him from even thinking about the subject.

He says:

> My wife has been depressed for years, she is on medication and has completely abandoned me; she is fat, disheveled, does not take care of the house, works only part-time and does not take good care of the child.

I ask him if this situation makes him angry as well as sad, and he tells me that it makes him angry.

> I feel that she has no consideration for me, that she doesn't care about me; she, as a woman, rejects me as a man, it's like living with a roommate.

He tells me that

> [I have] to take care of the girl's things, insist that she bathe, brush her hair: these are tasks that should be done by the mother, not by me; but if I don't do it, she can go a week without bathing and go to school without brushing her hair and in pajamas.

At this moment, I feel angry listening to the way he refers to his wife, his style of communication creating a visceral rejection in me. Faced with the worrying situation of caring for his child and the obviously poor psychological state that his wife is in, he does not show the slightest concern, but rather expresses

a feeling of rejection and betrayal. I have to do my own psychic work in order
not to react to his expressions and to continue listening.

Mariano tells me that he is the son of Venezuelan parents who, during his
childhood, always had a solid economic position, supported by his father's
work in the oil business. His mother was a housewife, and Mariano being the
elder of two brothers. The two brothers were always the pride of his mother,
who used to say that in "her time" it was always better to have male children
than female, that women who gave birth to male children were better.

At the same time, Mariano tells me that he has only recently learned that his
father was always a violent man with his mother:

> they always argued very loudly, it is not strange to think that my dad hit
> her, but I was never able to think about it until she told me some time ago.

He remembers his father with fear and admiration, as a kind of "monster to
whom we owed everything."

His childhood was marked by academic achievement, as he felt the need to
be an example to his brother and to comply to his family's demands. He does
not remember having many friends, as they moved around a lot. His erotic
life as an adolescent came "a bit late" in his view, he was not interested in
girls until he was 17 or 18.

It was at this time in his life that his younger brother fell ill with cancer and
died within a year. This event marked the beginning of a period of enormous
family turmoil, which exacerbated his parents' marital problems and largely
determined Mariano's need to emigrate, not only from his country, but also
from his family. At that point, he had had about two years of analytical
treatment with an analyst who encouraged him to emigrate and helped him to
work out the guilt of leaving his mother "without a son" and in the hands of
his father. At the time, his mother was undergoing psychiatric treatment for
suicidal thoughts, a situation that had been going on for several years.

The balance of a split sexuality, the price to pay

During the first few months of treatment, not only does the rigid splitting of
paternal and maternal duties became apparent, but also the deep anger Mariano
felt at having to take care of the things of the "woman of the house." He adds:

> even though I escaped from my parents' house, even though I did not put
> up with the violent relationship we all had there, everything seems to be
> repeating itself. I find myself saying some of the things my father said to
> my mother, and I hate myself for it. I am trapped. But what makes me
> most angry is that I live with this woman who is not a woman. I play the
> role of man and woman in my house.

Mariano is a lucid man, used to associating, to expressing himself; in fact, his previous analytical experience simplifies my work as an analyst. He tends to progress in his associations almost without my intervention. He develops a confident, open style of transference that allows us to dialogue and even use humor as a vehicle for thoughts and reflections. However, whenever he brings up one of his "gender" statements, his ideological rigidity and my difficulty in accommodating his stereotypes become apparent.

Faced with his statement about the annoyance of "playing both man and woman," I ask him if the fact that his wife is not "woman enough" does not make him "man enough." After another long silence, he adds:

> Our life as a couple was never great, we started dating because I was alone, had just arrived in Germany, and she somehow protected me, made me feel accompanied. We never had a very satisfying sex life, but enough, she was never my type of woman – I like sexier women, who dress up, wear high heels and make-up – but we were within a reasonable limit. There are some things I haven't said here, about my sexuality, about my habits, that I'm ashamed of, but I have to say them. I fear your gaze, your judgment, but if I'm not honest, there's no point in this analysis. I know I should have said it before, but I feel so ashamed.

A long silence follows. He becomes desperate, and tells me that he has a private routine regarding his sexual repertoire. Two or three times a year, he goes to the mountains alone, where he locks himself up to take a stimulant and engage in a series of autoerotic sexual practices. His wife is aware of this, but does not interfere; she allows these "escapades," as Mariano calls them, without asking too many questions. But it seems that this explicitness of the need to play a role more associated with the feminine stereotype, of home and childcare, has, in his words, "upset the balance."

He adds:

> I've never felt completely comfortable with my sex life, only when a woman is "magazine" I manage to connect, otherwise I feel a deep disinterest. It's like cartoons, the cover girl makes me feel like a complete man and then I function as such. When that doesn't happen, like now, when she's like an amoeba, I feel nothing, neither for her nor for myself, I feel nothing. I depend in everything on what she provokes in me. And that's how it has worked. I felt like a man because she was a woman.

To this I said:

> So on the one hand you have this experience of being the woman of the house, of not feeling like a man because she's "not a woman," and on the

other hand you have a private refuge for your sexual pleasure that you can only inhabit alone.

At this point, Mariano reflects on his "double life"; not that he has a double social life, but that he has a double sexual life. He explains that he has always believed that he is not man enough, that he has "something homosexual" hidden inside him, which is where he feels most authentic and at the same time most ashamed. But that he will never "go further" down this road, that he must keep life as it is, where he is a "normal man" with a "normal family," otherwise the chaos that would break out inside him would be unbearable. "They would never forgive me"; "Who?" I ask. "My parents. I would never be able to look them in the face again." Although he considers himself to be flexible and open to other people's private lives, he cannot imagine putting together these two aspects of himself, but he does not yet know why.

The revealing and integrating dream

A few months after, Mariano came to the session with a dream he wanted to share.

M: I had a dream last night that I want to tell you about. My daughter was driving a steamroller, she was a child, like today, and she was crushing a house, which I understood to be the house of my childhood, with a machine. I remember the dust, the feeling of surprise, I could hear the sound of the walls falling and the wooden ceiling creaking. She was silent and did not look at me, I looked at all the work she was doing, I had entered a few minutes before the demolition, as she had given me permission to take out what I thought was important, when I looked at what I had saved, I had in my hands a box with photos of my brother. I saved my brother in the dream [...] It is so obvious that I feel stupid.

A: What is obvious?

M: The time I've spent talking about my sexuality, what I'm hiding and what I'm "officially" living, I'm questioning who I am, I'm hiding from other people, I want that safe house back that gave me peace of mind. I think that breaking out of this mold would be a great betrayal to my parents, they have already lost one child, to reveal myself, to confess, would be like making them lose another child. I can't bear it.

A: I imagine that the arrival of your daughter has tipped the scales a bit, pushed your wife out of her previous role as a woman, submerged her in a maternal position – which is also very difficult for her – and taken you out of that arrangement where she had the primary function of supporting you.

Masculinity as scaffolding and absolution

I understand that Mariano's story reflects one of the challenges of masculinity today, where social stereotypes, patriarchal demands, and patriarchal forms, conveyed through parental discourse, impose extraordinary challenges and enormous sacrifices on women, but also on many men.

In this case, the trauma of Mariano's mother, immersed in a violent environment at the hands of the "man" who is also the source of all dependence and admiration, cannot but have encouraged Mariano to consolidate a masculine position full of contradictions. Conflicts in which he takes the path of renunciation, paying the price to avoid being expelled, to avoid being executed by a family that cannot bear any more losses.

Although the Oedipal exit always implies a certain renunciation, singular renunciations always have their own trajectories that give each subject their own drama and constitute their own modes of suffering. Oedipal mourning, the constitution of a subject's masculine identity, leads to the renunciation of their sexual *jouissance*, which remains crystalized in a private, shameful and detached practice from their everyday life.

It is their body, which at the same time exhibits their appearance and denounces their suffering, that forces them to find escape strategies in order to continue maintaining the scaffolding that enacts in them their entire family history.

Thinking about this history through the concepts of psychic bisexuality and mental bisexuality allows me to understand the psychic transactions that Mariano has constructed over the years as possible unconscious strategies for dealing with dilemmas between identifications and modes of satisfaction. The collage of messages and internal objects is understandable if we can think of the subject as always inhabited by both sexual positions, both types of goals and objects. It is in this singular map that one can imagine the ways of relating to others, to otherness, to social discourse, to previous generations and to oneself.

In Mariano's life, this possibility of articulating the different masculine and feminine positions and goals that make up the network of identifications that create the mental space of psychic bisexuality, and which allows the "other" to be housed within oneself, which allows one to recognize as one's own that which is experienced as alternative or different, does not manage to be integrated or incorporated into the experience of one's own sexuality. This form of sexual jouissance, the singular modalities of pleasure linked by Mariano to the feminine sexual position – as receptive – are split and are in permanent tension with the social discourse, its links, and family mandates. The expectations that Mariano fantasizes that the external world, his parents, and "the others" have for him as a "man," the masculine role that he must fulfil and that he pretends to assume without fissures or contradictions – heteronormative and cisgender – collapse with his sexuality. Mariano has no choice but to "choose" one pole of this binarism that should be integrated in the process of psychic maturation. Traumas, unconscious debts, compel him to incarnate a semblance, an appearance, a role that he plays, but which he lives as a masquerade where he renounces his "subjective truth" in order not to be rejected, finally to avoid the fantasied castration.

References

Baranger, M., Baranger, W. , & Mom, J. (1988). The infantile trauma from us to Freud: Pure trauma, retroactivity and reconstruction. *International Journal of Psychoanalysis*, 69, 113–128.

Bion, W.R. (1962). *Learning from experience*. Karnac Books.

Birksted-Breen, D. (1996). Phallus, penis and mental space. *International Journal of Psychoanalysis*, 77, 649–657.

Freud, S. ([1905] 1981). Three essays on the theory of sexuality. In *The Standard Edition of the Complete Psychological Works of Sigmund Freud, Volume 7* (pp. 123–246). Hogarth Press.

Freud, S. ([1917] 1981). Mourning and melancholia. In *The Standard Edition of the Complete Psychological Works of Sigmund Freud, Volume 14* (pp. 237–258). Hogarth Press.

Freud, S. ([1923] 1981). The ego and the id. In *The Standard Edition of the Complete Psychological Works of Sigmund Freud, Volume 19* (pp. 1–66). Hogarth Press.

Freud, S. ([1930] 1981). *Civilization and its discontents. The Standard Edition of the Complete Psychological Works of Sigmund Freud, Volume 21* (pp. 64–145). Hogarth Press.

Gampel, Y. (2006). Duelo, cuerpo, trauma. *Revista de la Sociedad Argentina de Psicoanálisis*, 9, 115–132.

Houzel, D. (2005). Splitting of psychic bisexuality in autistic children. In D. Houzel & M. Rhode (Eds.), *Invisible boundaries: Psychosis and autism in children and adolescents* (pp. 75–95). Karnac Books.

Hurwood, J. (2009). Psychic and mental bisexuality in the development of a sense of self and mind. *British Journal of Psychotherapy*, 25, 520–532.

Laplanche, J. ([1987] 1992). *Novos fundamentos para a psicanálise*. Martins Fontes.

Lévinas, E. (1996). Substitution. In A. Peperzak (Ed.), *Basic Philosophical Writings* (pp. 76–96). Indiana University Press.

Perelberg, R. (2018). *Psychic bisexuality: A British-French dialogue*. Routledge.

Pontalis, J. (1973). *Bisexualité et différence de sexes*. Gallimard.

Chapter 10

Psychic bisexuality and its pulsional vicissitudes

Luz María Abatángelo Stürzenbaum

Introduction

The question of bisexuality is of interest for at least two reasons. First, because, as Freud ([1905] 2010) himself pointed out, it is one of the presentations of the sexed experience of the human being that most challenges the theory he developed. Both the constitution of the psyche, taken through the bias of the choice of object, and the end of analysis, assuming that the bedrock of castration operates as the ultimate limit in a differential way for men and women, are prevented from the possibility of being resolved in a strictly binary way if bisexuality exists as a phenomenon.

On the other hand, the clinical practice of our time confronts us precisely with the inadequacy of binary thinking to address some manifestations of psychic suffering or, at least, invites us to question some elements of the theory. In no way does this imply the need to dynamite Freudian psychoanalysis and invent a new one, but it is true that manifestations such as transsexualism, bisexuality, and gender fluidity, among others, constitute interpellations to the theory that, rather than an obstacle, should be thought of as a fertile field. Ultimately, these phenomena force us to develop within psychoanalysis one of the points that emerge from Freudian elaboration, namely complex thought. Considering a multiplicity of operative variables simultaneously, and even (and above all) paradoxically, can allow us to expand the boundaries of psychoanalytic theory in order to understand and address accordingly the forms of suffering present in our clinical practice. To put it another way, the fluidity characteristic of our time can hardly be taken as an object of reflection through the use of categories whose central characteristic is fixity, i.e. the unequivocal reference of the term to that which it describes. The commitment of psychoanalysis to singularity is intimately linked to the interiority and is, in short, what should guide complex thought within the clinical field.

Taking up the question of bisexuality, then, has here, we might say, an epistemological status. When Freud develops the importance of thinking about the symptom in its overdetermination, he is merely proposing a way of

DOI: 10.4324/9781003584483-12

conceiving the subject of our intervention, that which justifies the analyst's interpretation. If in the symptom there is a convergence of diverse and even opposing meanings, with drive motions of different signs, it is because binarism as a modality of organizing thought is clearly insufficient to carry out a treatment of these symptoms. Moreover, the fact of granting it a satisfactory character displaces common sense as a lens for interpretation and places it in a complex relationship between the human being and his pleasures.

Our Western thought usually works in terms of binary opposition, something that Freud himself questioned. Faced with this scenario, psychoanalysis, which is committed to the production of an *in-between* in thinking about the analyst's work, can perhaps approach bisexuality by dispensing with the obligatory choice of a love object with unique characteristics, especially bearing in mind that the subject is inhabited by both hetero- and homosexual motions, that there are both masculine and feminine components in him or her. This raises the question that we will try to address in the following pages: is bisexuality a choice of object in itself, does it correspond to the classical idea that it implies a non-renunciation, a non-positioning in the face of the problem of sexuation, or is it instead the contingent implementation of hetero- or homosexual motions?

Perhaps the epistemological importance of bisexuality allows us to provide psychoanalysis with an edge through which to complexify the thinking about the relationships between human beings, their culture, and their time. If we understand bisexuality as the co-existence of feminine and masculine attributes in the psyche of all people, it is undoubtedly a concept that gives us a broader view to reflect on the choice of object, the processes of identification, masculine and feminine roles, and the way in which all these elements are articulated in different ways over time and in different cultures.

In order to develop the above, we will first present a brief overview of Freudian approaches to bisexuality. They constitute, in our opinion, both the cornerstone for thinking about the question, as well as an impasse in itself, since the phallus/castration binarism seems to have left bisexuality the only possible place for questioning, trying to maintain a tension between the classical Freudian concepts and the possible questionings that arise in the light of our time. We will then try to provide an insight into the way in which sexual difference is inscribed and the implications that this has for the psyche. Finally, we will investigate a case that aims to show some possible coordinates for thinking about the presentation of bisexuality within the analytic setting.

It should be added here that analytical work is approached in the following process from a complex perspective that we consider to be bidirectional. In the case that we will develop, this aspect is evident to the extent that, on the one hand, a modification of a theoretical nature is produced in the analyst, if we take into consideration that the decantation of the analytical process that we will expose has, as a corollary, some ideas about bisexuality that seem to transcend to some extent the classical conceptions of the subject within the psychoanalytic field. On the other hand, the case's description gives an account of the effects produced by the analytic experience in the patient. In short, the case, as a complex construction, shows this double movement.

Freud and bisexuality

In "Three Essays on Sexual Theory" ([1905] 2010), Freud presents his concept of bisexuality, linking it to repression, identifications, and object relations. He stresses that our libido oscillates between male and female objects, and that puberty defines an object choice that represses homosexual or heterosexual aspirations, as the case may be. Freud suggests that in male homosexuality, the chosen object integrates characteristics of both sexes, illustrating the constitutive bisexuality of human beings. He further distinguishes three senses of the terms masculine and feminine: biological (sex glands), psychological (active/passive, with the libido being always active), and sociological (mixture of sexual characteristics and behaviors).

In "The Ego and the Id" (Freud [1923] 2010), bisexuality is used to explain the resolution of the Oedipus complex, where identifications and object choices reflect the combined sexual dispositions. Freud notes that this complex oscillates between a normal Oedipus and its inverted version, depending on the strengths of the sexual dispositions. For his part, in "The Malaise in Culture" (1930), Freud asserts that men and women possess both masculine and feminine tendencies, and that the association of activity with the masculine and passivity with the feminine is not universal. He also discusses how social mores reinforce passive roles in women.

Finally, in "Terminable and Interminable Analysis" (1937), Freud reflects on the differences between bisexuals, homosexuals, and heterosexuals. He proposes that the limited libido forces the rival drives to compete, although they are not always divided proportionally. Freud raises questions about why some manage to integrate both tendencies while others do not. This approach does not seek to uphold a specific social order, but to pinpoint key elements of the patient's speech, especially in the articulation between sexuality, gender, and identity.

Further considerations on psychic bisexuality

Today, gender studies and other fields of knowledge have taken Freudian theory as an object of critique, especially with regard to the consequences of positing the constitution of the psyche in binary masculine/feminine terms. Taken to its extreme, this critique locates in psychoanalysis a normalizing therapeutics, that offers the subject a path with only two possible routes. In other words, the device invented by Freud would be a kind of agency of patriarchy insofar as it would allow the social relations of power that constitute it to be reproduced at the singular level.

However, our reading of Freud's ideas about sexuality in its broadest sense, including bisexuality, allows us to infer that Freud subverts the idea that anatomy and psyche are directly related. For, although he seems to put it in these terms, and even goes so far as to do so explicitly by quoting Napoleon in the text 'Some Psychical Consequences of the Difference Between the Sexes" – where he states that "anatomy is destiny" (Freud, [1925] 2010, p. 185) – this same text, to take just one example, clearly shows that, in reality, work is necessary on the part of the subject to enable him to take a position in relation to his own anatomy, which will eventually be articulated with an analogous taking of a position in relation to the choice of object. To put it another way, it is necessary for the subject to inscribe in his psyche that which nature provides, leaving a vacant space in the theory that, with Lacan, can be named "the bottommost decision of being"[1] (Lacan, [1946] 1966, p. 175), where what is summoned is the subject as the agent of these crucial decisions for the structuring of the psyche. It could even be thought that transsexualism, which is presented as an impasse of the masculine/feminine binarism, is precisely an account of the fact that anatomy is not destiny, but that there is a subject carrying out a work of inscription of the body itself that, in the symbolic, runs along different paths to those of anatomy.

The question then arises: is this subject, as a psychic instance, comparable with his/her identity? Here it is useful to take Jessica Benjamin's distinction between identity and subject ([1995] 2006). The subject is not subject to his/her identity. It is not a matter of the subject sinking its roots in that to which it is identical, for, in that line, one would be going down the path that indicates that Freud places anatomy in a relation of contiguity with the psyche. That is to say, the subject is not the mental version of what the biological body determines someone to *be*. Identity, thus conceived, would be a datum inherent to anatomy: each body would be identical to the male or female pattern and, from there, its subjectivation would be produced. On the contrary, the subject must be thought of as an agent, the one who can give an account in the analytical device of those bottommost decisions that constitute his or her identity, that is, that image that the subject assumes as his or her own and that serves, to put it metaphorically, as a face, as a facade with which he or she unfolds in the social field, which is, in these terms, a field of encounter and mis-encounter of identities.

If we can assume a subject's decision with respect to what he or she shows as identity, and we affirm, following Freud, that a work of inscription and symbolization of corporeality is necessary on his part, it is then appropriate to review the character we assign in the theory to the concept of original bisexuality. We have mentioned above that, thanks to this concept, Freud manages to locate that the choice of object somehow constitutes a renunciation, or at least a departure from conscious goals, of a part of his sexual aspirations. This positioning of the subject leads, as we mentioned recently, to an identitarian positioning, that is to say, in relation to others.

However, original bisexuality is not a verifiable fact. Only the Freudian logic of the *nachtraglich* allows us to locate *a posteriori* that, thanks to the existence of repressed or desexualized homosexual motions, some tendencies of the other sex inhabit each individual. However, the fact that it is not a verifiable fact except by its effects would allow us to situate original bisexuality in the place of a principled request. We know that the mythical in Freud has an important value in theory: let us think, for example, of the father of the horde, which, far from having a character of historical validity, constitutes a plot that allows us to investigate the function of the father in the analytic device.

A similar character must be attributed to constitutional bisexuality: the different sexual motions that inhabit the same person and that unfold within the framework of the transference do not confirm that the origin of sexuality is bisexual, but rather imply the need to find an origin that, strictly speaking, is an empty point. And it is on this empty point that Freud locates the original bisexuality, an idea that, moreover, is already present in Agathon's discourse in Plato's "Banquet": the human substance is composed of two parts, once united, that were separated by divine intervention and seek to be reunited. In Freud, the myth prescribes something similar, but in the opposite direction: both currents exist in the individual, but one has taken precedence over the other, condemning it to manifest itself only as an unconscious expression.

What are the consequences of thinking of constitutive bisexuality as a principled request? It allows us to approach the clinical phenomenon of bisexuality in a different light than that of non-decision-making. If we were to situate the Freudian approach in terms of a reliable origin on which the subject must resolve, and not as a work, as the emergence of a process of symbolization of the body and its location in a libidinal relationship with others, the choice of object would be, precisely, a choice and, therefore, a renunciation; bisexuality, in this scenario, is thought of as a non-taken-decision, a repression of homo- or heterosexual motions that was not done, making them co-exist in the conscious mind.

On the other hand, if it is thought of as a principled request about the choice of object, constitutional bisexuality may help us think about the way in which the subject carries out the work of inscription to which we have been referring. This work implies, first and foremost, the inscription of the similar and the different. And this is not something that is done in solitude, but necessarily involves others: it is there that we find what is similar and what is different. It is not so much a question of the intrinsic existence in the body of two tendencies, one masculine and the other feminine, but rather that the subjective constitution is built on the basis of the appropriation of the similar and the different of the other.

To put it another way, when the analytic setting summons the subject to account for his or her choice of object, this does not lead toward a taking of a position that does or does not coincide with anatomy and with the biological destiny of bodies (reproduction and death). On the contrary, what we find are the traces that were taken from the significant others who libidinized this body and, ultimately, through this sexualizing intervention, led the subject to carry out the work of inscribing this sexuality. Sexuality only becomes one's own, and eventually identity, to the extent that the subject inscribes it, but, strictly speaking, it always comes from the other, and therefore carries at its core something of that other, which will be inscribed as similar or as different. And the choice of object will be made precisely on the basis of these similarities or differences. The subject's position, in short, will be to accept what is different from the other, eventually taking him or her as an object of love, and thus becoming his or her similarity, or to reject what is different and condemn him or her to repression. It is in this sense that bisexuality can be thought of as part of the sexuation of the subject, as the acceptance of difference in the identical and of the identical in the difference.

It is through the intervention of otherness and by compelling the subject to take a position in the field of sexuality that the way is opened for the inscription that Freud states as defining sexuation: the difference of the sexes. In the approach we have been taking, the difference of the sexes is only inscribed as such to the extent that it implies the inscription of differences and similarities.

The opposite of this is the difference of sexes, where we find ourselves in a purely identitarian terrain: the other is different from us, belongs to another gender, is simply an other with whom there is no possible encounter insofar as there is no lack at stake, because the other is what it is. To inscribe the difference of the sexes is to be able to abandon the bias of having or not having a phallus and to be able to situate oneself in a field where what is inscribed, in short, is the radical alterity of the others, on the basis of which differences and similarities are established with them. In other words, the bedrock of castration is a limit only if it is thought of in binary terms.

On the contrary, it is openness insofar as it is the acceptance of the limit to the experience of fusion with the other, that is to say, to the fact that it is structurally impossible to make two differences into a similarity.

Regarding the Oedipus complex, paternal intervention is what prevents making two into one. The prohibition of incest must be thought of formally as the prohibition of imaginary identification with the maternal phallus, that is to say, it prevents a fusion between mother and child through the phallus as the element that brings them together. Now, if the oedipal resolution is indissoluble from paternal intervention, and leads to the possibility of the inscription of the difference between the sexes, it is extremely interesting to think about the implications of sexuation in a historical context marked by the fall of the paternal imposture.

Recalcati (2014) points out that the nodal consequence of this fall lies in the subject's relations with desire, which becomes impoverished, insofar as the rejection of castration implies, in short, the rejection of the contingent, the surprising, the different, and the diverse of the other. Articulating Recalcati's point of view with what we have been saying about the importance of the inscription of the difference between the sexes, we could affirm that bisexuality is a phenomenal emergent of our time, that is to say, an effect of the fall of the father as a social organizer. In this sense, bisexuality could be linked more to the difficulty of inscribing the difference between the sexes, especially if we understand it as a choice of non-choice.

In short, bisexuality is supported by anatomical bisexuality, as Freud puts it, but it does not stop there. On the other hand, it involves the subject as the agent of object choice, or it may be a non-choice, or the implementation of hetero- or homosexual motions. It may have to do not so much with the repression of certain motions in function of the identifications around the phallus and castration in the Oedipus, but rather with the possibility of making room for the otherness that inhabits the subject, found in the other at the moment of the encounter with them.

So, if bisexuality constitutes a position, is it the position that resolves neurosis, in the sense of transcending repression? We will say no, since we consider that in most cases it implies repression and not its lifting, but that it contains a subject bringing into play repressed motions at a given juncture.

The case we will see below shows this: there seems to be a homosexual choice of object, which does not prevent the putting into action of heterosexual motions (alongside with jealousy), that come to undermine the homogeneity that the choice of object implies at the egoic level.

Eugenia's decision

Eugenia was 35 years old at the time of the first consultation. She worked as a university lecturer, where she was well known for her academic work in the field of sociology. She had been in a relationship with Juliana for about three years. During that period, they had lived together at Juliana's house.

As she recounts from the beginning of her analysis, this relationship was for her both an emotional support and a real problem. Arguments were frequent, for various reasons, and usually escalated into really tense situations, characterized by insults and abuse. At the same time, Eugenia commented that she needed Juliana in her life and that, despite the arguments, she had never thought of separating; on the contrary, she went so far as to say in the first sessions that life with Juliana "is as necessary as it is suffocating."

These first sessions seemed to have a cathartic value, as Eugenia spent all the time recounting the disputes she had had with her partner during the week. However, after two months of treatment, she had a dream:

> I found myself in a big, open place ... like a park. I was a little girl and I was walking hand in hand with an older woman. The woman sat me on a bench and disappeared. I shouted at her not to go away, but her figure

became more and more distant. My anguish was enormous, until another girl approached and invited me to play. In the dream, this other girl was very sweet to me, but I was distant, distrustful. She asked me why I was there and I didn't know what to answer her, that was the most difficult thing.

The analyst points out that the distance she had with the girl in the dream was perhaps similar to that which existed between her and Juliana.

At that moment, Eugenia burst into tears and confessed that there was something she had been hiding from Juliana, and also from her analyst: for about four months, she had been in a parallel relationship with a man. She said it was something she was very ashamed of, and that it made her feel not only guilty but also deeply insecure, since she had never been attracted to a man before. However, she commented that what she liked about him was that he did not ask her questions, it was just about getting together and "having a good time without having to explain anything."

Eugenia considered that this relationship was a way of attracting Juliana's attention, to which the analyst replied:

> far from attracting attention, perhaps you are causing her to move further away, like the woman in the dream. Perhaps there is something of you in the girl who asks questions and gets no answers: you are also asking yourself what you are doing in the relationship with Juliana ... and with the man you are seeing.

A few weeks later, Eugenia recounted in a session that she had ended the relationship with the man she was seeing. She said that, since the dream, she had started to think about how valuable it was to find answers and that, through the relationship, she had only been putting off asking the necessary questions about her partner.

ANALYST: So you're not also leaving aside the question of your relationship with a man?

EUGENIA: I think it was a moment when I was looking for something different, really far away from Juliana, someone that didn't have her way of being, her way of walking, that didn't ask me any questions, that just saw me as a body ... that's what a man does.

A: It's a rather peculiar idea of what a man is. Especially because it leaves you in a place of pure object, one that is being used by the other.

E: I hadn't thought of it like that. During the first time with him, I think that's what I liked, that he treated me as a thing that he would call and I would appear there for him. And as I told you, it was just that, we hardly spoke when we met. On the other hand, Juliana is always attentive to me, she asks me how I am, she wants to know what's wrong with me while we argue, and my anger doesn't allow me to listen to her, I just want her to shut up and leave me alone. Sometimes I wonder why my reaction is to want to stay alone.

A: It seems that not only does so much anger not allow you to see Juliana and her good intentions, but you lose sight of the fact that through being attentive and telling you that she loves you deeply, she is giving you a place of importance in her life. She does not treat you as a thing, as an object. On the contrary, she wants you to be able to express yourself and that gives you a different place. You should think about what it is that prevents you from being able to take that place.

In the following session, Eugenia produced another confession:

... talking and talking about Juliana, I never told you that my mother died in a traffic accident when I was little. I was three years old. She went out to buy some things for me in her car and never came back. She had an accident and left.

She recounts this event in a disaffected way, as if it were a closed matter, as if there were no questions surrounding the event. Eugenia continued:

I don't have many memories of her, but dad used to tell me some things about her. What I remember most is that he used to say that she had gone to another place from where she looked after me. As a child I wondered what that place was like and why she had to leave without any warning. Then I realized that it was bad luck.

The analyst pointed out that her father used a euphemism to refer to this death, saying that she was gone, and that perhaps this was a way of making her death more tolerable for Eugenia and for himself.

A: Like the woman in the dream, according to your father's words, your mother is gone.

E: I never quite understood why he did that. He probably thought, as you said, that it would be easier for me that way. But, from what little I remember, I have a feeling of waiting, of thinking that at any moment, just as mum had gone, she could come back.

A: That is a way of dealing with loss, although it is perhaps a way that does not make it possible for that loss eventually to be processed. That was the way he found. We would have to see what is a possible way that could be more appropriate.

E: I think that was because he thought that mum had gone away and left him with me, that I was quite quarrelsome and troublesome.

A: As if you were a package ... or a thing. What you call being feisty and troublesome was maybe a way of finding a different place, other than being a thing.

E: Are you saying that my father is like all men?

A: No. I'm saying that your father is a man who has apparently been able to deal with his wife's death by pretending to you that it didn't happen.

The memory of Eugenia's mother's death was an important turning point, as it gave the relationship with a man a new colour. According to what was surmised in the course of the sessions, it could be an act that led, as in the dream, to the departure of a woman, leaving her full of questions, which were blocked by the paternal discourse that somehow proclaimed that her mother was still present.

In the light of what had been emerging in the sessions, probably a double movement took place after Eugenia's mother's death. On the one hand, the lack of grief-related coordinates on her father's side left some of that mourning work unfinished: if her father left, her mother could come back at any time, and if she could come back, she would not have died in the end. In this regard, Eugenia recounted that her father did not miss a day of work after the accident and that she had to go to kindergarten even though she felt very sad. This paternal position in the face of grief implies an obstacle to the unfolding of anguish. At the same time, it entails a de-subjectivized reading of the father's actions: how could he love his wife if, after her death, he could not devote a single day to mourning her death? From Eugenia's point of view, this was interpreted not so much as a lack of love, but as an action typical of men, namely treating women as objects.

Not finding an Other at fault at that fateful moment produced in Eugenia a remembrance that was actualized in her relationship with Juliana. Eugenia's refusal to talk to Juliana about what she, Eugenia, was feeling and what made her angry, as well as picking fights, bore the mark of the paternal refusal to talk about her mother's death. In other words, it had the form of refusing castration. Eugenia not only could not show herself at fault; proof of this is the time it took her to be able to talk about both her relationship with a male and her mother's death. In fact, she herself acknowledged that these elements took a long time to appear because she was too focused on talking about Juliana. One might think that to talk about Juliana was to put the fault on her side; Juliana would be the one with the problems, and not Eugenia, who was simply the object of what was happening to Juliana.

Some time later, in the course of a session, Eugenia stated the following:

E: Sometimes I feel that I don't deserve all the attention Juliana gives me. I know that sometimes I complain about it and I end up fighting with her about it, but it's her way of showing me affection, concern ... I reject that, it makes me feel very uncomfortable.

A: Feeling loved makes you uncomfortable, it seems. Maybe it's your way of shielding yourself from the pain that loving someone else can bring … someone else, like your mum.

Visibly distressed, Eugenia recalled that, as an adult, she argued with her father several times for referring to her mother as if she were still alive.

E: I know it's his way and all that, but it makes me very angry that he pretends it's nothing, that he doesn't want to talk about her, that he doesn't tell me things. In the end, he says so much that my mum is somewhere else looking after me, but he doesn't tell me anything about her … it's as if I've never had a mum.

A: Your father doesn't seem to be responding to your requests, which are nothing more than your need to have a memory of your mother. Perhaps it's not him you should ask for that memory, since he doesn't seem to be able to provide it. It seems that this request ends up making you feel like a thing, a burden that he has to deal with.

E: He just doesn't understand what it's like to lose a mother at such a young age. The only one who understands me is Juliana. Not long ago I started talking to her about it. She tells me to talk to my grandfather if I want to know more about my mum and that, for some reason, reassures me.

A: Maybe that means that there is a man willing to give you answers, to give you another place.

A few weeks later, Eugenia said she went to the village where her grandfather lived to spend a weekend with him. Her father had never got on well with him, so after her mother's death, she visited him only occasionally. Although they had little contact, she says, her grandfather was very attentive to her. He wrote to her regularly and, without fail, on every birthday he would send her several gifts.

E: During the weekend, he told me a lot of things. Not only about mum, about whom he told me some things I didn't know but a lot of things that, talking to him, I realized he just didn't have in mind, that he had forgotten. He also told me about himself, about his family history, about his friends from his youth and that one of them had recently passed away. It was strange, because at the same time that he seemed moved by that, I also noticed that he was cheerful.

A: The memory of someone who has died does not have to be exclusively solemn and painful. Your grandfather probably remembers his friend fondly because he remembers many pleasant things he shared with him.

E: There I had a familiar feeling. It reminded me of Juliana, who, whenever something bad happens to her, chooses to keep the good things that bad brings.

A: This is very interesting: a man can have something feminine as well ... or a woman, something masculine.

Months later, Eugenia reported that things with Juliana had improved. They no longer argued as much and had managed to reach a kind of agreement: if at any time Eugenia felt uncomfortable about questions her partner might ask her, she could say so through a code word and thus make her discomfort clear. "But I understand that her questions are well-intentioned and I often answer them even though I feel a bit weird about it," Eugenia said. "I think you have more answers to give now," the analyst replied.

Sessions later, she recounted a dream again:

> I was at school, but it was the me I am now. There was an exam, there were hundreds of questions. Despite being a sociologist and working in academia, that's something new, I think. I was never a great student, I had a hard time concentrating on exams. But in this dream, I did everything, I answered all the questions, although in some I cheated, I copied from my classmate.

The analyst interpreted that she was obviously finding it easier to answer, perhaps with the help of the analysis, but certainly with the help of her partner.

E: I just realized that I really care about her, and I think it's because she cares about me. Before, I saw Juliana as someone who had to carry me, but I didn't realize that it was something she chose to do. Now I see that, if she chooses, I don't have to be a burden. It's as if she is open to receiving me.

A: That same openness that you demanded from your father. Your grandfather has been more open and you accepted it. And now Juliana is the one who is open and you also allow yourself to accept it. And accepting that is openness on your part too.

Concluding remarks

In this chapter, we have addressed the question of bisexuality in two ways. In the first place, we have reviewed the Freudian approach, which places bisexuality as a central component in the psychosexual constitution of the human being. This constitutional character of bisexuality, as Freud puts it, can be thought of in terms of a request for principles, a sort of mythology about the origin of sexuality which, *a posteriori* in the analytic setting, would allow us to revise the choice of object and the drives at play in the symptoms. In fact, the reference to constitutional bisexuality in articulation with the Oedipus complex accounts for the way in which the foundation of neurosis must be thought through what Freud calls the complete Oedipus, thus crossing the limit imposed by the series that goes from anatomy to the psychic inscription of the body.

On the other hand, we approached bisexuality in connection with identity. In this sense, we proposed, first, that identity and what we could qualify as the position of the subject in relation to sexuality, are not homologous. That is to say, identity as a self-image put into circulation in social ties with others does not configure a reflection of the relationship that the subject has with the sexuality that inhabits him, as an effect of the libidinizing intervention of his significant others. In fact, the neurotic symptom shows how this relationship between subject and sexuality is problematized and does not have direct access to consciousness, but emerges through the symptom itself. In other words, human sexuality is driven and, therefore, the subject's satisfactions take forms contrary to those prescribed by society. Moreover, Freud makes it very clear how sexuality and community life enter into a conflict, in which the realization of the latter is conditioned by the repression of the former; the symptom is, in short, the outcome of this conflict.

Therefore, there is a distance between identity and subjectivity. The above case serves as a way of thinking about how the choice of object implies in terms of identity (in Eugenia's case, her homosexuality) runs parallel to the way her drives are brought into play. We have seen how the relationship with a man calls into question her identity in terms of choice of object and yet does not imply either a necessarily bisexual position, nor a non-assumed heterosexuality; it is, on the other hand, the putting into action of repressed motions. This enactment takes place within coordinates that must be thought of in a complex way, involving a series of variables that the analysis helps to elucidate: an Other who shows himself to be complete by not being able to mourn a death, the impossibility of situating desire in his relationship as a couple, and the question of his own sexuality based on this heterosexual relationship.

Finally, we would like to add a consideration about the psychoanalytic clinical practice of our time. We have already noted in passing that there is an integrationist tendency of social trends in gender, which may (but does not necessarily) result in work centered on ideals and images, rather than in the field of sexuality. In other words, it may transform the psychoanalytic experience into an agent of subjectivity production, rather than a field of openness to the subject's choice (which, by the way, produces subjectivity).

In the same vein, we consider that the current clinical practice seems to have a certain apprehension for the manifest content, dismissing the other scene. Is it perhaps a defense of the analyst against sexuality, a nodal component of this other scene? We believe that the question is valid, especially considering that the transference is, as Lacan (Lacan, [1946] 1966, p. 152) states, the actualization of the sexual reality of the unconscious. In this sense, to focus on the manifest without risking a reading of the latent could mean dispensing with the analyst's fundamental tool: interpretation. The case presented here shows a possible path: from something that could obviously be sexual, one can get to the scene that is being repeated, which is part of the patient's history and has traumatic value, as it is articulated with a mother's castration and with her desire. And it is in relation to this that the question that gave rise to this work arises: what place does the scene in which she had sexual relations with a man occupy for Eugenia?

Eugenia's presentation of this experience raises for her the question of a possible bisexuality, or of heterosexual experience that puts in tension her choice of homosexual object. This clarification takes on a relevant clinical value insofar as it invites us to think about the analyst's position, character-ized by non-judgment, that is, by not putting a predetermined knowledge before listening. In terms of Eugenia's case, judging would imply labeling the patient by virtue of her actions and not by virtue of what she says. In other words, if she has sex with a woman, she would be a lesbian, and if she enga-ges in a similar practice, but with a man, it would be a case of bisexuality. This quickness to catalogue what is found in the clinical field obstructs lis-tening. In our case, labeling Eugenia as bisexual obscures the conflict that the patient presents, namely the tension between desire and identity. Where a repressed emotion finds a channel in a single experience, the sanctioning of this at the level of identity is precisely a barrier to the unfolding of the anguish that Eugenia's choice of object, and what she represents in terms of identity, has produced when her choice of object is called into question.

Following David ([1975] 2018), the analysis focuses on the way in which sexuality is represented, the way in which the patient elaborates these con-tents, and not on the analyst's sanction as an element that defines the char-acter of this elaboration. "The economy of each person's sexuality is based on an always fragile relationship between the affirmation of bisexuality and the affirmation of sexual specificity" (David, [1975] 2018, p. 78). This is evidenced in Eugenia's case, where, precisely, this oscillation is evidenced, which is put in suspense and problematized in analysis. In a similar vein, Jacqueline God-frind points out that bisexuality implies the free use of attributes associated with both male and female genital identifications, a level at that analysis focuses on the conflict between the two, in light of the Oedipus complex (Godfrind, 2018).

In other words, designating Eugenia as bisexual at the identity level, or as a pure object choice, prevents the meaning given to her heterosexual experience from being developed in connection with the concept of psychic bisexuality. In the case presented, Eugenia's homosexual object choice is put in tension when the patient mentions having intercourse with a man. What the analysis allows us to locate is that this link is produced as an action directed toward her partner, seeking to pierce in her a lack that, in her history, she had not found in her father after the death of her mother. In fact, these two elements could only be connected some time after the beginning of the treatment, when Eugenia recounted the death of her mother at an early age. From that point onward, the analytic conjecture was that this movement in relation to her partner's desire was supported by the acting out of repressed heterosexual emotions, which found the occasion to express themselves in the aforementioned coordinates, which endorses the principled request that Freud introduces in relation to bisexuality.

Note

1 Translated by the author.

References

Benjamin, J. ([1995] 2006). *Sujetos iguales, objetos de amor: Ensayos sobre el reconocimiento y la diferencia sexual*. Paidós.

David, C. ([1975] 2018). The beautiful differences. In R. Perelberg (Ed.), *Psychic bisexuality: A British-French dialogue* (pp. 58–80). Routledge.

Freud, S. ([1905] 2010). Three essays on sexual theory. In *Obras completas tomo VII* (pp. 123–210). Amorrortu.

Freud, S. ([1923] 2010). The ego and the id. In *Obras completas tomo XIX* (pp. 1–66). Amorrortu.

Freud, S. ([1925] 2010). Some psychical consequences of the difference between the sexes. In *Obras completas tomo XIX* (pp. 267–276). Amorrortu.

Freud, S. ([1930] 2010). The malaise in culture. In *Obras completas tomo XXI* (pp. 65–140). Amorrortu.

Freud, S. ([1937] 2010). Terminable and interminable analysis. In *Obras completas tomo XIII* (pp. 219–254). Amorrortu.

Godfrind, J. (2018). From bisexuality to the feminine. In R. Perelberg (Ed.), *Psychic bisexuality: A British-French dialogue* (pp. 122–132). Routledge.

Lacan, J. ([1946] 1966). Acerca de la causalidad psíquica. In *Escritos 1* (pp. 151–190). Ed. Siglo XXI.

Recalcati, M. (2014). *¿Qué queda del padre?: la paternidad en la época hipermoderna*. Editorial Herder.

Chapter 11

When I look into your eyes

An approach to psychic bisexuality in the case of role reversal

Nadja Tröger

Introduction

In his BBC broadcast series titled *The Ordinary Devoted Mother and Her Baby*, Winnicott ([1949] 1991) said in the talk "A Man Looks at Motherhood":

> A mother's love is a pretty crude affair. There's possessiveness in it, appetite, even a "drat the kid" element; there's generosity in it, and power, as well as humility. But sentimentality is outside it altogether, and is repugnant to mothers.

It is curious to note that this more visceral description of motherhood combines opposite facets and conveys at the same time feminine and masculine aspects of human psychic life.

Keeping the crude affair of mother's love in mind, one might wonder what drives a woman in wanting to be a mother? Is it due to her biological nature, her instinctual life, or quite on the contrary, could the motivation derive from a loved partner's dear wish or even from social expectations? Or all of these together?

Whatever unfolds inside the mother's psychic space is a very subjective "affair" and will provide a unique experience with that particular baby she gets in contact with, as each baby corresponds to a new encounter, a new "affair." Nevertheless, a mother never is just a mother, as her identity entails different aspects of her existence, which involve her desires and needs, her femininity, and her perception as woman, ultimately, her drives and unconscious fantasies. In addition, she carries inside her the transgenerational maternal lineages that will link her to her descendants and that contain various aspects of identification with the maternal figure (Mariotti, 2012). Furthermore, there is to be considered the presence of the third hidden inside the maternal figure as the testimony of the ongoing transgenerational parental union. Ultimately, on the symbolic level, mother and father figures dwell as guardians of psychic bisexuality.

DOI: 10.4324/9781003584483-13

In relation to the transgenerational process, it is possible to imagine a phenomenon of repetition, but also of transformation, as each new relationship entails complex new inter- and intrapsychic dynamics, in which the presence of the third is acknowledged since the beginning of the dyadic relationship between the mother and her infant. If maternity is seen in a line of ancestral and cultural logic that crosses the symbolic maternal function and is pre-existent to the concrete experience of being a mother, it is equally relevant to consider the mother's individual unconscious desires that will have an impact on the way she communicates with her infant. In that sense, not only the mother's actual state of mind is significant, but perhaps even more so, the unique configuration of her internal space that harbors different parts of her identity and where traces of the communication with her own mother can be found.

Regarding the generational, hence the maturational differences between the mother and her infant, it is important to keep in mind the contrast of psychological conditions that exist between both, for the mother can be predisposed for identification, but in the early stages of life, the infant is before everything dependent and in a state of symbiosis (Winnicott, [1956] 2018). As mother and infant form a psychological entity, the development of this unit is not only related to primitive psychological organization, but also to a relatively mature one (Ogden, [1985] 2012).

For Mariotti (2012), the distinction between the symbiotic fusion and the identification with a maternal image is particularly important in the development of maternity, and she proposes to differentiate between motherhood and maternal function, relating the latter to the symbolic level as an essential component of maternity. In this context, the author concludes that even a woman with many children can have difficulties in her capacity to be a mother, as well as to feel authentically creative, and I would add, to be aware of those difficulties.

But what might have happened in the unconscious communication between mother and infant, when the roles were inverted, particularly, when a daughter prematurely took over the emotional care for her mother? And then, what might have happened to that mother to spark off that kind of phenomenon? Taking into account the mediating function of psychic bisexuality, what could be at stake in relation to the daughter's integration process of psychic bisexuality?

To shed more light on this complex matter, some preliminary thoughts will contribute to weave the *fil rouge* of the succeeding lines.

First, it seems necessary to circumscribe the meaning of role reversal regarding parent and child. The role reversal is related to a premature adaptation on behalf of the child that can be linked with Winnicott's concepts of true and false self, whereby the creation of a false self refers to the mother-child unit. Therefore, the occurrence of failures during the separation-individuation process and (unavoidably) during the phase of transitional phenomena has to be contemplated.

In this context, psychic bisexuality plays a central role in its mediating function and is examined in the frame of primary maternal preoccupation, as well as in the light of the transitional oedipal relationship in female development. It is suggested that an emotional care needing mother must have had difficulties in integrating psychic bisexuality, moreover that these difficulties reveal themselves as ambiguous parts, which make the mother less capable to mediate between symbiosis and relatedness and, furthermore, to offer herself as a paradoxical object, as we will see further below.

Who is who? About role reversal

Role reversal, also called parentification, refers to a severe disruption of psychological boundaries between parent and child that takes place when a parent seeks instrumental or emotional nurturance and support from his/ her child; the child, in turn, endeavors to guarantee the parents' wellbeing, preserving hereby a favorable environment at home (Engelhardt, 2012; Mello et al., 2015; Goldner et al., 2022). These parent-child relationships are marked by a subjective distortion that promotes the transformation of the child into an "imaginary adult" so that generational boundaries get blurred, and the child is taken as equal (Mello et al., 2015). Consequently, this boundary confusion implies the loss of psychological distinctiveness between parent and child, resulting in the child's sacrifice of their own needs for validation, guidance, and security (Goldner et al., 2022).

It is possible to distinguish adaptative and destructive role reversal. Whereas adaptive role reversal is less severe and might be connected with cultural norms, the destructive one is identified with poor parental care, in addition to the attribution of emotional responsibility and instrumental caregiving to the child (Mello et al., 2015; Goldner et al., 2022). Many situations can give rise to this kind of relationship, but it is noteworthy that role reversal can appear masked, especially when a child is voluntarily assuming emotional care and responsibility for a parent – as might be observed, for example, in several cases of parents' depression, chronic disease, or single parenting (Engelhardt, 2012; Goldner et al., 2022).

Role reversal is not only complex because it manifests itself in different forms and is frequently denied by parents, but also due to the individual family dynamic that depends on that particular family configuration (Mello et al., 2015). In this context, a secondary gain for the child might play an important role, above all when the performed adult role is acknowledged to be crucial to the family. The child may then experience feelings of grandiosity and embrace the caregiver role without any manifest complaints (Jurkovic, 1997). However, the reported outcome for these children shows evidence of a correlation between childhood parentification and psychopathology (Hooper et al., 2011).

In relation to the psychoanalytic understanding of this generational reversal, a reference to Ferenczi is fundamental, as he introduced the metaphor of the *wise baby* that refers to the child's desire to be wiser than the adult as a way to overcome dependency from the adult (Ferenczi, [1923] 1969). The *wise baby* is also the child using wisdom as a defense against emotional collapse in the situation of the adult's neglect and abuse. As the child is traumatized into precocious wisdom – whereby the adult's denial corresponds to the secondary and more traumatic experience for the child – he/she withdraws and removes his/her own subjectivity through the process of autotomy. Ferenczi's concept of autotomy (Ferenczi, [1930–1932] 1949) allows the understanding of how a rupture is caused between intelligence and feelings, aggravated by the condition that the child uses this defense in a sense of "whatever it takes," thereby producing an omnipotent intelligence as a healing agent. That intelligence is firmly held in the place of an absent connection between thought and affects. This development relates also to the "baby meteo" – children who analyse the fluctuations in the family environment in order to adapt adequately, just as meteorologists do (Mello et al., 2019).

From the parents' point of view, various kinds of factors can build the ground for parentification, and frequently these parents themselves were subjected to role reversal (Mello et al., 2015). The obligatory acceleration of the maturation process that is inherent to role reversal inhibits psychic growth in its required time, so that from the transgenerational perspective the "adult child" is built upon an immature adult.

In particular, the mother-daughter relationship can be more predisposed for role reversal due to the intensity and potential confusion that can take place in the relationship between a mother and her same-sex baby. The potential difficulties are naturally revealed in the course of the separation process, whereby psychoanalytic literature has emphasized the complexity of the mother-daughter relationship in terms of its strength, intimacy, and emotional power, on the one hand, and ambivalence, tension, and even conflictual potential, on the other.

As Guignard (2020) states:

> The mother is the first identificatory object for both daughters and sons – the boy will have to change his identificatory object, but for the girl, the mother is also the reference marker for her sense of identity through all the stages of her development and throughout her life as woman and mother.
>
> (p. 97)

If the separation process demands from the mother the capacity to accept otherness, as the daughter is becoming "her own person," it can represent for the daughter a response to the mother's unconscious communication. In fact, the daughter might be carrying out the mother's repressed fantasies and desires, or in contrast, the daughter might be trying to create a distance from her mother, as she fights against her own regressive wish to remain forever exclusively close to her (Mariotti, 2012).

Taking adolescence as a second separation-individuation process into account, Goldner et al. (2022) studied and elaborated on mother-daughter parentification and focused on the difficulties of separation-individuation in adolescent girls, with special attention to the consequences for the development of an authentic and true self and, by extension, of adolescent self-silencing. The results point to difficulties in the separation-individuation process in adolescent girls, when role reversal in the mother-daughter relationship is considered to be existent:

> When adolescent daughters engage in providing for their mothers' needs, they are absorbed within the maternal internalized object and conditioned to relinquish the possibility of acting congruently with their own voice, desires, and needs so as to provide their mothers with support.
>
> (p. 170)

The dilemma consists in the impossibility of creating a balance between the desire for autonomy and the need to maintain a connection with the mother, as the provision of care for the mother reduces the anxiety of abandonment, yet produces separation anxiety at the same time. Either way, the separation process is repressed, thereby reducing and restricting the authentic self. As the daughter complies with the mother's needs, she not only denies aspects of her own self, but also tends to silence certain feelings and thoughts in order to maintain other intimate relationships (Goldner et al., 2022).

From these considerations, it can be concluded that role reversal has its roots in child development. If the daughter's role of an emotional caretaker is conceived as a disturbance of the true self, the line must be traced back to the earliest stages of separation. Following Winnicott's concepts of true self/false self as crucial to identity development, it is relevant to reflect on the continuous disruptive movements that begin in the frame of the environmental mother.

Shaping a joint space

During the transition from the inter- to the extra-uterine life, the mother is consciously confronted with a real, existing baby, undergoing at the same time a complex process of unconscious communication, as she is navigating through the beginnings of the separation from her baby. It is the time of *holding*, the time of undifferentiated texture and the time of omnipresence of the feminine, as all human beings are born of a woman's womb, of a feminine body.

The separation-individuation process is a delicate venture, and, as Pines indicates, it corresponds to a woman's lifelong task to separate herself from the mother (Pines, 1982). On the other hand, and according to Winnicott ([1952] 2018), it is impossible to assert what occurs by reference to the infant alone, as at that stage the infant is not the individual, but rather a unit – that is, an environment-individual set-up. In this merged state undifferentiation prevails that can develop to a "not-me" position toward differentiation of a separate personal self.

Within this encounter, mother and baby begin to shape the unique space they share, where the baby will gradually internalize the experience of protective boundaries that the mother provides due to her capacity to understand her baby intimately (Mariotti, 2012). According to this author, the mediation of boundaries corresponds to a transgenerational process, as the aspects of symbiosis – equal to lack of boundaries – and relatedness – which requires flexible boundaries – reach back to the mother's relationship to her own mother and forward to the future generations through the internalization of her baby. Additionally, as both parents convey to their children their unconscious image of a parental couple, the maternal image can be complemented and enriched or, conversely, undermined by the father's unconscious representation of his own femininity and its relation to his male identity (Mariotti, 2012).

In relation to the symbiotic bond between a mother and her baby, it is important to introduce Bleger's[1] concept of *ambiguity*, since it relates to this symbiotic interdependence. While symbiosis is silent and only revealed when it is disturbed, ambiguity is defined by Bleger (2013, p. 165) as:

> (a) a specific type of identity or ego organization, characterized by the co-existence of a multiplicity of nuclei that have not integrated and consequently may co-exist and alternate without involving confusion or contradiction for the subject; (b) each nucleus of this "granular ego" is characterized in itself by a lack of ego/non-ego discrimination or, in positive terms, by a syncretic organization. We can synthesize these two characteristics as belonging to a very primitive or very regressive ego (or identity).

Bleger (2013, p. 164) clarifies further that

> ambiguity is not confusion, but the persistence of or a regression to a state of primitive fusion or undifferentiation, which characterises the adumbrations of psychological organisation (glischro-caric position).[2]

Regarding the unconscious communication along the maternal lineages, it is important to note that, for Bleger, this primitive undifferentiation, the symbiosis, does not refer to a state, but rather to a different structure, always including the subject and the subject's environment as non-differentiated entities. Consequently, the remnants of the nuclei of this primitive undifferentiation in an adult personality (the psychotic part) are responsible for the persistence of symbiosis, that is, ambiguity. Bleger (2013) considers that this unconscious phenomenon exists and pre-exists in unconscious form.

In that sense, ambiguity could play a key role, when a mother has difficulties in mediating between symbiosis and relatedness.

While in Bleger's theoretical conceptualization the glischro-caric position constitutes the cornerstone for the paranoid-schizoid phase, Winnicott conceives the holding environment as preceding the paranoid-schizoid phase by stating that the baby is coupled with the object of maternal care and does not exist all by himself (Green, [1975] 2012).

On the other hand, and with respect to the uniqueness of each human being, Winnicott ([1960] 2011) describes a core of the personality that is the centre of the self – the true self – that is conceivable as the heritable potential, a potential individuality at birth. It appears as soon as there is any mental organization at all, and it represents the summation of the sensorimotor aliveness. This *heritable potential* experiences a continuity of being and acquires, in its own way and at its own speed, a personal psychic reality and a personal body-scheme. According to Ogden:

> This state of being that lies at the core of the self constitutes an impenetrable (utterly unknowable) mystery that is the source both of lively communicating and absolute silence … Silence that is neither verbal nor non-verbal is beyond human comprehension.
>
> (2022, p. 17)

Winnicott describes this absolute personal mystery poetically as the "music of the spheres."[3]

The true self is the source of the spontaneous gesture, as well as of personal ideas, and only the true self can be creative and feel real. At the stage of first object-relationship, the infant's gesture will periodically give expression to a spontaneous impulse that comes from the true self. It quickly develops complexity and relates to external reality, leading to the infant's ability to react to stimuli without trauma, as they have a counterpart in the infant's inner psychic reality. Moreover, the infant holds the stimuli for being projections, what will – if everything goes well – enable the infant to retain a sense of omnipotence (Winnicott, 1965).

Winnicott states also that, at this stage of development, "fusion of motility and erotic elements is in process of becoming a fact" (Winnicott, 1965, p. 154).

The mother's capacity to be and to use her imagination allows her to attune to her baby and to tolerate its spontaneity, thus providing the possibility for the infant to retain her/his sense of omnipotence, but also to tolerate frustration and to comply. The latter corresponds to the unavoidable development of a false self that can correspond either to a healthy compromise with external reality or to the formation of a split-off, pathologically compliant false self.

Winnicott emphasizes that the concept of the true self precedes the concept of an individual inner reality of objects. The mother-infant unit shelters two relational aspects, namely the aspect of mother as a holding environment and the aspect of mother as object. Although the former aspect is dominant in early infant experience, it becomes a silent background of object-related experience, as the balance is shifting during the infant's psychic development. For Ogden, that silent background constitutes the "matrix of the mind" (Ogden, 1987). Through the mother's capacity to "feel" herself into her baby's place, that peculiar state of mind described by Winnicott as "primary maternal preoccupation," the mother is able to create the illusion that internal and external reality are one and the same, that is, the illusion of the "subjective object." The mother's task consists in not interfering with the baby's spontaneous development that is depicted as a "going on being" and that guarantees the unfolding of the infant's individuality (Ogden, [1985] 2012).

Following Ogden, it is important to emphasize that this process of "invisible oneness" refers to the illusion that needs do not exist, hence needs cannot become desire, thus providing the possibility of delaying the infant's awareness of separateness. Naturally, some amount of frustration will exist, and thus need is unavoidable and necessary.

Nevertheless, as Winnicott stated ([1960] 2011), the true self is strengthened through the mother's tolerance of her baby's spontaneous gestures, that means, through her implementation of the infant's omnipotent expressions. But if the mother is not able to tolerate her baby's spontaneity – most probably due to failures in early object-relationship with her own mother – and if she replaces the baby's gesture by her own instead, the baby tends to comply and to accept this environmental demand. The persistence of this unconscious communication leads to disruption of the infant's sense of "going on being" with serious implications. As Green (1975) states:

> The mother/object's intolerance of the baby's spontaneity can bring about in the baby a dissociation between psyche and soma, or between the two components of bisexuality, or between one aspect of the drives (e.g., the destructive drives) as against the other. The creation of a false self, conforming to the image of the mother's desire, allows protection to the true self, which is kept in secrecy.
>
> (p. 190)

Consequently, the infant's compliant false self takes over the caretaking function of the mother. According to the degree of compliance and of imitation as its inevitable companion, significant aspects of individual evolvement are compromised, thus impeding the development of what someone could have become. Considering the mother's difficulties in seeking to meet her baby's spontaneity, it is essential to search for an understanding of her psychic space that harbors the capacity to mediate in the multi-layered separation-identification process and where ideally an interplay of mutual investment and discovery between mother and child would take place as transitional phenomena come into play. This aspect is even more important if we consider the mother's role in the continuous integration process of her daughter's psychic bisexuality.

Psychic bisexuality for two as one: a focus on the mother-daughter unit

Since Freud, the concept of psychic bisexuality has been enriched through different perspectives (David, [1975] 2018; Birksted-Breen, 1993; Ferraro, 2003; Perelberg, 2018). Considered as indispensable for psychic and sexual integration, bisexuality is related to psychic organizations that depend on many variables and cannot be reduced to the residual traits of one sex within an individual.

David ([1975] 2018, 1992) introduces the idea of an unconscious bisexualization process, which refers to the early internalization of sexual differentiation. This pre-Oedipal concept highlights the positive and creative aspects of bisexuality that emerge as part of the maturation of desire, fantasy, and internal objects within the mother-infant dynamic.

Various authors (André, 2011; Fiorini, 2018; Gibeault, 1993, cited by Marta, 2024) suggest that psychic bisexuality is understood within a pre-genital framework, rooted in the primal homosexual mother-daughter bond. In this context, a binary logic plays a role in shaping psychic bisexuality, manifested through rhythms of coming and going, inside and outside, receptivity and penetration, which develop in the early mother-infant relationship.

For Winnicott ([1960] 2011), at the beginning, the baby's body is undifferentiated from the world. When body image and awareness begin to develop they are not gendered, although the body is always sexed insofar as bodily attributes are socially ascribed on a sex basis. Bisexuality is understood as a quality of the whole self. According to Winnicott, pure female and masculine elements exist in both sexes and fulfil their functions in the context of object relating. The female elements are present from the very beginning of life and provide the baby with the possibility "to be," and to weave a seamless tissue where the baby becomes the breast (or mother). "To be" in the sense of "being" is the ground for the development of a sense of self that links to the development of mechanisms of projection and introjection. On the other hand, male elements are associated with "doing" and require separateness. They are object-relating, implying complex mental mechanisms that still need time to appear. However, female as well as male elements within the baby contribute to the development of a sense of self.

Ferraro (2001; 2003) employs Winnicott's concept of pure female and male elements and articulates it with Freud's conceived instinctual drives:

> The relationship of the female element with the breast entails the identity of subject and object and constitutes the basis of the capacity for being, whereas the male element's relationship with the object presupposes separateness from it and is maintained by the instinctual drive
>
> (Ferraro, 2001, p. 489)

The female elements refer to the breast (the mother), more specifically, the child becoming the breast (the mother), the object is the subject, and instinctual drive takes no part, for the female element *is*. In turn, the male elements are related to an active or passive relationship that is backed by instinct drive, hence the male element *does* (Ferraro, 2001).

By offering this theoretical perspective, Ferraro (2003) not only articulates Winnicott's and Freud's ideas, but places also femininity and masculinity in early mental life, therefore allowing distance from sexual typification, as bisexuality becomes an essential component of identity. For Ferraro, the bisexual nature in psychic space is constant and predisposes the primitive psychic organisation toward triangulation.

This basic identity is initially marked by an omnipotent fusion with the object as a prelude for the drive investment, yet to come to the fore. The male elements involve object relating backed by instinctual drives and open space for drive satisfaction and frustration, thus sustaining further development of identity, in particular, the capacity for distinguishing between me and not-me (here, we are reminded of the gradual dissolving of the "invisible oneness," as awareness of need and emergence of desire develop during the separation process).

It is important to note that fundamental bisexuality is formed by the primal bisexuality that derives from the sensory register and that results from an integration process at the heart of the primary relationship (primary maternal preoccupation). This integration process depends on the supply of female elements (*being*). On the other hand, the bisexual disposition of the drives produces an interplay of identifications with the parental couple, as it

> induces both sexes to alternate between homoerotic and heteroerotic – originally paternal and maternal – objects, allows changes in their identificatory qualities and attributes which, when laid down in the pre-oedipal relationship, receive their definitive organisation from the overcoming of the Oedipus complex. This double movement is crucial to the constitution of identity.
>
> (Ferraro, 2001, p. 494)

Therefore, according to this perspective, psychic bisexuality takes part in the modulation of the separation-individuation process and is a quality of the self (Ferraro, 2001; 2003).

As the unconscious communication of the mother-infant entity is the object of the present reflection, it is necessary to think about the mother's psychic space, as it is suggested that the role-reversal promoting mother reveals difficulties in the separation-individuation process.

Taking Ferraro's proposal into account, thus linking psychic bisexuality to the development of an identity, the mediation of psychic bisexuality can be conceived as the adequate interaction between early female and male elements inside the baby's psyche and in the mother, that is, the breast or the maternal container. Following Ogden (1985), and as shown above, the baby's matrix exists initially within the mother's matrix, whereby the baby can react to stimuli, as in her/his inner psychic reality exists a correspondent. Inter- and intrapsychic interaction will become more differentiated over time. *Mutatis mutandis*, it could be stated that the pre-existing pure female and male elements in the baby will articulate with those existing inside the mother's breast/container, because there is a correspondence. For this to happen, it is necessary that an integrated psychic bisexuality exists in the mother container, so that the self of the baby is strengthened and able to form an inside and outside (Hurwood, 2008).

But if the mother herself had difficulties in integrating her own psychic bisexuality, thus in forming her own sense of self and identity, her matrix, that breast container in her psychic space must be marked by an inadequate articulation of female and male elements, which results in a failure or weakening of the triangulation process. This aspect raises questions about the identificatory processes the mother underwent and that refer to the mother's identification with the internal parental objects. This will be contemplated in the context of the transitional oedipal relationship.

If the female and male elements could not interact sufficiently, there could be an excess of undifferentiated parts. In this case then, and taking up Bleger's concept of ambiguity, it would be possible to imagine a structure that comprises the co-existence of a multiplicity of nuclei that lack me/not-me, ergo ego/non-ego discrimination. As Bleger states, these nuclei can co-exist and alternate without confusion or contradiction for the subject. In the inter-psychic communication, thus in countertransference too, ambiguity produces confusion due to feelings of uncertainty and the impossibility of defining (differentiating) clearly what the person is thinking.

In this context, it should be noted, though, that a certain amount of ambiguity promotes the continuity of internal growth of the self. Ambiguity is equal to undifferentiation, but undifferentiation produces also ambiguity (Ferreira, 2024), representing ambiguity as the capacity to sustain the paradoxes that constitute building blocks for complex thought. Therefore, one can view a well-balanced tension between undifferentiated and differentiated parts of the self as an important ingredient for individual creativity and exploration/elaboration of the unknown/unconscious. These aspects are indispensable for the development of individuality and for thinking with one's own mind. In a more mature and integrated psyche, ambiguity corresponds to the psychotic part that exists split-off and that Bleger called the *agglutinated nucleus*.

Nevertheless, considering the importance of the mother's mental space in the context of the invisible oneness, if the mother is significantly inhabited by ambiguous parts, she will (paradoxically) be less able to sustain the illusion that both needs and, in a broader sense, desires do not exist, as the increased fusion of ego and non-ego parts will hinder the mediation between symbiosis and relatedness.

Mariotti (2012), describes the positive outcome of such mediation capacity as follows:

> The mother on her part needs to be able to use her imagination at the level of transitional processes (Winnicott, [1951] 2011) in order to relate to her baby as part of herself, "*created*" by her, invested with all the narcissistic attention that can be reserved to one's body-mind, and also to see the child as "*found*", to be discovered in his or her intrinsic, unknown individuality.
>
> (p. 15)

Created and yet *found* describes the paradox that one can re-experience in dreams. It comprehends the coexistence of oneness and separateness, thus the coexistence of contradictions, that means, without conflict, that is the reign of ambiguity (Ferreira, 2024).

When generational boundaries are blurred and a mother seeks emotional care in the relationship with her daughter, a regressive ambiguous structure is most likely to be at work. In this context, it might be noteworthy that role reversal does not imply a clear pathology, as it is observable, for example, in psychotic mothers, although one could suppose the existence of a narcissistic logic in the mother.

The concept of ambiguity is pertinent in the sense that the psychological organization of ambiguous structures does not refer to a lack of identity, but to a different type of identity and a different sense of reality. These features could explain not only the frequently observed transgenerational persistence of role reversal, but also the parent's denial of this condition. Additionally, and with reference to the transgenerational process, there is to be considered the factor of maternal lineage (Mariotti, 2012): the mediation between symbiosis and relatedness is directly linked to the quality of psychic boundaries and thus crucial for the blurring of the generational boundaries.

An important short detour through the routes of linking

Returning now to the mother container and to the hypothesis of a weak articulation of female and male elements in the integration process of her psychic bisexuality, it is interesting to think about how this mother container might be structured. In fact, a mother may struggle to balance symbiosis and relatedness, and therefore have difficulties in being receptive to the baby's spontaneity, or being empathic, but, at the same time, she may or may not be aware of her difficulties.

For this matter, Birksted-Breen's (1993) differentiation of the phallic position and the "penis-as-link" offers possibilities of understanding the complexity of the interaction between female and male elements inside the mother container.

Taking up Bion's concept of prototypes for all links – the primitive breast or penis – Birksted-Breen conceives the breast in its function of being with, thus referring to the link between self and other, whereas the penis has the function of giving structure and is related to the link between parents, introducing thereby the notion of triangulation from the start.

For the author, the mother's bisexual mental functioning involves the maternal function of "being with" and a structuring function that is accomplished through the paternal function of observing and linking. Therefore, the mother's capacity for containment already implies psychic bisexuality. Birksted-Breen explains further that containment implies for a mother receiving the projections empathically (the maternal function) and being able to take a perspective on this (paternal function). This configuration corresponds to mental bisexuality.

Whereas the phallic function exists in the unconscious as a basic position and is based on a binary logic through the distinction between being and not being/having and not having, Birksted-Breen conceives the "penis-as-link" in a configuration that contemplates the vagina, allowing thereby the linking between two objects, thus viewing the self (of the mother) as a tripartite world that involves the knowledge of difference and therefore the perception of incompleteness and need for the object (Birksted-Breen, 1993).

> While the phallus belongs to the mental configuration that allows only for the "all or nothing" distinction, hence to the domain of omnipotence, and is an attempt away from triangulation, the penis-as-link, which links mother and father, underpins oedipal and bisexual mental functioning and hence has a structuring function which underpins the process of thinking.
>
> (p. 655)

Birksted-Breen considers the phallus position to be problematic, especially for the girls, insofar as that the phallus is possessed by nobody, thus expressing a lack, leaving no place for femininity. Whereas the boy's penis still can promote the (omnipotent) illusion of possession, so that this illusion facilitates the psychic integration into his internal object-relationship. On the other hand, the identification with the phallus may be necessary in order to cope with the lack and the concomitant feelings (helplessness, fear, envy, guilt), but, according to the author, the phallus is ubiquitous and belongs to a binary vision that leads to a rigid and restrictive mental organization. However, Birksted-Breen considers the co-existence or alternation of both the phallic position, as well as the "penis-as-link" configuration in the unconscious. She even postulates that they refer to specific symbolic functions or organizations.

Consequently, the author relates the phallus to a pre-symbolic way of thinking that refers to symbolic equation, and the "penis-as-link" to true symbolic function. This perspective can also be linked to Mariotti's (2012) reference to a maternal function that relates to the symbolic level.

Drawing the strands together

From this detour it is possible to conclude that a baby needs to meet a mother container who withholds psychic and mental bisexuality. Whereas psychic bisexuality refers to an initial sense of self and internal space, mental bisexuality encompasses further development that allows for space between internal objects, and self and others through the "penis-as-link" function. The latter provides fertile ground for thinking in a three-person dimension and contributes to the second phase of bisexual development, that is, the development of a sense of gender and sexual orientation (Birksted-Breen, 1993; Hurwood, 2008). As psychic and mental bisexuality are dynamic in progressive and regressive ways, and go along with each other, both developments can harmonize or overlap, so that it is possible to develop, for example, a strong sense for gender and/or gender option, but a weak sense of self.

Ideally, the good-enough environmental mother is able to "be with," as well as able to think about herself and her baby through the capacity of a third-party perspective. In analogy, this capacity can be seen as inherent to psychoanalytic function too, and is therefore also applicable to the psychoanalyst.

But if, as already mentioned, the mother could not develop a strong sense of self and identity herself, she is less able to meet the baby empathically. Unavoidably, the mother interferes too much with the spontaneous development of her infant, as she experiences difficulties in attuning to her infant and needs her/him to adapt to her. Not being able to have a perspective on this points to a weak internalization of the "penis-as-link" function, whereby the increased regressive nature of the mother's structure – due to predominance of undifferentiated parts – makes her essentially ambiguous, hence more susceptible to the symbiotic position, than receptive toward otherness/relatedness. The risk of seeing the daughter as a part of herself is even increased because of the same sex/same body, whereby the real individual child goes unrecognized, and is therefore neglected.

However, taking the natural maturation process of the girl's matrix into account and as transitional phenomena come into play, once again, the mother's integration of psychic bisexuality is at stake, as it propels the identificatory processes of her infant.

What father awaits the daughter?

> Maternality is also the expression of a profound and multilayered wish structured within the Oedipal configuration: in the space between mother and baby the father may be hidden, sometimes himself a "dark continent" in the background – and yet inescapably present.
>
> (Mariotti, 2012, p. 3)

In his paper, "The Transitional Oedipal Relationship in Female Development," Ogden (1987) reflected about how the infant can realize the shift from
protective illusion of the *subjective object* to experiencing objects as separate
from him in a non-traumatic way, proposing that the relationship with the
mother mediates this internal reorganization.

The author postulates that the mother serves as an oedipal transitional
object insofar as she allows herself to be loved as a man through her own
unconscious identification with her own father.

Therefore, while the mother is still the centre for affectionate interplay,
before the little girl is falling in love with the (external) father or the
mother, she falls in love with the "father as mother" or the "mother as
father." The mother's internal configuration of oedipal object relations
provides the girl with the possibility of triangulating the object relations in
the context of a two-person relationship, hence preparing the daughter for
the later oedipal phase.

Naturally, the mother's capacity to "perform" the transitional role depends
on the relationship with her own oedipal father. In fact, the mother's mediation
of psychic bisexuality that underlies her own identification process is put to the
proof through her capacity to sustain the dialectical structure inherent to transitional phenomena, since the mother ought to support the psychological state
created from paradoxes, so that

> reality enters into a mutually defining and enriching relationship with
> fantasy. It is only in the space between reality and fantasy created in this
> way that subjectivity, personal meaning, symbol formation and imagina-
> tion become possible.
>
> (Ogden, 1987, p. 487)

Again, ambiguity can show its creative or confusing face while the mother
offers herself to her daughter as a paradoxical object, as oneness and separateness, me and not-me, reality and fantasy co-exist.

For the development of the girl's identity, the opening of the symbolic
space is absolutely essential to get involved gradually in the meaningful symbolic play. Mariotti (2012), describes the interchangeability at the service of
self-exploration.

> The symbolic space of the play allows the young child to be no longer (only)
> her mother's child but, in her identification with the maternal figure, she has
> become her own child's mother. The little girl needs to be potentially ready
> to relinquish her exclusive position as daughter in order to integrate her
> identity as potential mother. This she does in her play with dolls, which
> offers her a space where she will not be asked "Are you a mother? Are you a
> daughter?" In the transitional space of play (Winnicott, [1951], 2011) she
> can elaborate very many interesting questions – where the babies come

from, where am I situated in the context of this question? Am I the same as my mother or can I be different?

(p. 29)

At this point, and drawing the strands further together, a brief clinical vignette may help to continue the line of thinking that leads to what could be at stake for the daughter in her own psychic bisexual development.

Searching for Leila

When Leila came to see me, she was a young woman who had just moved to Portugal to participate in a scientific project for at least two years. She thought that this project would give her the opportunity to finally find more time for herself. But instead of feeling more relaxed, she felt sometimes overwhelmed by an acute state of anxiety, without understanding what caused these sensations she was experiencing. Suddenly, her heart would start racing badly and she would feel dizzy and nauseous.

At a first glance, Leila appeared to me as a sweet teenager with an open smile. Wearing casual clothes, she seemed to me as more girlish than a young woman enhancing her femininity. Although she talked in a very eloquent way about how she got my contact through a colleague of hers, she revealed a certain hesitation. There was a certain shyness that was not congruent with what seemed to appear as an extroverted attitude.

As she began to explain why she decided to search for help, her voice got so soft that I had difficulties in understanding what she was trying to tell me. She could describe quite well the symptoms she observed in herself, but the more she tried to explain what she felt, the more she searched for words. Her body seemed tense, her hands were shaking, and her voice trembled through long silences, in which her facial expression indicated the enormous effort she was making to find words for what was going on inside of her. She stumbled and could not finish most of the sentences. At the same time, she seemed to contain herself in a suspenseful stillness.

During the first sessions, I often asked myself what she was trying to tell me and found myself lost and confused, almost stuck between unfinished sentences and moments of silence. I thought that the initial setting could inhibit Leila and I introduced the idea of her moving over to the couch, but Leila only smiled and her eyes wandered, as if she would be lost. Without her saying "No," it became clear to me that she needed to *see* me.

There were two Leilas. One coming through the door with a firm handshake and a lovely smile. The other began to exist while sitting on the chair and attuning to the session. She always looked around, as if she would make sure that nothing changed and although she seemed at the beginning to struggle with how to begin, I gained the impression that she was enjoying the arrival and the joint silence. Strangely, from time to time, I felt that I could accommodate Leila at my home and not at my office.

As we worked through these first encounters, Leila began to speak of her new life far away from her family and that she felt the need to be on her own, but she did not know what to do with herself, feeling sometimes overwhelmed by anxiety.

Being one of three children, Leila began from early on to be asked to accompany her siblings to different activities, thus having less time for herself. Her mother and her father, both ambitious hard workers, did not need to tell Leila what to do. Somehow, for Leila it was self-evident to take care of her room, do homework, help her siblings with clothing and breakfast, get involved in school activities, etc. Her mother would ask her to take care of the siblings, when they were ill. Although the mother worked in a studio on the ground floor, and on such occasions would provide food and medicine, Leila would spend time with her ill sisters. Sometimes, when her mother became nervous and irritated about a scheduled task, Leila would calm her down and solve the "problem."

When I asked Leila at some point if she remembered what she *liked* to do, she was surprised with herself, as she could not recall anything. She seemed disturbed, as she left. Countertransferentially, I felt that this simple question had done something violent to her, as if I had frightened her by reminding her of her own existence. Somehow, a new perspective had appeared. We had shifted from the joint (parental) look at her family to look together at Leila. This new perspective had placed Leila at the centre.

The next session, she was silent for a while and then she said in a very disjointed way:

> I have been thinking since our last session … and it came to my mind … I am not sure and I don't know if this makes sense, but I thought that I know about my life … I have my work, my friends … but perhaps, I don't really know who I am. I thought about what you asked me, what I liked to do when I was young … After leaving the session, I kept thinking and it came to my mind that I enjoyed reading. The more I thought about it, the more I remembered that I used books to not be available for others. I even remembered reading without taking any interest in the story.

Leila's insight opened a new space for elaboration and the following months were fruitful but difficult for her. She did not feel dizzy and nauseous anymore, but restless and anxious, and from time to time she would feel low. Far from being angry or irritated, she began to think about her relationship with her parents. She described her relationship with her mother as difficult, as she felt that she was needed. Her mother did not approve of Leila's decision to live for a while somewhere else, whereas her father was absent most of the time, although easier to talk to. The psychoanalytic process made Leila curious about her family history, and she began to feel intrigued.

Little by little, she came to realize that, on her mother's side, a maternal lineage was marked by successive abandonments or alcohol abuse by the fathers. Despite feeling disturbed by her findings, she began to link certain of her parents' life events, and searched for her place in the family constellation.

Leila is still working through her internal world. She does not feel prepared for a love relationship, but she expresses great enthusiasm in coming to the sessions and presenting her thoughts about things in her life, though according to her, they are nothing special!

Concluding remarks

This little résumé of Leila's experience is intended to illustrate the features of masked role reversal, which can be extensive as it crosses generations.

Following the transgenerational perspective (here the mother's mother is referred to as the grandmother), it can be suggested that the oedipal father that inhabits the unconscious of the mother is not suitable for a healthy identification process for the infant, because the oedipal father was unconsciously experienced as absent, or perceived as sinister, or even as terrifying, acquiring thereby a traumatic quality. Both possibilities would then be a consequence of the early object relationship between the mother and the grandmother and/or through the identification process with the real existing oedipal father. This condition would represent a cross-generational factor that travels through unconscious communication and thus affects the female-male-element-dialectic by weakening the male elements that are essential for the modulation of the separation-individuation process.

As already mentioned, the loss of psychological distinctiveness in relation to the child, especially to the daughter, points to the persistence of a symbiotic bond that often appears masked insofar as that these children seem to accept and perceive their condition as normal. They may even consider themselves lucky, as they occupy a special role in the family constellation. This feeling of grandiosity can be linked to the reinforced omnipotence gained from the symbiotic bond with the mother. On her side, the mother maintains this bond through the projected unconscious desires that relate to her internal oedipal object-relationship, for it seems that the role reversal pursues the fulfillment of the mother's (profound and unconscious) desire to be taken care of, thus unconsciously putting her own daughter in the position of her own mother (the grandmother). As the "caretaker child" complies and protects the adult, it could be also suggested that, through caretaking, the child also embodies the idealized oedipal father.

The subjective distortion that underlies the development of the child as an "imaginary adult" is linked with the projective identifications of the mother whose internal space seems to be marked by ambiguity. The care needed by the mother reveals an immaturity that calls for adaptation on behalf of the child. This immaturity is not necessarily related to some incapacity to function in the occupational routine and in everyday life. Instead, it reveals itself especially in the emotional context in which the child and later the adolescent is supposed to contain the feelings of the adult and/or even the siblings.

It can be concluded that the disruption of the sense of "going on being" due to the mother's inadequate bisexual mediation contributes to the development of a weak sense of identity and, simultaneously, of the formation of the false self, through premature taking on of the care function. On the other hand, precocious wisdom serves to overcome the increasing gap between the objective world and subjectivity. Insofar as it is possible to imagine that a lack of *being* is compensated by precocious wisdom that, in turn, is associated with *doing*.

A patient who was repeatedly sought out by his family members for help remembered from his childhood that his mother responded to his pleas by saying to him: "Just do it! I don't care how, just do it!" As a result, in adulthood, as the patient began to distance himself from family, feelings of paralysis, anxiety, and panic began to appear, whenever the patient did not feel able to "do" something in order to change a situation. In fact, it takes a good quality of being to do well.

Notes

1 In the present text, ambiguity is not taken in terms of ambiguous personality; however, it should be noted that, according to the author himself, Winnicott's concept of "false self" is different from this concept of ambiguity, which allows for recognition of different types of personality organization.
2 The glischro-caric (glischro = viscous or agglutinated; caric = nucleus) position refers to a psychic structure that precedes the paranoid-schizoid position that holds the "agglutinated nucleus" together. Projective Identification cannot occur due to the undifferentiation between self and object.
3 Music of the spheres (*musica universalis*) refers to Pythagoras' philosophical conception of the music produced by the celestial spheres that is in perfect harmony and inaudible to humankind.

References

Birksted-Breen, D. (1993). *The gender conundrum: Contemporary psychoanalytic perspectives on femininity and masculinity*. Routledge.
Bleger, J. (2013). *Symbiosis and ambiguity: A psychoanalytical study*. Routledge.
David, C. ([1975] 2018). The beautiful differences. In R. Perelberg (Ed.), *Psychic bisexuality: A British-French dialogue*. Routledge.
David, C. (1992). *La bisexualité psychique*. Éditions Payot.
Engelhardt, J. (2012). The developmental implications of parentification: Effects on childhood attachment. *Graduate Student Journal of Psychology*, 14, 45–52.
Ferenczi, S. ([1923] 1969). The dream of the "clever baby". In J. Rickman (Ed.), *Further contributions to the theory and technique of psychoanalysis* (pp. 349–350). Hogarth Press.

Ferenczi, S. ([1930–1932] 1949). Notes and fragments. *International Journal of Psychoanalysis*, 30, 231–249.

Ferraro, F. (2001). Vicissitudes of bisexuality: Crucial points and clinical implications. *The International Journal of Psychoanalysis*, 82, 485–500.

Ferraro, F. (2003). Psychic bisexuality and creativity. *The International Journal of Psychoanalysis*, 84, 1451–1476.

Ferreira, A. (2024). A ambiguidade e o feminino. In A. Melícias & A. Ferreira (Eds.), *Paula Rego: Ensaios psicanalíticos* (pp. 35–46). Freud & Companhia.

Goldner, L., Jakobi, C. D., Schorr, S., Dakak, S., & Shawahne, N. (2022). Keep it quiet: Mother-daughter parentification and difficulties in separation-individuation shaping daughters authentic/true self and self-silencing: A mediation model. *Psychoanalytic Psychology*, 39 (2), 165–174.

Green, A. ([1975] 2012). Potential space in psychoanalysis: The object in the setting. In J. Abram (Ed.), *Donald Winnicott Today* (pp. 183–204). Routledge.

Guignard, F. (2020). Maternity and femininity: Sharing and splitting in the mother-daughter relationship. In M. Alizade (Ed.), *Motherhood in the twenty-first century* (pp. 97–110). Routledge.

Hooper, L., Decoster, J., White, N., & Voltz, M. (2011). Characterizing the magnitude of the relation between self-reported childhood parentification and adult psychopathology: A meta-analysis. *Journal of Clinical Psychology*, 67 (10): 1028–1043.

Hurwood, J. (2008). Psychic and mental bisexuality in the development of a sense of self and mind. *British Journal of Psychotherapy*, 25 (4), 520–532.

Jurkovic, G. (1997). *Lost childhoods: The plight of the parentified child*. Brunner/Mazel.

Mariotti, P. (2012). *The maternal lineage*. Routledge.

Marta, R. (2024). Integração da bissexualidade no feminino. In A. Melícias & A. Ferreira (Eds.), *Paula Rego: Ensaios psicanalíticos* (pp. 101–119). Freud & Companhia.

Mello, R., Ferés-Carneiro, T., & Seixas Magalhães, A. (2015). Das demandas ao dom: As crianças pais de seus pais. *Revista Subjetividades*, 15 (2), 213–220.

Mello, R., Ferés-Carneiro, T., & Seixas Magalhães, A. (2019). Trauma, cleavage and intellectual progression: A study of the Ferenczi's wise baby. *Psicologia em Estudo*, 24, 1–12.

Ogden, T. ([1985] 2012). The mother, the infant and the matrix: Interpretations of aspects of the work of Donald Winnicott. In J. Abram (Ed.), *Donald Winnicott today* (pp. 46–72). Routledge.

Ogden, T. (1987). The transitional oedipal relationship in female development. *The International Journal of Psychoanalysis*, 68, 485–498.

Ogden, T. (2022). *Coming to life in the consulting room: Towards a new analytic sensibility*. Routledge.

Perelberg, R. (2018). *Psychic bisexuality: A British-French dialogue*. Routledge.

Pines, D. (1982). The relevance of early psychic development to pregnancy and abortion. *The International Journal of Psychoanalysis*, 63, 311–319.

Winnicott, D. ([1949] 1991). A man looks at motherhood. In D. W. Winnicott, *The child, the family and the outside world* (pp. 3–6). Penguin Classics.

Winnicott, D. ([1951] 2011). Transitional objects and transitional phenomena. In L. Caldwell & A. Joyce (Eds.), *Reading Winnicott* (pp. 99–103). Routledge.

Winnicott, D. ([1952] 2018). Anxiety associated with insecurity. In D. W. Winnicott, *Through paediatrics to psychoanalysis* (pp. 97–100). Routledge.

Winnicott, D. ([1956] 2018). Primary maternal preoccupation. In D. W. Winnicott, *Through Paediatrics to Psychoanalysis* (pp. 300–304). Routledge.

Winnicott, D. ([1960] 2011). The theory of the parent-infant relationship. In L. Caldwell and A. Joyce (Eds.), *Reading Winnicott* (pp. 147–152). Routledge.

Winnicott, D. (1965). *The maturational process and the facilitating environment: Studies in the theory of emotional development.* International Universities Press.

Chapter 12

Of gender and bisexuality

Ângela Vila-Real

Introduction

This chapter focuses on thinking about the relation between gender and bisexuality based on the clinical experience with two patients who, very different from each other, allow a deeper reflection around questions often seen as essential. The issues they bring about in the transference-countertransference field are very specific and have, therefore, different theoretical and clinical stimuli.

Psychoanalysis was grounded on the discovery of the unconscious, infantile sexuality and the difference between female and male. But it was also discovered very early on that bisexuality existed in both males and females. Even with the disclosed difficulty in grasping what is masculine and feminine, several authors tried to pursue the essence of the feminine, which turned out to be an inglorious task.

Ashley and the analyst's countertransference

Ashley turned up with a male name and a boyish look and declared himself as trans. He was depressed, and during the first months his purpose in treatment was to stop crying. After a while, he asked me whether I would see him more as a male or as a female. This question made me go back to when we first met. Ashley triggered a paradoxical impact in the analyst by presenting himself as male, despite being felt countertransferentially as female. What should I choose, what I saw or what I felt? It looked like there was a disharmony, or a contrast, between the superficial contact and the internal aspect, between male and female features. The issue of discontinuity was established from the start, which in my view indicates that sex and gender are conceptually different: they often coincide, but not always, as many authors (Freud, [1920] 1957; Butler, 1990; Suchet, 2011) have shown. But, more recently, in the social context, trans people have started to assert their personal worth, their identity, and their visibility, and the perception of such a discontinuity is more present, which may sound like a mismatch. And, as we well know, the impact of this visibility on the social context is not always peaceful.

DOI: 10.4324/9781003584483-14

The body surface is not always the basis for gender perception. So, there is no material basis for the statement or for the conscious or unconscious definition one might assign to an individual. The physical appearance, based on body materiality, may not be significant as a guidance principle of relational approach. But it also causes an effect of covering up the subtleties of an identity organization. The trans subject might also unconsciously camouflage his/her identity behind a gender definition – or un-definition.

The impossibility of finding a grounded and pattern-following support places us in a fragile position, which comes from the fact that we are facing the person, and at the same time facing ourselves, through the unknown/unfamiliar, which usually brings about a disturbing uncanniness (Freud, [1919] 1957). The social pressure to rush into a defined gender within the binary system is shown by the persistence on which differences are practiced and underlined (Butler, 1990), as, for instance, in ritual practices. Without such repetitions, without this performed practice, gender itself would no longer be branded by binary opposition, which demonstrates how fragile it really is. And that is why dichotomy has a tendency to present itself on a saturated form, so that doubts and disturbance will not rise.

Nowadays these differences are less obvious, as gender roles are less split, which could indicate that splitting is not so necessary and that roles are less rigid. Nevertheless, differences are maintained in terms of inequality and of hierarchy of social value.

Such persisting inequalities seem to correspond to intense internal needs that are related to the superlative and fearful status attributed to the woman-mother. During the first period of life, the mother is the object of love and phallic power (Lacan, [1966] 1991) and every human being needs to distance himself from her in order not to fall into her dominion once again. Therefore, her power is unconsciously felt throughout time, feared, and rejected. This connection is deeply rooted, intense, and determinative for the desire, gender, and identity organization, that is, of everything related to archaic roots.

Gozlan (2008) claims that gender's archaic nature pressures us to choose between male and female. Precociously, an impossibility of bearing ambiguity, doubt, and ambivalence imposes itself, which makes it painful to maintain un-definitions, especially those that relate to our identity organization. We tend to categorize in extremes to contrast them and, as a consequence, to eliminate the anxieties stirred by ambiguity. "Outside this splitting it is extremely difficult to talk about gender" (Gozlan, 2008, p. 541). "There is something unintelligible and traumatic in gender which provokes anxiety and inhibition, leading us to an act of 'forgetting' what we are not through a fixation or splitting of gender identities" (Gozlan, 2008, p. 544). Therefore, facing the difference is always traumatic. But the difference surpasses gender and everything that concerns it, and its resolution varies.

Throughout the relationship with patient Ashley there was a counter-transferential perception of a constant changeover between male and female.

Could this truly correspond to changeovers within the subject's internal and relational world, or could it be attributed to the usual way we organize our perceptions, that is to the gender's indicators that we use to position ourselves in relation to others? How can we define male and female? We grasp the idea of a man or a woman through stereotyped references, on which we support our judgments. The insertion in a cultural medium requires a reciprocal adaptation: the subject assimilates the rules and obeys rituals and, beforehand, the medium constitutes itself as a continent, that is, an extension of the maternal continent. But, as referred by Butler (1990), an individual inside a binary system who does not define his/her allegiance to a gender does not exist, for there are no cultural references to read him/her. Therefore, this feeling of uncanniness, of paradoxality, which we find mentioned by other authors (e.g., Harris, 2009; Suchet, 2011) may truly come from the fact that the organizing parameters of the patient's identity do not coincide with ours. However, the world organizes itself in a binary manner, and although it constitutes a ground support for most of the time, it could constitute itself as an obstacle for analyzing the internal world of a trans patient. The routine of finding grounded markers for diminishing doubt-related anxieties is a sort of blind screen upon which every gender-attributed shadow is projected. The same goes for homosexuality, which is frequently seen by clinicians and patients as the identity's major organizer.

The cultural stereotypes and also all the theoretical-clinical research history have a tendency to establish an immediate equivalency between sexuality and gender. As a matter of fact, in common fantasy there is indeed the tendency to think about the sexual life of the individuals with gender non-conformity as if it would be the touchstone of his/her dynamic organization. This is the mistake that often obscures the possibility of discovering an identity that is not defined by or that surpasses sexuality.

For Freud ([1920] 1957), the sexual body characteristics, masculinity or femininity, and the type of object choice vary independently from one another. But still today, against all our research, the tendency to overlap sex and gender in a rigid manner does not let one embrace the non-binary organizations, and it hinders their conceptualization. The abjection mentioned by Kristeva (1982) as a natural movement of distancing the other in an effort of separation and of creating a self is also the same movement for treating the other as a stranger or, in extreme, as non-existent. The same goes for non-conforming gender identities. They can be the foreigner, the stranger, the bizarre, the target of our projections.

In transgender, without continent or reference supporting any comprehension, there is an ambiguity and an unbearable doubt, which, in social context, might trigger violence. In a clinical relationship it might trigger the abjection, side by side with the consequent inability to relate to and understand that patient. The ambiguity seems unbearable because it relates to defining identity, its boundaries, and its comprehensibility.

Patricia Elliot (2016) reports the legal conflict in Canada in the 1990s between Kimberly Nixon and the Vancouver Rape Relief Centre, a feminist organization. This clearly shows the body's importance when one defines gender identity. Kimberly Nixon, a male-to-female transsexual individual, after having undergone a sexual reattribution operation, was excluded from the center, while wanting to collaborate in its work. The reason was because Nixon was not born a woman.

Halberstam (1998) mentions the life-and-death struggle around gender definition which transsexual individuals have to face to get an inscribed material definition.

This author's conceptualization seeks to define a "feminine masculinity" without the use of body as a reference or comparison with what is masculine. However, it never defines masculinity or femininity, or feminine masculinity for that matter. Establishing degrees of masculinity, Halberstam cannot help but implicitly summon the stereotypical references we know, and that experience within a social context will progressively and slowly transform. Several biographies of female-born individuals living as men, often successfully, are mentioned. Nevertheless, the reference is always the male stereotype. They are female, but do not feel themselves as women.

This summons Freud ([1920] 1957) when he refers to "a feminine personality, which therefore has to love a man, unhappily attached to a male body; or a masculine personality, irresistibly attracted by women, unfortunately cemented to a female body" (p. 172). Obviously, we do not know what a female personality or a masculine personality really is, but we also do not know what we refer to when we find, in countertransference, what we designate as masculine or feminine traits.

Back to the patient Ashley. In the beginning, male and female seemed clearly differentiated, contrasted but paradoxical, because we could not find correspondence between what is visual and what is intimate. The masculinity revealed on the surface seemed to be a reaction to an undisturbed latent femininity. Freud wondered ([1920], 1957), when he realized that psychic bisexuality existed, what we really repress in bisexuality. Why we would repress certain impulses or dispositions and not others is also hard to explain. Assuming there is a repression of one part of sexuality, without which bisexuality would be possible, the reason or perhaps reasons why we repress it would have to be common to many human beings in whom the gender obeys the binary logic. But also, in many cases, it reveals itself to be too saturated. That is, it renders impossible the configuration of an unsaturated gender expression or experience. It could be that such saturation arises as a reactive formation related to a too-fragile gender experience. That is what it sounds like whenever Ashley summons painful memories of his experiences as a girl. A similar configuration was suggested in the past by other authors (e.g., Harris, 2009; Suchet, 2011).

At other times, Ashley seemed to change over between male and female, indicating a gender variance within a changing body. Such dynamics naturally suggest a greater freedom of statement of a subjectivity that does not relate to any sort of binary reference. However, such shapes of coherence, unreferenced, can easily fall into feelings of helplessness, brought forth by the individual's experience of repulsion-led abjection from the social context. The trans person risks feeling expelled to a ghetto that could be the source of a precarious identity.

Francis and repetition

Francis sought therapy because of an obsessive idea that he is gay. He is a young man, at the beginning of his working life, belonging to a religious family to which he is very attached. Although in other aspects evolution in the analytic process takes place, eventually, from time to time the preoccupation with sexual orientation reappears, as if to reaffirm the anxiety that brought him to treatment in the first place, but he claims not to be homophobic.

In the sessions, he often refers episodes of masturbation while watching "shemale" porn, for him the most arousing type of porn. Soon afterward, he mentions invasive thoughts of death, establishing therefore a connection between both.

He referred to "shemales" as women, and his logic was founded on the fact that they had breasts. The fact that they also had a penis appeared not so relevant. In this way, he emphasized the presence in shemales of the anatomical element that he lacked. His shemale fantasies, as well as the time he spent watching porn, involved mixed feelings of sexual arousal, pleasure, pain, and fear. This mix of pleasure and terror suggests an infantile stance toward sexuality. In fact, this mix of sensations and emotions, as well as the death-related ideas, place this configuration as an Oedipus-castration impasse.

In his narrative, Francis emphasizes the idea that it's a pleasure and a punishment altogether. Every time he masturbates, Francis comes to me sulking, as if he's hoping for absolution. After the fear and shame with which he recounts what happened, he calms down because there is no condemnation from the analyst's side. His fantasy, which requires watching/projecting, is of a sexual relation where the materially shaped bisexuality is evident. Both erotic scene partners have male and female anatomic components, in which both sexes are condensed, and therefore delivering a castration-free completion.

Castration is felt as incompleteness and shame on two levels: the fear of punishment due to his uncontrolled impulses, for which Francis asks for absolution, and shame due to envy at not having breasts and all the characteristics attributed to women, whom he considers powerful and fearsome. It is not only sexuality that is at stake here; there is also a search for definition of the self through the object of desire.

But its elusiveness is maintained through the materialization of bisexuality through repetition. It could be said that the fact of being absolved gives him a feeling of lightness that allows him to start again and, to that extent, to repeat something. Repetition can be observed in time, as the cycle begins again, but also in space, as the partners he chooses repeat themselves in each other, in this way rejecting otherness.

The evolution of the analysis leads to awareness of his unconscious fear of homosexuality and also his fear of women, who are both exciting and powerful.

For Ashley, the fantasy of having children one day or, in his own words, "to make a family," becomes increasingly present. It is a sweet fantasy in which, with a subtle smile, he states his wish of being permanently around his children. He suddenly refers to this fantasy as taking care of children, using the words "my children," excluding his lover from his family life. He is concerned and blames himself, feeling this exclusion is not fair. Ashley was conceived on a holiday adventure, had very little contact with his father, and often regrets having an incomplete family. Sometimes he gets angry against his father, or against his mother, or both, for not having been protective or understanding enough. At first, his wish to build his family and stay at home watching over his kids, is seen as a form of repairing the mother/child bond. Nevertheless, I end up realizing Ashley wants to be both the mother and the father of his children, fantasizing that he will love them and provide all the attention he never had. Within this repetition/reparation, this family with mother and father, both male and female in its evidence/performance of a perfect union, never existed in his childhood. As such, he rejects the splitting between male and female and seeks the perfect/complete continent for his children, who would also be the grounded material reparation of his own early childhood and his deprivation of both motherly and fatherly love. Seeking perfection and completeness, he renders inexistent the splitting between father and mother, between male and female.

Concluding remarks

In both cases, the bisexuality is obvious, but, in Francis, the problem lies in the sexual difference; setting it aside by introducing the penis in both participants of a sexual scene that, apparently, puts away the castration anxiety present in the foreground. We are therefore within binary logic, in which the penis represents desire and power. Within this system, the threat of castration becomes concrete and sets aside the differences through insisting on the representation of a penis, which repeats itself opposing the dreaded imaginary absence as real. But at the same time, feminine attributes are also absent, and this is also felt as insufficient. This results in an impasse, a dead-end.

In Ashley, it seems that the organization takes place on a different level, which pretends to merge father and mother, male and female, in an undifferentiated whole that sets aside splitting and conflict. Therefore, it is not about phallic power nor about castration, which, in this case, organizes or polarizes the gender for the primary scene's function to create a wholeness which does not exist, but it is fantasized as perfect.

In both cases, we realize how traumatic difference can be. In both cases, gender issues are placed in a different manner. Regarding Francis, gender issues seem to arise secondarily to a castration anxiety rendering the difference to be solely on a basis of a sexual materiality which he sets aside. In the patient's point of view, he turns men into women, and through such process, there is no more difference.

Within binary logic, the identities define themselves and organize themselves initially with a reference to an infantile fantasy related to a specifically invested part of the body, forcing the child to face not only the difference, but also the absence and the failure. As such, the difference between the sexes shows up as a hierarchized relation, in which the feminine corresponds to failure, absence, passivity, castration. It seems rejected by the hysterical dynamic in which the conflict is staged, simulating a primary scene where both roles are symbolically performed in a rape scene. The same goes for Francis, who places both participants in an erotic scene in complete equality and continuity, with the particularity of preserving the fantasy of the sometimes overwhelming feminine power.

One of the reasons these differences manifest themselves so permanently and are so resistant to transformation resides in the fact that they are seen as symbolic sexual concepts. In fact, early on, identity, desire, and the erotic inscribe themselves directly in the body through early contact, in which the adult transmits to the child his/her enigmatic messages. These unconscious messages are directly inscribed within the soma, and are manifested afterward, interpreted, and symbolized by the child as if naturally and originally his/hers. What is apparently natural is actually a primitive bodily inscription, which is afterward a basis for evolution and sexuation: the symbolic inscription applied to the gender's identity basis (Laplanche, 2007).

We cannot forget that the abjection mentioned by Butler (1990) and Kristeva (1982) as an element of an identity that excludes others who differentiate themselves from us is frequently served by the view that when it does not exclude another, it could exclude some parts of a self that are alienated or foreclosed, and maintained as strange bodies. Therefore, some parts of one's identity may be secret from the subject him- or herself throughout his/her whole life, even if they wake up feelings of uncanniness, of unreality – feelings that the subject has no clue where they came from. The gaze of the person themselves or the gaze of others might, then, be constitutive, organizing, or aggressive and destructive when it segregates the self's completeness. Suchet (2011) approaches the trans sensitiveness as an aggressive-felt gaze, because of its excluding character. Lemma (2010) underlines the importance of the maternal look over the child's body as the first organizer of desire, of bodily boundaries, and the identity's core, including, naturally, gender identity. This look is sought for or rejected by the others we cross throughout all our life.

Suchet (2011) also mentions the aggressiveness, which may be within the look of surprise or curiosity when facing a trans person, and the manner in which the therapist's look may be of major importance. Such a look may confirm an identity, especially during moments of crisis present in trans people's lives.

But the infantile body does not take shape solely through the parent's look. The body, erogenous, takes shape through contact with the adult and his/her body from the start. Laplanche (2007) developed the theory that the adult sends unconscious messages to the child implanting a sexuality that, because of its enigmatic character, the child must decode. The mother, or the primary love object, causes many bodily feelings in the baby, which are marks of pleasure or pain, bringing forth sexuality and therefore creating an erotic body. But at an extreme, the unconscious message the child perceives from the adult implies a decoding activity that creates a sexual body and the unconscious. The erotic body and the self both take shape from the start (Dejours, 2019).

Implanted in this early dynamic are not only sexuality but also psychic bisexuality, which is decoded and possibly symbolized by the child through his/her development and his/her life circumstances. Gender's early organization, as well as the psychoanalytic clinical approach of psychic bisexuality, lead to new conceptual possibilities.

According to what we have said, it does not seem maintainable to think of gender organization as something totally separate from sexuality. Nevertheless, it does not seem adequate, according to the patients' experience, to consider binary organization alone. This serves mainly as an organizer, avoiding powerful anxieties. However, new identity configurations, as well as major social transformations, force the need to explore other routes. There is no doubt that experiences are inscribed in our bodies. But they are elaborated and symbolized throughout life, integrating all data we have access to in every moment. There is no point in considering that we should elaborate all data in a sequential manner.

References

Butler, J. (1990). *Gender trouble, feminism, and the subversion of identity.* Routledge.

Dejours, C. (2019). Les deux corps: Le corps biologique et le corps érotique. Conference presentation. Annual Conference of Fedération Européenne de Psychanalyse, Madrid, 30 March–1 April.

Elliot, P. (2016). *Debates in transgender, queer, and feminist theory.* Routledge.

Freud, S. ([1919] 1957). The "uncanny". In S. Freud (Ed.), *The standard edition of the complete psychological works of Sigmund Freud, Volume 17* (pp. 217–256). Hogarth Press.

Freud, S. ([1920] 1957). The psychogenesis of a case of homosexuality in a woman. In *The standard edition of the complete psychological works of Sigmund Freud, Volume 18* (pp. 147–172). Hogarth Press.

Gozlan, O. (2008) The accident of gender. *Psychoanalytic Review,* 95(4), 541–570. doi:10.1521/prev.2008.95.4.541.

Halberstam, J. (1998). *Female masculinity.* Duke University Press.

Harris, A. (2009). *Gender as soft assembly.* Routledge.

Kristeva, J. (1982). *The powers of horror: An essay on abjection.* Columbia University Press.

Lacan, J. ([1966] 1991). La signification du phallus. *Écrits II.* Editions du Seuil.

Laplanche, J. (2007). Gender, sex and the sexual. *Studies in Gender and Sexuality,* 8(2), 201–209. doi:10.1080/15240650701225567.

Lemma, A. (2010). *Under the skin: A psychoanalytic study of body modification.* Routledge.

Suchet, M. (2011). Crossing over. *Psychoanalytic Dialogues: The International Journal of Relational Perspectives,* 21 (2), 172–191. doi:10.1080/10481885.2011.562842.

Chapter 13

A chronicle of mother-daughter envy

Dana Amir

Introduction

Gender dichotomy is probably the primary dichotomy internalized in human thinking. It acts as a prototype for all the later dichotomies, in a sense inaugurating dichotomous thinking in general – first within the imaginary of the parent who holds the soon-to-be-born infant in their mind – and afterward within the infant's mind. As with any dichotomy, it may collapse into a saturated state, becoming fixated in a way that enables it only a minuscule degree, if any at all, of transformability – or it may remain unsaturated and, in this sense, contain movement, richness, and layered meanings.

In my book, *On the Lyricism of the Mind* (Amir, 2016), I suggested a "lyrical dimension" of mental space, which is in charge of the integration of two experiential/perceptual modes: the continuous mode, which perceives the world as predictable, explainable, and logical, and the emergent mode, which perceives the world as unpredictable, unexplainable, and constantly changing. The integration of these two modes of experience, which Bion ([1970] 1984) initially identified as constituting the container/contained interaction, yields the capacity to presuppose constancy and continuity on the one hand and to tolerate severe deviations from that constancy and continuity without losing one's sense of identity on the other hand.

Formulating his notion of the *container-contained* interaction, Bion ([1970] 1984) pointed at three possible types of this interaction, of which the one with the most powerful capacity for change is the *symbiotic* interaction, while the one with the most destructive power is the *parasitic* (in between these two, Bion posited a somehow neutral interaction he entitled "*commensal*"). If we formulate the interaction between the emergent and the continuous principles of the self in Bion's terms, we may suppose that wherever the interaction between the emergent and the continuous is parasitic or takes the form of a "malignant containment" (Britton, 1998, p. 28), one of two things might happen: the continuous self may smother the emergent self, leaving the latter no space for movement or development; or the emergent self might stretch the continuous self beyond its breaking point, crashing through its boundaries.

DOI: 10.4324/9781003584483-15

Bion ([1970] 1984) argued that the sense of catastrophe that attends such an interaction between the emergent and the continuous is related to the fact that the psychic space cannot supply an experience of constancy beyond change. This constancy is the primary condition for change. When the continuous principle prevails, the psychic space becomes lacking in depth and resonance, but when the emergent principle takes over the psychic space becomes a terrifying nightmare. If, by contrast, the interaction is compatible, integration may occur, inaugurating the lyrical dimension of the psychic space. The emergent is the force that preserves things in their unsaturated condition, whereas the continuous is the saturated state.

The more fertile the interaction between the two, the more likely one is to experience oneself as owning a historical and biographical continuum on the one hand – and as being a singular individual whose creativity is allowed to interrupt this continuum, on the other hand. One can formulate gender excess in terms of the relationship between the continuous and the emergent: for example, an excess of a "continuous" gender experience as opposed to an "emergent" gender experience could damage the possibility of establishing a "gender space," which holds the continuous and the emergent in a fertile dialectic relation. On the other hand, an excess of "emergent" gender experience, in which every shift threatens to change the deep nucleus of identity, may undermine the possibility of a cooperative relationship between the two poles of gender dialectic (the actual and the phantasmatic). Gender is constantly emerging. Yet every emergence needs a continuous container for its forcefulness and volatility. When there is a "continuous" gender that can contain the various gender emergences in a way that does not force the self to undergo a catastrophic identity change – "a lyrical gender space" (Amir, 2018) is created. However, where the continuous (which manifests itself, for example, in the prior propensity toward saturated dichotomies) is too fragile and rigid, and its encounter with the volatile and powerful emergent threatens breakdown, parasitical relations may form between the actual and the phantasmatic gender, resulting in anxiety that further builds up fragility and rigidness.

One can think of Leda, the protagonist of Elena Ferrante's *Lost Daughter*, as a woman trapped in the excesses of gender dichotomy. She is capable of choosing either total dedication to traditional female gender roles or total abandonment of these roles without any capacity to create a lyrical gender space that allows free and creative internal and external movement. The entrapment within gender dichotomy is, in many ways, what underlies the occurrence described in this book.

The Lost Daughter

Elena Ferrante's novel *The Lost Daughter* (2008) centers on an egregious deed: one morning, Leda, the book's protagonist, inexplicably steals a doll belonging to a little girl. In doing so she wrecks both the little girl's relations with her mother and her own vacation. This chapter focuses on the vicissitudes of envy in the relationship between mothers and daughters, and their psychotic potential, using Ferrante's extraordinary tale to examine their early roots and cast light on certain dimensions of these relations in general.

Leda is the mother of two adult daughters who live in Toronto with their father. When they left, she recounts, all she felt was relief, a kind of release from a protracted imprisonment. It took her some months to shed the layers in which motherhood had wrapped her and restore her youthful looks. It is in this state, which she describes as exceptionally comfortable, that she decides to take some time off.

As soon as she heads out to her vacation let on the beach, she grows anxious that this break may have been a mistake. For many years, all vacations were planned with her daughters in mind, and when they grew older and started going on vacations of their own, she would stay home just in case they might need her. But this total availability in fact masked its opposite: she tells us about her fear of ending up being blamed for what she really was, distracted, absent, trapped inside herself. As her vacation unfolds, she realizes that she knows everything about her daughters and nothing about herself. Everything she experiences, she observes through their eyes. But it is a perspective that does not really reveal her closeness to them, as one might be tempted to conclude, but rather reflects her alienation from herself. She might have been set free of *their* burden, but this does not mean she has found *herself*. In fact, she is situated in relation to herself as she is to her vacation rental. She finds herself dwelling somewhere that is neither alien nor familiar: the domain of the uncanny (Freud, [1919] 1953), in the sense that this site captures Leda's childhood scene and language – her deepest roots, that is – along with her alienation from these origins and their associated memories.

Into this territory barge a mother and her young daughter, part of a large Neapolitan family who happen to be spending their time near her on the beach. In many ways this family reminds her of her own original family: the same jokes, the same sticky sweetness, the same arguments. The young mother (Nina) is barely 20, and she and her daughter (Elena) appear to Leda to be living in a perfect world of their own. Leda envies the easy-going relations between them – which she compares both to her relationships as a mother to her daughters, as well as to her own mother's attitude to her when she was a child – a blend of aggression and absence. Much of the mother and daughter's play happens with and around the child's doll, Nani, whose name significantly resembles Leda's mother's name.

We are encouraged to think of the doll as a transitional object (Winnicott, [1951] 1982), charged both with the mother's qualities as well as with the child's. Their play with the doll creates a zone of caring, concern, and physical connection, as mother and daughter treat the doll as if it were a child they shared. Leda spends hours watching their effortless closeness. A day later, the damage sets in: everything that appeared tempting and attractive the day before is now felt to be exorbitant. Nina and Elena's play appears artificial to Leda, and she is maddened by how they make the doll speak in a double voice, a mixture of the girl's pretend-adult speech and the mother's quasi childish prattle. From this point on, Leda is overtaken by an urge to cause harm, to poison the mood, to disfigure the idyl. Her own mothering of her daughters, which she describes as the insertion of a poisonous insect into her bloodstream, a slow stripping away of her soul, her body, and eventually of her own daughters too, who preferred their father – all this rallies against her as she witnesses Nina and Elena's enactment of perfect closeness, accumulating into unbearable anguish.

The incident of the lost daughter enters this dense, explosive inner texture. Though Leda finds Elena and brings her back to her mother and aunt, the little girl remains inconsolable because she has lost her doll. Later it transpires that Leda has found the doll, hidden it in her bag and taken it. This cruel and disgraceful deed, which is baffling to Leda herself, is the crux of the story.

The night after she steals the doll, Leda recollects another doll, one she owned when she herself was a child. One reason she loved it was because it functioned as a substitute for the body of her mother who, recoiling from the child's need for physical closeness, would not let Leda "play" with her. So, when Bianca, her own first child was born, Leda threw herself fully into the role of being her "doll," allowing the child to treat her as she liked in the hope of giving her what she herself had lacked. But this demanding, unbounded, constant intimacy was exhausting.

One day she decided to give Bianca her own childhood doll so that it would serve the child as a substitute the way it had done for her, and to release herself. But to Leda's surprise the girl was not impressed by the doll, preferring one her father gave her. Leda describes the child sitting on the doll, using it like a pillow, a lifeless object rather than a creature onto which she projects human traits, while she treats the doll her father gave her with loving care. Asking Bianca to get up to remove the doll from underneath her, Leda sees that the child has spoilt the doll by having scrawled all over it with a marker. Leda throws the doll from the balcony and, together with her little girl, spends a long time watching how the passing traffic crushes it.

This scene can be understood in many ways: given to Bianca as a substitute for the maternal closeness she craves, the girl cannot but hate the doll. She treats it as an object without human attributes much like she treats her mother: as an object rather than a subject, as a function rather than a human creature. This mode of conduct, though, has been elicited by the very way in which she was given the doll in the first place: by way of a substitute to unavailable motherly love. Unlike Nani, the doll that functions as a kind of playful transitional space – charged by both the mother (Nina) and daughter's (Elena's) intimacy, which at the same time also allows for a certain distance between them (situated as it is, as a kind of "third" between the two of them, who "look after it") – Leda's childhood doll, which she later gave

Bianca, has been invested with the hatred, rather than the love, of mother and daughter, and so it ends up disfigured and mangled by both of them. It is the inverse of Nani, the other doll, much like the relations between Leda and Bianca are the inverse of those between Nina and Elena.

The theft of the doll can be thought of as an act of envy if we consider it in Klein's ([1957] 1975) terms. Its appropriation from the little girl involves no desire for the doll itself but results from the wish to spoil the connection the doll stands for (and enables) between mother and daughter. When it is taken away, their intimacy, previously described as delicately balanced, turns insufferable. Once the doll is gone, both mother and daughter confront intensities of demandingness and dependency that threaten to ruin their bond. The deed, over and beyond exposing Leda's hatred, also brings out into the open Nina's hatred, who suddenly transforms from being an ideal of perfect motherhood into its miserable opposite.

As the story unfolds, the reader witnesses a grievous dynasty of mothers and daughters: in Leda's dense inner theater, her daughters serve both as witnesses to her failure to repair, by means of them, her own failed relationship with her mother, as well as another iteration of her own mother's rejection of her, as they eventually reject her and choose their father. The appropriation of the doll itself takes part in this chain of events: Leda, in taking away the doll, takes sadistic revenge on Elena, standing for all daughters, as well as on Nina, representing all mothers. At the same time, she masochistically punishes herself, her theft turning her into the evil fairy of children's tales, bringing tidings of death to the scene of celebration.

Aulagnier (2001) has argued that the potentially psychotic child is born into the scene of their mother's non-desire for it. Sometimes this non-desire is conscious, then again it may be camouflaged and reveal itself in a variety of violent acts. The mother's non-desire for the child originates, according to Aulagnier, in a unique type of desire, namely the mother's desire to revisit the pleasure of her own birth, that is: to be reborn herself by means of – and in the place of – the child she delivers. Aulagnier claims that the child, in this sense, is the product of the mother's covert incestuous relations with her own mother: she wishes to give this child, who is in fact herself, to her own mother. The mother's desire to give birth to herself equals a death wish for the new-born infant, because rather than a subject with a life and future of their own, her desire aims for an object by means of which she reproduces her own past (Aulagnier, 2001).

Leda's motherhood does indeed include a death wish of the kind Aulagnier described. Not only because she wishes to give her daughters to her own mother (she consciously wishes to keep them away from her mother who represents, as far as she is concerned, everything she herself has tried to escape; unconsciously, however, she gives her daughters to her mother when she abandons them for three years and lets her mother take care of them), but rather because it is through them that she herself attempts to be reborn or restored to herself. Instead, time and again, she finds herself being taken away from her own self and the life she wants to be living. Possible reparation transforms into a repeat of the damage.

The doll is a metaphor for this confusion between damage and reparation. Leda's theft of the doll enacts, with a hint of psychosis, an attempt at controlling, in the concrete world, the internalized negative representations and internalized negative objects. Simultaneously, the theft of the doll constitutes an envious enactment of an unconscious phantasy of total fulfillment, reparation, unification without lack. Leda, in this sense, realizes two unconscious phantasies at once: one is the envious phantasy of destroying Nina's good mothering, and the other is the greedy phantasy of appropriating this mothering.

When Leda runs into Nina in the toyshop, she confesses to her that she abandoned her own daughters for three years. Like stealing the doll, this confession is itself a mixed sado-masochistic act of vengeance: while it masochistically exposes Leda, to whom Nina until then has looked up, as a bad mother – prompting and endorsing Nina's aggression (who, as said, identifies with Leda) toward her daughter, it also damages the former's good mothering (and in that way expresses Leda's sadism). More than that: Nina has treated Leda as a role model, a promise of release from the entanglements of family and the prison of motherhood. Leda later denies her this identification when she tells her about having stolen the doll. At the same time, however, Leda restores Nina's responsibility for herself and her own life by means of this negation.

This book presents us with a dynasty of women, each of whom represents a different dimension of femininity: From Rosaria, Nina's sister-in-law who carries her pregnancy as a power, a weapon, a type of superiority, to fragile, easily influenced Nina, who shifts between her perfectly inhabited motherhood and her urge to escape this illusory paradise it provides her.

As said before, being trapped in a gender dichotomy is, in many ways, what drives the events described in this book. Not only Leda but all women in the book range between total devotion to motherhood, alongside the inevitable ambivalence it consciously and unconsciously arouses, and various forms of abandonment of the maternal role, an abandonment that is not experienced as freedom but rather as a failure. Lacking the ability to integrate the different gender roles and the freedom to move between diverse expressions of masculinity and femininity, or, in my terms, between diverse expressions of "gender continuous" and "gender emergent," these women remain isolated between two difficult choices, each of which deprives them of themselves in a different way.

The envy Nina arouses in Leda is the same envy Leda experienced with her own daughters: it is connected to a profound implication of her own alienation and expropriation from herself, something that prompts her to enact another expropriation: of herself from her daughters' dominion, of the doll from Nina's control, and of Nina from her own control.

The path toward psychosis that Aulagnier drafts may expose some dimension inherent to this very trap of motherhood. This dimension relates to the gap between the desire for a child the mother can give her total care, investment, and dedication to – and the unconscious phantasy behind this overt desire, namely, the young mother's phantasy of *being that child herself,* and receive herself the care she gives that child. The mother's envy – perhaps all mothers' envy – could be said to be directed at their own dedication, a dedication which, beyond taking their time and energy, also erases the illusion that they might be on its receiving end. Giving her child what she would want for herself, the mother not only gives herself what she was denied as a child, but also once again deprives herself of it. Leda's urge to spoil her image in Nina's eyes can also be considered an enactment of the envious urge to spoil herself as a valuable gift she presents to the other. In this sense, it is through this act of wreckage or spoilage that she restores herself to herself in the only way she knows: by damaging herself. It is only by this self-inflicted damage that she escapes the other end of compulsory dedication. The tragedy of this story however is that this escape does not set her free from repetition. On the contrary: it sends her straight into its tight embrace.

References

Amir, D. (2016). *On the lyricism of the mind: Psychoanalysis and Literature.* Routledge.

Amir, D. (2018). The two sleeps of Orlando: Transsexuality as caesura or cut. In O. Gozlan (Ed.), *Current critical debates in the field of transsexual studies: In transition* (pp. 36–47). Routledge.

Amir, D. (2023). A chronicle of mother-daughter envy: Elena Ferrante's Lost Daughter. *Fort-Da,* XXIX (2), 43–47.

Aulagnier, P. (2001). *The violence of interpretation.* Routledge.

Bion, W. R. ([1970] 1984). Container and contained transformed. In *Attention and interpretation.* Karnac Books.

Britton, R. (1998). *Belief and imagination: Explorations in psychoanalysis.* Routledge.

Ferrante, E. (2008). *The lost daughter.* Europa Editions.

Freud, S. ([1919] 1953). The uncanny. *The standard edition of the complete psychological works of Sigmund Freud, volume 17* (pp. 217–256). Hogarth Press.

Klein, M. ([1957] 1975). Envy and gratitude. In *Envy and gratitude and other works: 1946–1963* (pp. 176–235). Delta.

Winnicott, D. W. ([1951] 1982). Transitional objects and transitional phenomena. In *Through paediatrics to psychoanalysis.* Hogarth Press.

Index

For Product Safety Concerns and Information please contact our EU
representative GPSR@taylorandfrancis.com
Taylor & Francis Verlag GmbH, Kaufingerstraße 24, 80331 München, Germany

www.ingramcontent.com/pod-product-compliance
Lightning Source LLC
Chambersburg PA
CBHW050656280326
41932CB00015B/2928

*9 7 8 1 0 3 2 9 5 3 5 5 7 *